Capitalism as Religion?

A Study of Paul Tillich's Interpretation of
Modernity

HARVARD THEOLOGICAL STUDIES
59

CAMBRIDGE, MASSACHUSETTS

Capitalism as Religion?

A Study of Paul Tillich's Interpretation of Modernity

Francis Ching-Wah Yip

DISTRIBUTED BY

HARVARD UNIVERSITY PRESS

FOR

HARVARD THEOLOGICAL STUDIES

HARVARD DIVINITY SCHOOL

Capitalism as Religion?
A Study of Paul Tillich's Interpretation of Modernity

Harvard Theological Studies 59

Series Editors:
François Bovon
Francis Schüssler Fiorenza
Peter B. Machinist

The Greek font, Symbol Greek II, used in this book is available from Linguist's Software, Inc., P.O.B. 580, Edmonds, WA 98020-0580, USA, tel 425.775.1130.

Managing Editor:	Margaret Studier
Copy Editors:	Eve Feinstein, Richard Jude Thompson, Keith Stone
Typesetter	Richard Jude Thompson
Proofreader:	Keith Stone
Index:	Caramon K. K. Lee, Francis Ching-Wah Yip

Yip, Francis Ching-Wah, 1967-
    Capitalism as religion? : a study of Paul Tillich's interpretation of modernity / Francis Ching-Wah Yip.
        p. cm. -- (Harvard theological studies ; 59)
    Summary: "Examines Paul Tillich's critical interpretation of capitalism and cultural modernity, highlighting the context of his theology in relation to the Critical Theory of the Frankfurt School, and finally drawing on Jürgen Moltmann and Émile Durkheim to develop Tillich's insights into a critical view of capitalism as a global religion and as the culture of modern society"--Provided by publisher.
    Includes bibliographical references and index.
    ISBN 978-0-674-02147-1 (alk. paper)
    1. Tillich, Paul, 1886-1965. 2. Christianity and culture. 3. Capitalism--Religious aspects--Christianity. I. Title.
    BX4827.T53Y57 2009
    261.8'5092--dc22
                    2009009038

To

my father and mother

and to

Miranda and Amos

Table of Contents

Chapter Two
Tillich's Critique of Capitalist Modernity

Acknowledgments

This book is a revised version of my doctoral dissertation. The writing process, from initial research to final publication, has taken more than ten years. I am indebted to many persons. My deepest gratitude goes to Francis Schüssler Fiorenza, my *Doktorvater*. Without his responsive advice, insightful comments, and very helpful suggestions, as well as his unfailing support, encouragement, kindness, patience, and contagious sense of humor, the publication of this book would not have been possible. My profound gratitude also goes to Gordon Kaufman, who raised crucial and penetrating questions, gave thoughtful comments, helped me engage critically with Tillich's thought, and encouraged me to go beyond the cultural parameters of Western theology. I owe my special thanks to the anonymous reviewer, who, as a critical and constructive interlocutor, has given me extremely perceptive, helpful, and detailed comments and suggestions, including those penciled on numerous pages of my manuscript. I am also indebted to Harvey Cox for his stimulating questions and his thought-provoking analysis of the Market God; to Sarah Coakley, Ronald Thiemann, and other members of the Theology Colloquium for constructive comments; and to Cornel West for his advice and encouragement at the initial stage of research. Special thanks are due to Kwai Hang Ng for his helpful comments on the manuscript, which he brought in person from San Diego to Hong Kong.

Earlier versions of chapters two and four were presented, respectively, at the "Paul Tillich and Sino-Christian Theology" conference held in Hong Kong in 2005 and at the annual meeting of the North American Paul Tillich Society (NAPTS) held in Washington, D.C. in 2006. I am very grateful to the participants for their comments, encouragement, and friendship. I am also grateful to The Chinese University of Hong Kong for a grant which supported the research related to chapter four and my participation in the NAPTS meeting in 2006.

I thank Frances O'Donnell, curator of manuscripts and archives, Andover-Harvard Theological Library, for granting permission to publish short quotations from three unpublished documents archived in the Paul Tillich papers quotations from three unpublished documents archived in the Paul Tillich papers collection, and to the former curator,Tim Driscoll, for granting access to the collection.

I wish to express my gratitude to the series editors of the Harvard Theological Studies academic book series and other faculty members of the Harvard Divinity School for making it possible to publish this book in the HTS series. The HTS editorial team has done an excellent job in improving my manuscript. I am especially indebted to Margaret Studier for managing the whole publication process with professional proficiency and gracious patience, and for her experienced editorial advice and careful proofreading. I am also indebted to Eve Feinstein and Richard Jude Thompson for the earlier phase of copyediting and to Keith Stone for the latter phase of copyediting and initial help in indexing. Considerable work in indexing has been done in Hong Kong by Caramon K. K. Lee. I am grateful for his timely assistance amidst his busy schedule.

Colleagues, friends, and students at The Chinese University of Hong Kong have been supportive of me in many ways. I am especially indebted to Rev. Lung-Kwong Lo for his sympathetic understanding, timely encouragement, and indispensable help. My thanks are due to Tobias Brandner and Chi-Ho Chan for advice in translation. I am also grateful to other colleagues at the Divinity School of Chung Chi College and the Department of Cultural and Religious Studies for their intellectual stimulation and cordial encouragement. I wish to mention in particular Wai-Yin Chow, Lap-Yan Kung, Simon Kwan, Chi-Tim Lai, Pan-Chiu Lai, Laikwan Pang, Milton Wan, and Gustav Yeung. I thank my students for sustaining me by their encouragement and prayers and by providing me with the opportunity to experience the joy of teaching.

Many persons have helped, sustained, and facilitated me directly or indirectly throughout the long journey of research and writing. I am indebted to the late Professor Philip Shen for his personal encouragement and for sharing with me his wisdom as a Christian scholar and educator; to Susan Abraham, Peter Chang, Nami Kim, Laura Nasrallah, and Ivan Petrella for their intellectual and moral support and for lively discussions; to Kathryn Kunkel, Jeffrey Kinnamon, Taylor Petrey, and the late Kin-chun Lee for their practical advice, help, and support; and to Kwok Pui-Lan, David Pao, Nancy and Stewart Sanders, Kam-lin Lam, Sze-Kar Wan, Annia Giger, Rev. Carol Stine, and members of the Quincy Community United Methodist Church for their hospitality, friendship, care, and assistance. I am also grateful to the Harvard Divinity School as well as the General Board of Global Ministries of the United Methodist Church for their financial support, and to the Andover Newton Theological School for short-term accommodation and library access.

Words are never sufficient to express my profound gratitude to my wife Miranda, who unfailingly supported me in countless ways, who readily took up extra duties (on top of her already heavy workloads) when I excused myself from many responsibilities as husband and father, and who lovingly accompanied me and experienced together with me all the stress, relief, disappointment, hope, anguish, joy, *angst*, and grace in the twists and turns of this unexpectedly long journey. My son Amos has literally grown up with this book. He often invigorates me with his relentless curiosity, enthusiasm in discussion, and perseverance in asking for bedtime story-telling. Last and most important, I owe my special thanks to my father (葉焯南) and mother (莫錦薇) for everything they have given me, for their care and concern, and for patiently awaiting the completion of this book during seemingly unending years. To these four significant persons in my life I affectionately dedicate this book.

Abbreviations

Abbreviations of Tillich's Works

CEWR	*Christianity and the Encounter of World Religions*
CTB	*The Courage to Be*
ERQR	*The Encounter of Religions and Quasi-religions*
GW	*Gesammelte Werke*
HCT	*A History of Christian Thought*
IH	*The Interpretation of History*
IRCM	*The Irrelevance and Relevance of the Christian Message*
MSA	*My Search for Absolutes*
MW/HW	*Main Works / Hauptwerke*
OAA	*On Art and Architecture*
OB	*On the Boundary*
PE	*Political Expectation*
PTC	*Paul Tillich on Creativity*
RS	*The Religious Situation*
SD	*The Socialist Decision*
SSOTS	*The Spiritual Situation in Our Technical Society*
ST	*Systematic Theology*
TC	*Theology of Culture*
TP	*Theology of Peace*
TPE	*The Protestant Era*
UC	*Ultimate Concern*
VS	*Visionary Science*
WR	*What is Religion?*

Journal Abbreviations

ChrCent	*Christian Century*
CRDSB	*Colgate Rochester Divinity School Bulletin*
Daed	*Daedalus*
EJST	*European Journal of Social Theory*
HPolEc	*History of Political Economy*
HTR	*Harvard Theological Review*
JAAR	*Journal of the American Academy of Religion*
JChS	*Journal of Church and State*
JCQ	*Japanese Christian Quarterly*
JESHO	*Journal of the Economic and Social History of the Orient*
JHI	*Journal of the History of Ideas*
JR	*Journal of Religion*
ModTh	*Modern Theology*
PCul	*Public Culture*
RelLife	*Religion in Life*
RelSRev	*Religious Studies Review*
RRelRes	*Review of Religious Research*
SocAn	*Sociological Analysis*
SocRS	*Sociological Review*
SPhilSocS	*Studies in Philosophy and Social Science*
Th11	*Thesis Eleven*
TT	*Theology Today*
ZNeuerThG	*Zeitschrift für neuere Theologiegeschichte*

Introduction

While I am putting the final touches on the manuscript of this book, Americans are facing the worst economic crisis since the Great Depression. Once the most stable ground of capitalism, the United States has become the epicenter of an earthquake that generated a financial tsunami which brought devastation to countries around the world. Stock markets have plummeted. Investment banks have collapsed. American and European governments have deployed huge amounts of money to save their once powerful financial institutions from bankruptcy. Politicians who used to support laissez-faire capitalism have called for more regulation of the financial markets. People are discussing whether the global financial turmoil means the end of American-style capitalism. Some are proclaiming that unregulated capitalism, styled as the god of the conservative intellectuals, is already dead.[1] Others, such as the outgoing President George W. Bush, hold on to their faith in capitalism: "Despite corrections in the marketplace and instances of abuse, democratic capitalism is the best system ever devised." That is to say, we need to preserve "the foundations of democratic capitalism—a commitment to free markets, free enterprise, and free trade."[2]

At the other side of the globe, many people in Hong Kong share this faith in free-market capitalism, despite the fact that Hong Kong arose as a modern metropolis in southern China as a result of capitalistic aggression. Britain, the pioneer in industrial capitalism, took possession of Hong Kong

---

[1] Harold Meyerson, "Gods That Failed," *The Washington Post*, 15 October, 2008, http://www.proquest.com/ (accessed 15 November, 2008).

[2] Associated Press, "Text of President Bush's speech on economic crisis," *Boston.com,* 24 September 2008, http://www.boston.com/news/nation/washington/articles/2008/09/24/text_of_president_bushs_speech_on_economic_crisis/?page=full; Deb Riechmann [Associated Press], "Bush to host global financial summit," *Boston.com,* 19 October, 2008, http://www.boston.com/news/world/asia/articles/2008/10/19/bush_to_host_global_financial_summit/?s_campaign=8315.

Island after defeating China (at that time under the imperial Qing dynasty) in the First Opium War (1839–1842) in retaliation for China's attempt to stop the opium trade. Subsequent waves of British military aggression, in which the French also participated, resulted in China's cession of the Kowloon Peninsula in 1860 and the 99-year "leasing" of the New Territories to Britain in 1898.[3] The acquisition of Hong Kong was driven primarily by the interest of the British in opening up the market of the world's most populous nation for trading.[4] John Bowring—who helped initiate the Second Opium War (1856–1860) and was later governor of Hong Kong and superintendent of trade in China[5]—believed so zealously in free trade, which he deemed a trend no nation could resist, that he once said "Jesus Christ is Free Trade and Free Trade is Jesus Christ."[6]

While few people in Hong Kong would equate free trade or any other aspect of capitalism with Jesus Christ, they maintain a strong confidence in capitalism. Research in the mid-1980s showed a "pervasive normative support" for capitalism in Hong Kong.[7] The successful performance of the capitalist economy of Hong Kong wraps "an aura of sacredness around it."[8] Even after the economic downturn following the 1997 Asian financial crisis,

---

[3] For the history of the British acquisition of Hong Kong, see John M. Carroll, *A Concise History of Hong Kong* (Hong Kong: Hong Kong University Press, 2007) 10–16, 21–28, 67–72; Steve Tsang, *A Modern History of Hong Kong* (Hong Kong: Hong Kong University Press, 2004) 3–23, 29–41.

[4] As a historian observes, "the British Empire acquired Hong Kong first and foremost to promote its economic interests in China, and only secondarily to support diplomatic contacts for which naval and military backup was often required" (Tsang, *A Modern History of Hong Kong*, 21). Another historian remarks that Hong Kong was "the British headquarters for the China trade" and "founded primarily for trade" (Carroll, *A Concise History of Hong Kong*, 33). In fact, from the very beginning of Hong Kong as a Crown Colony, the governor of Hong Kong was the same person as the British plenipotentiary and superintendent of trade in China (ibid.).

[5] Carroll, *A Concise History of Hong Kong*, 21–24; Tsang, *A Modern History of Hong Kong*, 30–34.

[6] Ronald Hyam, *Britain's Imperial Century, 1815–1914* (Basingstoke, U.K.: Palgrave Macmillan, 2002) 113, quoted in Carroll, *A Concise History of Hong Kong*, 23.

[7] Lau Siu-kai and Kuan Hsin-chi, *The Ethos of the Hong Kong Chinese* (Hong Kong: The Chinese University Press, 1988) 63. Their study indicates that the people of Hong Kong have a preference for opportunity, freedom, and individual competition, in spite of the inequalities the capitalist system would bring (ibid.).

[8] Lau and Kuan, *The Ethos of the Hong Kong Chinese*, 63.

there was still "solid support" for the capitalist system.[9] "The free market is still an article of faith for Hongkongers."[10] In 2004, following the horrendous outbreak of Severe Acute Respiratory Syndrome and the ensuing economic downturn, the people of Hong Kong still "espouse[d] some of the core values of capitalism," although they were aware of the problem of social injustice.[11] The actual and perceived economic benefits of capitalism do not fully explain such a strong, even quasi-religious, support for capitalism. For the people of Hong Kong, capitalism means more than just an economic system. It means also a way of life which is different from—and often in stark contrast to—the way of life in mainland China. It constitutes the identity of Hong Kong vis-à-vis socialist China and thus must be vigorously guarded against any erosion. Remarkably, the capitalist system of Hong Kong has been given constitutional protection by the Chinese communist government.[12] There is hardly another place in the world where capitalism has been given such a guarantee that adopting socialism or any other noncapitalist system would be unconstitutional.[13] Capitalism is sacrosanct in Hong Kong.[14] One might even

---

[9] In a 1999 survey, a majority of respondents agreed that Hong Kong's capitalist system was a good system, that it provided for equal competition, and that everyone will benefit if business people are allowed to make the maximum of money. Many respondents did not think that workers should go on strike for the sake of higher pay or improved working conditions. Lau Siu-kai, "Confidence in the Capitalist Society," in *Indicators of Social Development: Hong Kong 1999* (ed. Lau Siu-kai et al.; Hong Kong: Hong Kong Institute of Asia-Pacific Studies, The Chinese University of Hong Kong, 2001) 98–99.

[10] Ibid., 113.

[11] Ng Chun-hung, "After the Crises: Changes in Social Ethos," in *Indicators of Social Development: Hong Kong 2004* (ed. Lau Siu-kai et al.; Hong Kong: Hong Kong Institute of Asia-Pacific Studies, The Chinese University of Hong Kong, 2005) 280.

[12] Article 5 of the Basic Law of the Hong Kong Special Administrative Region of the People's Republic of China stipulates: "The socialist system and policies shall not be practiced in the Hong Kong Special Administrative Region, and the previous capitalist system and way of life shall remain unchanged for 50 years." The full text of the Basic Law can be found at http://www.info.gov.hk/basic_law.

[13] The other place is Macao, a former Portuguese colony which was returned to China in 1999. Its Basic Law is modeled on that of Hong Kong.

[14] While the economic situation of Hong Kong has influenced my concern and thus my choice of topic, I am not writing from a specifically Hong Kong (or Chinese or Asian) perspective. I am concerned with capitalism and modernity as global phenomena. The capitalism and modernity of Hong Kong do not differ so greatly from those of New York, London, Frankfurt, or Tokyo. Cultural variations do exist, but they are variations within a global capitalistic modernity.

regard it as a religion. In fact, as I will argue later in this book, capitalism can and does function as a religion.

This book attempts to develop a theological response to global capitalistic modernity by means of a critical interpretation of capitalism as a quasi-religion. Global capitalistic modernity is arguably still the most decisive aspect of the contemporary situation even after the global financial crisis. It affects virtually everyone in the world. If theology seeks to articulate an understanding of faith that is relevant to the contemporary situation[15]—for the task of systematic theology is "the reinterpretation of the tradition for the present situation"[16]—it should take global capitalistic modernity seriously. Equally important, theology cannot be constructed in an ahistorical vacuum. It must involve "the reinterpretation of the tradition."[17] As there are various traditions in Christianity, and each tradition is so rich, any reinterpretation of the tradition must be highly selective. I will develop my response to global capitalistic modernity on the basis of a reconstruction, examination, and evaluation of Paul Tillich's interpretation of capitalism and modernity. Before explicating my choice of Tillich, I will comment briefly on the notion of "global capitalistic modernity."

In using the term "global capitalistic modernity" in the singular, I am not unaware of the discussions of "multiple modernities" that stress cultural and geohistorical differences.[18] However, one should not emphasize such cultural differences to the point of obscuring the commonality that these "modernities" share. As Arif Dirlik says, "Recognition of difference is important, but it is equally necessary to recognize that contemporary differences derive their meaning from a common experience of modernity; indeed, it is often quite difficult to distinguish differences that define trajectories of modernity from

---

[15] Christian theology often seeks relevance by relating to the contemporary situation in three moments: interpretive, critical, and therapeutic. It tries to show that Christian faith (as interpreted by the theologian) can make sense of and throw light upon the situation, that it can confront and critique the social, cultural, and existential problems in the situation, and that it can address, answer, and heal these problems, leading to their transformation. The interpretative moment is particularly crucial, for any theological response to the situation (whether critical or therapeutic) presupposes and depends upon the interpretation of the situation.

[16] David Tracy, *Analogical Imagination: Christian Theology and the Culture of Pluralism* (London: SCM, 1981) 64.

[17] Ibid.

[18] See, for example, S. N. Eisenstadt, "Multiple Modernities," *Daed* 129 (2000) 1–29.

differences produced by modernity."[19] My qualifier "capitalistic" points to the inseparability of capitalism and modernity.[20] Modernity is capitalistic, not just in its origins but also in its subsequent development.[21] Characterized by the general dominance of the market in society and the unlimited accumulation of profit, capitalism is, according to Christian Comeliau, "a pillar of modernity" and "the most thorough institutional expression of modernity."[22]

Relevance of Paul Tillich

Paul Johannes Tillich (1886–1965) is one of the most renowned Christian theologians of the twentieth century. Born on 20 August, 1886 in Germany, Tillich studied at several prominent European universities. After serving as an army chaplain during the First World War, he held academic positions at Berlin, Marburg, Dresden, Leipzig, and Frankfurt. An active advocate of "religious socialism" and a pioneer in "theology of culture," he wrote extensively on issues related to religion, culture, and politics. His critique of the political ideology of National Socialism in the book *The Socialist Decision* led to his suspension from his teaching post in the University of Frankfurt in April 1933; he was the first non-Jewish German scholar to be suspended under the Nazis. Later in the same year, he came to New York at the invitation of the Union Theological Seminary and taught there for twenty-two years. After his retirement in 1955, he was honored with an appointment as University Professor at Harvard University (1955–1962). Subsequently

---

[19] Arif Dirlik, "Global Modernity? Modernity in an Age of Global Capitalism," *EJST* 6 (2003) 288–89.

[20] This is a position both Marx and Weber would agree on, albeit for different reasons. For the views of Marx and Weber on the significance of capitalism in modernity and their close connection, see Derek Sayer, *Capitalism and Modernity: An Excursus on Marx and Weber* (London: Routledge, 1991). For the affinity between Marx and Weber on capitalism and modernity, see Karl Löwith, *Max Weber and Karl Marx* (ed. Tom Bottomore and William Outhwaite; preface by Bryan S. Turner; London: Routledge, 1993).

[21] For the historical connection between capitalism and modernity, see Luciano Pellicani, *The Genesis of Capitalism and the Origins of Modernity* (trans. James G. Colbert; New York: Telos, 1994). Pellicani observes that the genesis of capitalism up to the Industrial Revolution shows a close correlation between the expansion of the exchange logic of the market and modernization (ibid., 203).

[22] Christian Comeliau, *The Impasse of Modernity: Debating the Future of the Global Market Economy* (trans. Patrick Camiller; London: Zed Books, 2002) 28, 32.

he joined the University of Chicago and remained there until his death on 22 October 1965.[23]

As Christoph Schwöbel has noted, "Unlike Karl Barth, Tillich was from the beginning intent on relating theological thought to non-theological reflection and seemingly non-religious spheres of culture."[24] The success of this approach can be seen in the extent of Tillich's influence, which reaches beyond church and academy. For example, his concept of "ultimate concern" was cited by the Supreme Court of the United States as a criterion by which beliefs may be judged religious.[25] "His public lectures and books reached large audiences who did not usually show an interest in religious questions."[26] His more popular books, such as *The Courage to Be* and *The Dynamics of Faith*, "reached a circulation of more than 100,000 copies each."[27] Thus it is not an exaggeration to call Tillich "the first (and only) 'pop' theologian of the twentieth century."[28]

I have decided to draw on Tillich because of his theological perspective on social and cultural phenomena. For example, he sees modernity in terms of autonomy, which falls short of theonomy; he sees capitalism in terms of the demonic, which is an evil structure with an ambiguous mix of creativity and destructiveness. Moreover, Tillich has made significant contributions toward a critical interpretation of capitalism and modernity. For some people this is not so obvious. While they know that the religious-socialist writings of the "early Tillich" were critical of capitalism, they would regard these writings

[23] Walter Leibrecht, ed., *Religion and Culture: Essays in Honour of Paul Tillich* (Freeport, N.Y.: Books for Libraries Press, 1972) xi; Christoph Schwöbel, "Tillich, Paul (1883–1965)," in *The Blackwell Encyclopedia of Modern Christian Thought* (ed. Alister McGrath; Oxford: Blackwell, 2005) http://www.blackwellreference.com/subscriber/tocnode?id= g9780631198963_chunk_g978063119896322_ss4-1 (accessed 20 September 2008). For a full biography, see Wilhelm Pauck and Marion Pauck, *Paul Tillich: His Life and Thought* (New York: Harper & Row, 1976; repr., San Francisco, Calif.: Harper & Row, 1989).

[24] Schwöbel, "Tillich, Paul (1883–1965)."

[25] See James McBride, "Paul Tillich and the Supreme Court: Tillich's 'Ultimate Concern' as a Standard in Judicial Interpretation," *JChS* 30 (1988) 245–72.

[26] *Encyclopædia Britannica Online*, s.v. "Tillich, Paul," http://search.eb.com/eb/article-7267 (accessed 13 September 2008).

[27] Wilhelm Pauck, "To Be or Not to Be: Tillich on the Meaning of Life," in *The Thought of Paul Tillich* (ed. James Luther Adams et al.; San Francisco, Calif.: Harper & Row, 1984) 29–43, at 30.

[28] Peter McEnhill and George Newlands, "Tillich, Paul" in *Fifty Key Christian Thinkers* (London: Routledge, 2004) http://www.reference.routledge.com/subscriber/ entry?entry=w036_w036b44 (accessed 20 September 2008).

as outdated, for capitalism has undergone many changes since his death. At the same time, they would regard the "later Tillich" as an existentialist theologian,[29] whose magnum opus, the three-volume *Systematic Theology*, is a fine attempt to correlate an existentialist interpretation of the human situation with a modern reinterpretation of traditional Christian symbols. Such an existentialist perspective might seem of little relevance for the interpretation of capitalism and other aspects of modern society. It may also be seen as having limited usefulness for the interpretation of modernity, for we are, they might say, entering the postmodern era.

My perspective on Tillich is quite different from the above view. Instead of a discontinuity between the "earlier" and "later" Tillich, I find in many of his works—from his early writings on religious socialism to the third volume of *Systematic Theology*—a continuous concern with the critical interpretation of capitalistic modernity. We can say that Tillich was a prophetic, political theologian.[30] Informed by Marx's critique of capitalism, Weber's interpretation of the capitalist spirit, and his own critical concept of the demonic, Tillich's religious socialist writings offer a critique of capitalism and bourgeois society, seeking to transform society and culture into theonomy.[31] After his emigration to America, Tillich toned down his political criticism, including the direct critique of capitalism.[32] This seems to have

---

[29] For example, James C. Livingston, "Christian Existentialism," in *Modern Christian Thought* (ed. James C. Livingston et al.; 2d ed.; Upper Saddle River, N.J.: Prentice Hall, 1997–2000) 2:133–34, 140–53; John Macquarrie, *Twentieth-Century Religious Thought* (new ed.; Harrisburg, Pa.: Trinity Press International, 2002) 368–69.

[30] Langdon Gilkey observes that "Tillich began as a political theologian" (Langdon Gilkey, *Gilkey on Tillich* [New York: Crossroad, 1990] 3). See also Gary M. Simpson, *Critical Social Theory: Prophetic Reason, Civil Society, and Christian Imagination* (Minneapolis, Minn.: Fortress, 2002) 27–52.

[31] One should not underestimate the continuity of Tillich's thought. Many concepts that Tillich uses in his later writings (e.g., theonomy, kairos, demonic) come from his early writings on religious socialism. Even his concern for ontology can be traced back to his early, political thought. See James W. Champion, "Tillich and the Frankfurt School: Parallels and Differences in Prophetic Criticism," *Sound* 69 (1986) 521–22.

[32] The reasons for what may look like depoliticization will be spelled out in the next chapter. In spite of certain disappointments resulting from his political involvement, Tillich maintained that "politics remained, and always will remain, an important factor in my theological and philosophical thought" (*MSA*, 50). Indeed, just a few months before his death, he commented on the political view of the papal encyclical *Pacem in Terris* (Paul Tillich, "On 'Peace on Earth,'" in *Theology of Peace* [ed. Ronald H. Stone; Louisville, Ky.: Westminster/John Knox, 1990] 174–90).

resulted in a compensatory sharpening of focus on the cultural dimension of capitalistic modernity. This area of critique remained important for Tillich and in fact constituted a crucial part of his analysis of the "situation" in the method of correlation of his mature theological system.[33] For example, in part 1 of *Systematic Theology* he points out how technical reason leads to meaninglessness and how controlling knowledge brings objectification and dehumanization.[34] This shows similarities to the critical social theory of the leading members of the Frankfurt School, who were good friends of Tillich and shared with Tillich a heritage of humanistic Marxism. In this connection, it is worth noting that Tillich regarded Marx as an existentialist.[35] For Tillich the term referred less to a philosophical school than to an attitude, the opposite of which is detachment. Part 5 of *Systematic Theology,* which correlates the ambiguities of history (including political problems) with the kingdom of God (which, as Tillich stresses, is political and social[36]), it is even farther away from existentialism (in the usual sense of a predominate concern with individual human subjectivity).

Moreover, Tillich's critical interpretation of modernity and capitalism is not outdated and irrelevant. While there have been changes in modern culture since his death, such as the widespread use of information technology, the characteristics of modernity remain basically the same as those which Marx

[33] For Tillich, theology moves between two poles: the eternal truth of the Christian message and the temporal situation which receives it. A good theological system must keep both poles together in balance. The "situation" he talks about is not the psychological or sociological conditions as such but the interpretation of existence in scientific, artistic, economic, political, psychological, and ethical perspectives (see *ST* 1:3–4). Concisely put, the situation is "the totality of man's creative self-interpretation in a special period" (*ST* 1:4). Tillich's method of correlation "makes an analysis of the human situation out of which the existential questions arises, and it demonstrates that the symbols used in the Christian message are the answers to these questions" (*ST* 1:62). While the content of the Christian answers, which rely on the revelatory events on which Christianity is based, are independent of the situation, their form are "dependent on the structure of the questions which they answer" (*ST* 1:64).

[34] Tillich borrowed from Marx's critique of objectification and dehumanization as part of Marx's critique of capitalism (*SD*, 171 n. 8; *MW/HW* 3:522–23); thus Marx's influence continued in Tillich's later writings (Brian Donnelly, *The Socialist Émigré: Marxism and the Later Tillich* [Macon, Ga.: Mercer University Press, 2003]). As Carey points out, Donnelly "demonstrates that Tillich drew heavily on Marx's thought for all of his career" (John J. Carey, *Paulus Then and Now: A Study of Paul Tillich's Theological World and the Continuing Relevance of His Work* [Macon, Ga.: Mercer University Press, 2002] 36 n. 49).

[35] *SSOTS*, 125–26. See also *ST* 2:25; *HCT*, 484.

[36] *ST* 3:358.

and Weber—to whom Tillich was indebted—have analyzed. Even features attributed to a dawning postmodernity are better seen as the radicalization and reflexive application of certain aspects of modernity.[37] For example, the instability, fluidity, and perpetual change often associated with postmodernity are actually characteristic of capitalism, which, as Marx says, is constantly revolutionizing the means of production and thereby all social relations, so that "all that is solid melts into air."[38]

Similarly, Tillich's critical interpretation of capitalism also remains current. It is true that capitalism has undergone changes and transformations in recent decades,[39] yet contemporary capitalisms, in their different varieties,[40]

---

[37] Anthony Giddens, *The Consequences of Modernity* (Stanford, Calif.: Stanford University Press, 1990); Ulrich Beck, Anthony Giddens, and Scott Lash, *Reflexive Modernization: Politics, Tradition, and Aesthetics in the Modern Social Order* (Cambridge: Polity, 1994).

[38] Karl Marx and Friedrich Engels, "Manifesto of the Communist Party," in *The Marx-Engels Reader* (ed. Robert C. Tucker; 2d ed.; New York: Norton, 1978) 476. For perpetual change as a key feature of modernity, see Marshall Berman, *All That Is Solid Melts into Air: The Experience of Modernity* (New York: Penguin, 1988).

[39] These transformations include the change from Fordism (large-scale, mass production and mass markets) to "flexible accumulation" (small-batch production, subcontracting, and other flexible labor arrangements), from the material-dependent industrial economy to the information-dependent service economy, from manufacturing products to satisfy the demand of consumers to manufacturing needs to meet the supply of producers, and so on. See David Harvey, *The Condition of Postmodernity: An Enquiry into the Origins of Cultural Change* (Cambridge, Mass: Blackwell, 1990) 121–97; Benjamin R. Barber, *Jihad vs. McWorld* (New York: Ballantine Books, 1996) 59–87; Ernest Sternberg, "Transformations: The Forces of Capitalist Change," in *Twenty-First Century Economics: Perspectives of Socioeconomics for a Changing World* (ed. William E. Halal and Kenneth B. Taylor; New York: St. Martin's, 1999) 3–30.

[40] Richard Whitley, "The Institutional Structuring of Market Economies," in *Competing Capitalisms: Institutions and Economies* (ed. Richard Whitley; Cheltenham, U.K.: Edward Elgar, 2002) 1: ix–xxvii. For example, Hall and Soskice distinguish between "liberal market economies" (such as the United States) and "coordinated market economies" (such as Germany) which differ in corporate governance, intercompany relations, industrial relations, financial systems, and training systems. In the first ideal type, business firms relate to each other primarily by competitive market arrangements and formal contracting; in the second ideal type, firms rely more on cooperative and collaborative relations to build their competencies ("An Introduction to the Varieties of Capitalism," in *Varieties of Capitalism: The Institutional Foundations of Comparative Advantage* [ed. Peter A. Hall and David Soskice; Oxford: Oxford University Press, 2001] 1–68). Coates further differentiates the second type, arriving at a typology of three models of capitalism: market-led capitalisms in the United States and United Kingdom, negotiated or consensual capitalisms in Germany and Sweden, and state-led capitalisms in Japan and South Korea (David Coates, *Models of Capitalism: Growth and Stagnation in the Modern Era* [Cambridge: Polity, 2000]).

still share many common characteristics.[41] In Weber's view, the defining characteristics of capitalism include private enterprise, the pursuit of profit through exchange, capitalistically organized provision of wants, the rational organization of free labor, rational capital accounting, as well as formal, calculative rationality.[42] For Luciano Pellicani, capitalism is a "*self-regulated system of markets* that tends to extend the *catallactic* [i.e., exchange] *logic* to all distributive and productive processes."[43] Its unique spirit is the will to endlessly acquire, which drives its continuous transformation and expansion. While there is exchange in all societies, capitalism is distinctive for the centrality of the market, the rule of the law of supply and demand, and the extensive use of money, which makes possible the rational calculation of profits and prices.[44] Capitalism involves the competition of economic enterprises for the maximization of profit with the use of capital. In capitalism everything, including labor, is a commodity to be bought and sold. Thus capitalism entails not only the predominance of economic logic but also the primacy of economics over politics, religion, morality, and culture. Capitalism is therefore not just a mode of production; it is also a social order in which the market is prevalent and dominant.[45] Despite the transformations of capitalism, these characteristics persist.

Contributions

While there is currently a certain revival of interest in Tillich's thought,[46] little attention is being paid to his theological interpretation and critique of capitalism and modernity, even though these are important themes throughout his works.[47] I believe that this book is the first full reconstruction of this

---

[41] After giving an overview of three different forms of capitalism (merchant, industrial, and financial capitalism), one sociologist points out that, while their business activities are different, "all involve the investment of money in order the make a profit, the essential nature of capitalism" (James Fulcher, *Capitalism: A Very Short Introduction* [Oxford: Oxford University Press, 2004] 13–14).

[42] Sayer, *Capitalism and Modernity*, 92–95.

[43] Pellicani, *The Genesis of Capitalism and the Origins of Modernity*, 8 [emphasis original].

[44] Ibid., 8–9.

[45] Ibid., 10–11.

[46] See the examples mentioned in Robison B. James, *Tillich and World Religions: Encountering Other Faiths Today* (Macon, Ga.: Mercer University Press, 2003) 1 n. 2.

[47] The focus of this book is not Tillich's theology, although an understanding of his theology is indispensable, as it informs his critical interpretation of capitalism and modernity.

aspect of his thought. To be sure, there are studies on Tillich's critique of capitalism and his religious socialism—most notably the classic volume by John Stumme[48]—but they focus mainly on Tillich's early writings, while this book draws on both his early and later works. Ronald Stone's *Paul Tillich's Radical Social Thought*,[49] which looks at Tillich's social thought from his early years to his later writings, has a similar, though broader, theme, and its approach is primarily historical. Moreover, unlike this book, it does not focus on Tillich's critical interpretation of capitalistic modernity as a key to his social thought.

This book does not stop at reconstruction and interpretation. It makes further contributions to Tillich scholarship by critically assessing Tillich's insights alongside those of Jürgen Moltmann and Émile Durkheim. Tillich's dialectical, nuanced, and theologically informed critique of capitalism and modernity is commendable, yet his interpretation of capitalistic modernity is Eurocentric (overlooking the "others" of modernity), and his conception of religion is asocial (and ultimately inadequate for the critique of capitalism).[50] Offering a Durkheimian revision of Tillich, I propose a critical perspective that views capitalism as a quasi-religion (with its sacred things, beliefs, and practices) that functions as the civil religion of global modernity and as the religious substance of modern society. Thus I am not just concerned with the past, looking back to what Tillich did; I am also concerned with using my reconstruction and evaluation of Tillich as the basis for developing a new way for the theological interpretation and critique of global capitalistic modernity. So oriented, this book contributes not only to Tillich scholarship but also to constructive theology, as it articulates the relevance of theology to the contemporary situation.

---

[48] John R. Stumme, *Socialism in Theological Perspective: A Study of Paul Tillich, 1918–1933* (American Academy of Religion Dissertation Series 21; Missoula, Mont.: Scholars Press, 1978).

[49] Ronald H. Stone, *Paul Tillich's Radical Social Thought* (Atlanta, Ga.: John Knox, 1980).

[50] So far as I know, no previous studies of Tillich's concept of religion have focused on the asocial nature of Tillich's understanding of religion.

Overview of Chapters

Chapter 1 lays the groundwork for this book. It gives a brief overview of Tillich's critique of capitalism and tackles the question of whether the American Tillich discontinued his critique of capitalism. Also, I look at the place of his theology of culture in his religious analysis of the culture of capitalistic society; the analysis of capitalism as demonic constitutes an important aspect of Tillich's theological critique of capitalism. I will explicate the idea of the demonic and will show that this idea is more adequate than others for the critique of capitalism. I will also explore the possibility of using Tillich's notion of quasi-religion for a critical interpretation of capitalism.

Chapter 2 examines in detail Tillich's critical interpretation of cultural modernity. After introducing a few key concepts, including Tillich's concept of theonomy, I proceed with an overview of his interpretations of modernity and of the historical development of bourgeois society. This is followed by a thematic reconstruction and examination of Tillich's critique of and response to various aspects of cultural modernity, including autonomy, self-sufficient finitude, technical reason, controlling knowledge, objectification, and conformity. Tillich's similarities with the Frankfurt School will be mentioned and the distinctiveness of his critique will be highlighted.

Chapter 3 assesses Tillich's critical interpretation of capitalistic modernity. The first part of the chapter brings in the view of Jürgen Moltmann on capitalism and modernity as an alternative perspective. The second part brings in the insights of Durkheim's theory of religion to assess Tillich's idea of religion. I argue that Tillich's relevance for a contemporary theological response to global capitalistic modernity can be further enhanced by putting more emphasis on the material-economic dimension, by shifting from a Eurocentric to a global perspective, which remembers the victimized others, and by developing a more social conception of religion and quasi-religion.

Chapter 4 is the last chapter before the conclusion. Following a general assessment of the contributions and limitations of Tillich's response to capitalistic modernity, I put forward a constructive proposal that interprets capitalism as a quasi-religion, with its own beliefs and practices in relation to its sacred things. Finally, I argue that the capitalistic quasi-religion can be understood as a global civil religion and the religious substance of cultural modernity.

CHAPTER ONE

Tillich's Religious Critique of Capitalism

An Overview of Tillich's Critique of Capitalism

Although capitalism in its early inception can be said to have emerged from Christian soil, as Max Weber has suggested,[1] it was not welcomed by Christian thinkers. From the early-twentieth century onwards, many Christian theologians, including but not limited to those influenced by Karl Marx, have been critical of capitalism in one way or another.[2] In fact, as an economist observes, it is "difficult to think of a major Christian theologian who wrote from 1920 through 1960 who regarded capitalism with favor."[3] Paul Tillich, the renowned German-American theologian and philosopher of religion, was among the theologians critical of capitalism.[4] Like many critics of capitalism, Tillich supported socialism. Yet his socialism was not just a socialism that calls for the elimination of capitalism through revolution but was *religious* socialism that sought a radical transformation of bourgeois society *and* the inauguration of a new relation between religion and culture (which he calls "theonomy").[5] Seen in this light, it seems especially fitting that Tillich's ashes were finally interred

---

[1] Max Weber, *The Protestant Ethic and the Spirit of Capitalism* (trans. Talcott Parsons; intro. Anthony Giddens; New York: Routledge, 1992).

[2] In the first half of the twentieth century, notable theologians such as Karl Barth, Reinhold Niebuhr, William Temple, and Paul Tillich, among others, were critical of capitalism.

[3] Karen I. Vaughn, "Theologians and Economic Philosophy: The Case of Paul Tillich and Protestant Socialism," *HPolEc* 24 (1992) 1 n. 1.

[4] Tillich's view on economic issues "were fairly representative of a wide spectrum of theologians from the 1920s through at least the 1950s" (ibid., 4).

[5] Tillich's concept of theonomy will be explicated in the next chapter. Suffice it to say at this moment that "theonomy" in Tillich's writings is an ideal situation when culture is linked and transparent to its religious depth. It does not mean the imposition of divine law by an external religious authority. Tillich calls the latter "heteronomy."

in a park bearing his name in New Harmony, Indiana, a small town with both
a religious and a socialist legacy. The town was established in 1814 by a group
of German Rappites, a religious group named after their leader Johann Georg
Rapp, to be the site of their ascetic and eschatological community. Ten years
later it was sold to the Scottish industrialist and social reformer Robert Owen
to establish a utopian socialist community.[6] It was both the religious and social
dimensions, emphasized respectively by the Rappite and Owenist communities,
that Tillich sought to bring together in his religious socialism, especially in his
religious critique of capitalism.

Tillich's Critique of Capitalism: Marx and Beyond

Religious Socialism and the Critique of Capitalism

Tillich became a religious socialist and a critic of capitalism after the First
World War. Before that he was conservative, nationalistic, and quietistic.
The son of a Prussian Lutheran pastor, he volunteered to serve as a chaplain
shortly after the war broke out in 1914. As the war dragged on, the death of
comrades, mass burials, horrors of combat, widespread devastations, and his
own suffering and mental breakdown led to radical changes in his thought.[7]
During the collapse of imperial Germany and the revolution during the last
year of the war, Tillich "began to understand such issues as the political
background of the war, the interrelation of capitalism and imperialism, the
crisis of bourgeois society, and the schisms between classes."[8] He soon

---

[6] Gert Hummel, "Hope for a New World: The Rappites' Eschatological Settlements" in
Paul Tillich's Theological Legacy: Spirit and Community (ed. Frederick J. Parrella; trans.
Doris Lax; Berlin: de Gruyter, 1995) 1–17; Wilhelm Pauck and Marion Pauck, *Paul Tillich:
His Life and Thought* (New York: Harper & Row, 1976; repr., San Francisco, Calif.: Harper
& Row, 1989) 276–78; *Encyclopedia Britannica Online*, s.v. "New Harmony," http://search.
eb.com/eb/article?eu=56861 (accessed 26 July 2003); *Encyclopedia Britannica Online*, s.v.
"Owen, Robert," http://search.eb.com/eb/article?eu=59239 (accessed 26 July 2003).

[7] See John R. Stumme's introduction to *The Socialist Decision*, by Paul Tillich (New
York: Harper & Row, 1977) x–xi; Ronald H. Stone, *Paul Tillich's Radical Social Thought*
(Atlanta, Ga.: John Knox, 1980) 32–38; Pauck and Pauck, *Tillich*, 40–56. It should be noted
that Tillich's turn from the political right to the left did not occur until the end of the war. As
a study of his sermons during the First World War shows, Tillich's thinking during the war
fit into "the broad stream of war theology of the national-conservative Protestantism of that
time" (Erdmann Sturm, "'Holy Love Claims Life and Limb': Paul Tillich's War Theology
(1914–1918)," *ZNeuerThG* 2 [1995] 62).

[8] *OB*, 32–33.

joined a group of intellectuals known as the "Kairos Circle," whose members were concerned with the rethinking of socialism and became increasingly convinced that the First World War brought forth the opportune time—indeed a *kairos*, i.e., a significant moment for a breakthrough of the divine into history—for decisive transformations. Tillich's religious socialism, expressed in *The Socialist Decision* (*Die sozialistische Entscheidung*) and a few essays,[9] was developed through the discussions in this group.[10]

In Tillich's view, religious socialism was the concrete embodiment of the prophetic tradition in the Hebrew Bible. Like the biblical prophets, especially the eighth-century prophets, he interprets the historical situation from the point of view of the divine or the eternal, identifies the evils in society and culture, and looks forward to a transformation of the present towards the goal of theonomy. Tillich interprets the epochal transformations in Germany and elsewhere in the world after the First World War as a special historic situation, a *kairos*, the breaking through of the eternal into the temporal, judging and transforming the latter.[11] For him, one crucial aspect of this *kairos* is that capitalism as a social and economic order with all sorts of evils "has been shaken to its foundations" and is on the verge of collapse, just as Marx had anticipated.[12] With such a belief, Tillich's critique of capitalism involves what Seyla Benhabib calls a "crisis diagnosis."[13]

Tillich regards capitalism as the most significant demonic power in the modern world and believes that it has led to many problems and crises, as

---

[9] Some of these essays are collected in *PE*.

[10] Stumme, introduction to *Socialist Decision*, xv–xvi; Pauck and Pauck, *Paul Tillich: His Life and Thought*, 70–74. For an in-depth study of Tillich's religious socialism in his German years, see John R. Stumme, *Socialism in Theological Perspective: A Study of Paul Tillich, 1918–1933* (American Academy of Religion Dissertation Series 21; Missoula, Mont.: Scholars, 1978).

[11] *TPE*, 46–47. *Kairos* is "the fulfilled moment of time in which the present and the future, the holy that is given and the holy that is demanded meet" (*PE*, 61).

[12] *RS*, 116. Although Tillich's expectation of the imminent collapse of capitalism eventually proved to be mistaken, it cannot be regarded as naïve. As Karen Vaughn points out, the social situation of Germany and the United States—with hyperinflation and high unemployment rates exacerbated by the Great Depression—in the 1930s would have reinforced such an expectation. Moreover, the view that capitalism was headed for collapse was shared at that time even by notable economists such as John Maynard Keynes and Joseph Schumpeter (Vaughn, "Theologians and Economic Philosophy," 15 with n. 22).

[13] Benhabib delineates three levels of critique in Marx's critical theory of capitalism: immanent critique, defetishizing critique, and crisis diagnosis (Seyla Benhabib, *Critique, Norm, and Utopia* [New York: Columbia University Press, 1986] esp. 102–33).

he writes, "The fundamental demonic phenomenon of the present day is the autonomy of the capitalistic economic system, with all its contradictions, and the mass disintegration and destruction of meaning in all spheres of historical existence which it produces."[14] However, as I shall explain later in this chapter, Tillich's concept of "the demonic" does not refer to something purely devilish. "The demonic" is also greatly creative.[15] For Tillich, to call capitalism a demonic force means that capitalism is a structural evil with enormous power not just in destruction but also in creation. He recognizes that capitalism "is the most fruitful method for producing goods that has ever existed" and that the "mechanism of the free market is the most effective machine yet conceived for balancing supply and demand."[16] He acknowledges that the rationalization of economy, a key feature of capitalism, would guarantee "the best possible provision for the greatest number."[17] He also appreciates the fact that capitalism has brought significant technological achievements, which have emancipated the masses from bondage and subjection to nature.[18] He points out, however, that intense competition in capitalism forces the entrepreneurs to increase the use of technology in production, which causes chronic unemployment in a large labor force and the overproduction of products beyond the consumption capacity of the market. The result is frequent and serious economic crises, which lead to increasing poverty, insecurity, despair, and meaninglessness for the masses. This, in turn, leads to growing class struggles between the proletariat and the bourgeoisie. Further, he suggested, overproduction and the increase of unproductive capital in the banks could cause imperialistic wars.[19] Since these problems and crises are rooted in capitalism itself, they can only be dealt with by overcoming capitalism. Therefore, "the attack on capitalism (in the sense of an economically established system of domination [*Herrschaftssytems*], not in the sense of market economy) is the first and permanent task of the

---

[14] *TP,* 47.

[15] We may understand Tillich's concept of the demonic as combining two senses of the word "demonic": "1. Of, belonging to, or of the nature of, a demon or evil spirit; demoniacal, devilish. . . . 2. Of, relating to, or of the nature of, supernatural power or genius" (*Oxford English Dictionary,* 2d ed., s.v. "demonic").

[16] *PTC,* 88.

[17] *SD,* 89.

[18] *SD,* 156. See also *RS,* 107–8.

[19] *TPE,* 224; *SD,* 90, 156; *TP,* 130–31.

socialist formation of society."[20] In a nutshell, Tillich, as a religious socialist, is unrelentingly critical of capitalism. Yet he does not regard it as something entirely bad. Rather, it is highly ambiguous. He is able to perceive the positive, creative, and beneficial aspects of capitalism, in spite of his belief that capitalism will eventually be self-destructive. Tillich thus takes a quite nuanced—or what he would call a "dialectical"—view of capitalism.

A Holistic Perspective

Tillich was deeply influenced by Marx throughout his career.[21] In his critique of capitalism Tillich acknowledges his indebtedness to Marx's analysis of capitalistic society.[22] This includes the following: the recognition that contemporary society is determined by the capitalist economy having the market at its center; the inevitability of class struggle as a structural necessity; the dialectical tendency of capitalism to overthrow itself; and the solidarity with the proletariat.[23] His religious socialism also affirmed some philosophical principles of Marxism, given that their distortions are rejected. These principles include the demand for the unity of theory and practice (which Tillich calls "existential thinking"), historical materialism, and dialectical methodology. Shortcomings in Marx's analysis do not invalidate its insight into the contradictions in the structure of capitalism, and such insight was, in Tillich's view, "confirmed by the catastrophes of the present world."[24]

Nevertheless, Tillich does not subscribe to any economic determinism, which is often attributed to Marx, in his critique of capitalism. He rejects the distortion of Marx's materialism into a "mechanistic economics" or a "metaphysical materialism." He stresses that the economic sphere is interdependent with other social and cultural factors and is not isolated. "The economic sphere is itself a complex sphere, to which all other spheres essentially contribute, so that they

[20] *MW/HW* 3:199.

[21] As a recent study argues, the influence of Marxism continued in Tillich's later writings. While Tillich after his emigration to America became more reserved if not silent about Marxism, he had appropriated already Marxist ideas (such as the concept of ideology, the proletariat, the philosophy of history, the praxis of knowledge, revolution, and materialism), which affected, inspired, and shaped his later theological thought. Brian Donnelly, *The Socialist Émigré: Marxism and the Later Tillich* (Macon, Ga.: Mercer University Press, 2003).

[22] *PE*, 48. Tillich admits that religious socialism has "learned more from Marx's dialectical analysis of bourgeois society than from any other analysis of our period" (*PTE*, xvii).

[23] *PE*, 48–49.

[24] *TPE*, 258–59 = *MW/HW* 3:481–82.

cannot be derived from it, although they can never be separated from it."[25] Since capitalism is embedded in an all-encompassing system of life, it can only be overcome together with this system (that is, with various aspects of life).[26] Therefore, the critique of capitalism cannot be confined to the economic sphere alone but must include other spheres—social, cultural, and psychological. Thus socialism, the system that Marx projected to replace capitalism, is not just concerned with the reorganization of the economic system but is concerned with the transformation of society in all its dimensions: "Socialism was the symbol of a profound cultural rebirth based on radical change of bourgeois-liberal-competitive society into a more proletarian-collective-united society, a new society transformed in all realms. . . . It represented a comprehensive vision of a creative and meaningful society in which the destructive implications of modern industrial technology would be minimized or overcome."[27] Moreover, as we shall shortly see, Tillich's critique of capitalism and his vision for transformation focus more on the cultural-spiritual, rather than the economic-material, dimension. His holistic perspective and cultural focus should be borne in mind as we examine the alleged depoliticization of Tillich in America.

Sharpening of the Cultural Focus

The Alleged Depoliticization of Tillich

"It has been a widely held assumption in Tillich scholarship that after Tillich came to America in 1933 he essentially gave up his Marxian and political interests and turned to the writing of his *Systematic Theology* and other cultural interests."[28] Most of Tillich's treatises and essays on religious socialism were written before his emigration to the United States in 1933 in

---

[25] *TPE*, 258 = *MW/HW* 3:481. "Economics is an infinitely complex, many-faceted reality. *All aspects of human being must be considered when economics is considered*. The latter cannot be isolated and made the cause of that which in fact is intrinsic to it, and without which it cannot be conceived" (*SD*, 116 [emphasis original]). See also *OB*, 87–88 = *IH*, 65; *TPE*, xviii.

[26] *MW/HW* 3:199.

[27] *HW/WH* 3:522. The quotation is from *ChrSoc* 15 (1949–1950) 19–22.

[28] John J. Carey, *Paulus Then and Now: A Study of Paul Tillich's Theological World and the Continuing Relevance of His Work* (Macon, Ga.: Mercer University Press, 2002) 36 n. 49. Carey points out that Donnelly's dissertation (published as *The Socialist Émigré*, see footnote 21 above) "refutes that assumption and demonstrates that Tillich drew heavily on Marx's thought for all of his career" (ibid.).

view of the increasing hostility of the Nazis towards him.[29] His critique of capitalism can still be found in works written in the first few years after the Second World War.[30] After that period, there is seldom direct and explicit criticism of capitalism in his works. Meanwhile, it seems that he is turning more to existentialism, psychoanalysis, and philosophical theology. This might add credibility to allegations that the American Tillich abandoned his former social-political concerns and reduced politics to theology.[31] Moreover, such allegations would seem to be supported by Tillich's own admission that the expectation of a *kairos* was shaken by the victory of fascism. The situation after the Second World War led him to doubt the viability of religious socialism:[32]

> I do not doubt that the basic conceptions of religious socialism are valid, that they point to the political and cultural way of life by which alone Europe can be built up. But I am *not* sure that the adoption of religious-socialist principles is a possibility in any foreseeable future. Instead of a creative *kairos*, I see a vacuum which can be made creative only if it is accepted and endured and, rejecting all kinds of premature solutions, is transformed into a deepening "sacred void" of waiting. This view naturally implies a decrease of my participation in political activities.[33]

Allegations of Tillich's depoliticization are based on a distorted interpretation of Tillich's thought. They ignore the continuity that exists within the development of his critique of capitalism and prevent one from understanding

[29] For an account of the historical events leading to Tillich's emigration to the United States, see Pauck and Pauck, *Paul Tillich: His Life and Thought*, 123–38.

[30] For example, "Storms of Our Times" (1943) in *TPE*, 237–52 and "The World Situation" (1945) in *TP*, 111–57 and *SSOTS*, 3–40.

[31] "Tillich's political and socialist thought became 'frozen' and we can see from the late 1940s the theologizing of most of the basic concepts of the 1920s and 1930s, which was completed in the almost totally apolitical text of *Systematic Theology*. This is in true sense the reduction of politics to theology" (Terence O'Keeffe, "Paul Tillich and the Frankfurt School," in *Theonomy and Autonomy: Studies in Paul Tillich's Engagement with Modern Culture* [ed. John Carey; Macon, Ga.: Mercer University Press, 1984] 87). A similar allegation is this: "What Tillich did . . . was essentially to abandon his earlier preoccupations with the broad social-political dimensions of history in order to offer a formulation ('New Being') more open to individualistic applications" (David Hopper, *Tillich: A Theological Portrait* [Philadelphia: Lippincott, 1968], quoted in J. Mark Thomas, intro. to *SSOTS*, xiii n. 2).

[32] *MW/HW* 3:527. Speaking at the Deutsche Hochschule für Politik in Berlin in 1951, Tillich remarks that "today we live in a period in which the Kairos, the right time of realization, lies far ahead of us in the invisible future, and a void, an unfulfilled space, a vacuum surrounds us" (*PE*, 180).

[33] *MW/HW* 3:527.

his intellectual career as a lifelong effort in the critical analysis of and response to capitalistic modernity. As the opening sentence of the paragraph quoted above indicates, the American Tillich upholds the validity of religious socialism. This can also be seen in his objection to the title ("Beyond Religious Socialism") of the article from which the above paragraph comes.[34] He asserts: "If the prophetic message is true, there is nothing 'beyond religious socialism.'"[35] For him, the apparent irrelevance of religious socialism is due to the character of the period after the Second World War.[36] In an unpublished speech in 1955, Tillich points out that, while his earlier religious socialism and his "later point of view" differ in several ways,[37] he continues to believe in the need to participate in "the fight for the fragmentary realization of the kingdom of God in history," in the interdependence of individual and social healing, and in the task of "[revealing] the special demonic powers" in the West. He described the threats to human beings by "the spirit of industrial society," such as the misery and injustice in some groups and "meaninglessness in the production of means for ends which again are means." He discussed the negative aspects of accommodation for the process of production and the subjection to methods of consumption.[38] These examples show that Tillich continued the critique of capitalism found in his earlier writings, even though he does not explicitly mention the word "capitalism." This is true throughout most of his American writings.[39]

---

[34] Paul Tillich, "Beyond Religious Socialism," *ChrCent* 66 (15 June 1949) 732–33. Also in *MW/HW* 3:526–29.

[35] Paul Tillich, "Autobiographical Reflections," in *The Theology of Paul Tillich* (ed. Charles W. Kegley and Robert W. Bretall; New York: Macmillan, 1952) 12–13.

[36] Elliot H. Shaw, "The Americanisation of Paul Tillich, 1945–1955" (Ph.D. diss., University of Lancaster, 1993) 196.

[37] For Tillich, the later view of religious socialism differs from the earlier view in the following ways: not to seek a radical transformation or revolution; not to calculate in terms of historical necessities; not to see any saving group or class; and not to have a total world view comprehensively describing a coming economy (Paul Tillich, "Past and Present Reflections on Christianity and Society," transcript of notes for remarks to the New York Christian Action retreat, May 1955, box 409:005, Paul Tillich Archives, Andover-Harvard Theological Library, Harvard University, Cambridge, Mass.).

[38] Ibid.

[39] One possible reason, in addition to those discussed below, for Tillich's omission of the term "capitalism" in his American writings is his view that, partly under the influence of Marxism, capitalism has undergone many changes in the twentieth century. In the mid-twentieth century, Anglo-Saxon countries have "mixed systems": "a controlled capitalism

McCarthyism and Tillich's Suppression of Marxist Themes

Tillich had good reasons to avoid a direct and explicit critique of capitalism in America. As Elliott Shaw's study shows, anti-communism, exemplified by McCarthyism, was prevailing in the post-1945 decade in the United States. Tillich might reasonably view McCarthyism as a threat and would avoid social-political criticisms that could let people associate him with communism. Tillich had already been blacklisted by the United States Army in 1945 and was temporarily denied permission to travel abroad owing to his chairmanship of the Council for a Democratic Germany, which was perceived as having a pro-communist bias.[40] At the same time, a number of Tillich's contemporaries encountered trouble because of the anti-communist atmosphere in this period. For example, Bertold Brecht, who had worked with Tillich on the Council, was required to testify before the House Committee on Un-American Activities regarding the alleged communist infiltration within the movie industry.[41] In this hostile atmosphere Tillich said that it was "dangerous" to write about Karl Marx, because one would be called "a Communist by many, especially by professional red-baiters."[42] Out of apprehension, he objected to the publication of the essay (already translated by James Luther Adams) "Class Struggle and Religious Socialism" (*Klassenkampf und religiöser Sozialismus*) and said that "it would destroy me in this country."[43] Also, such reservations led to Tillich's tendency to suppress favorable references to Marx or Marxist themes when writing or rewriting his manuscript for publication in the 1950s.[44]

---

in the United States and a market socialism in Great Britain" (Paul Tillich, "Rejoinder," pt. 2, *JR* 46 [1966] 190).

[40] Shaw, "The Americanisation of Paul Tillich," 13, 139.

[41] Ibid., see also 198.

[42] Paul Tillich, "How Much Truth Is There in Karl Marx?" *ChrCent* 65 (8 September 1948) 906. Tillich often clarifies that religious socialism is not Marxism or communism. "This is especially necessary in a country like the United States, where everything critical of nineteenth-century capitalism is denounced as 'red' and, consciously or through ignorance, confused with communism of the Soviet type" (*TPE*, xvii).

[43] James Luther Adams, "Introduction: The Storms of Our Times and *Starry Night*," in *The Thought of Paul Tillich* (ed. James Luther Adams, Wilhelm Pauck, and Roger L. Shinn, with assistance of Thomas J. S. Mikelson; San Francisco, Calif.: Harper & Row, 1984) 18; Jacquelyn Ann K. Kegley, prefatory note to "The Class Struggle and Religious Socialism," in *Paul Tillich On Creativity* (ed. Jacquelyn Ann K. Kegley; Lanham, Md.: University Press of America, 1989) 93; see also the *Textgeschichte* of the article in *MW/HW* 3:167–68.

[44] Shaw, "The Americanisation of Paul Tillich," 268. For example, Shaw observes that

Another consequence of Tillich's apprehension of political dangers was "the displacement of political concepts into the language of psychoanalysis."[45] For example, Shaw observes that Tillich used the concept of neurosis in the postwar period in a way that paralleled his use of the concept of ideology in the 1930s. Thus, instead of his alleged depoliticization, Tillich politicized psychoanalytic concepts. "In doing so Tillich was able to pursue a Marxist critique of society without employing Marxist language and, thus, to avoid exposing himself to the kinds of difficulties that some of his contemporaries encountered."[46]

Tillich's Focus on the Cultural Dimension of Capitalism

Tillich's avoidance of a direct—much less an overtly Marxist—critique of capitalism corresponds with his sharpened focus on the cultural-spiritual dimension of capitalism. This was already a key aspect of the critique of capitalism in his religious-socialist writings in Weimar Germany. As we have noted, Tillich's critique of capitalism can be characterized as having a holistic perspective and a cultural focus.[47] He was more concerned with cultural-spiritual problems, such as meaninglessness and dehumanization, than with economic-material problems, such as poverty and injustice. One can see this already in his early writings on religious socialism. For example, when analyzing the situation of the proletariat, he focuses on their insecurity, social exclusion, and hopelessness: "All this leads the proletariat to be conscious of the utter *meaninglessness* of its existence." Such meaninglessness is "the result of the fading of the religious background of Christian humanism and the dominion of the capitalist system."[48] Thus, for Tillich the goal of (religious) socialism is a meaningful society (*sinnerfüllte Gesellschaft*) in which the power of life of every individual and every group can actualize itself.[49]

Tillich suppressed "sympathetic references to Marx or Marxist themes" when he rewrote his Terry Lectures for publication as *The Courage To Be* (ibid., 406). Shaw also discovers that Tillich's unpublished English writings "suggest that he was anxious about the reemergence of the right in the United States and the growing power of exploitative capitalism" (ibid., 397).

[45] Shaw, "The Americanisation of Paul Tillich," 14.

[46] Ibid., 15.

[47] See page 18 above.

[48] "Class Struggle and Religious Socialism," in *PTC* 101–4 [emphasis in original].

[49] *MW/HW* 3:198. "The development of a meaningful society, in which the possibility exists to recognize the meaningful power of being of another, or, what amounts to the same thing, the formation of a community as the unity of power and love, is the socio-ethical ideal of religious socialism" (*PE*, 53 = *MW/HW* 3:214).

This focus on the psychological and spiritual effects of capitalism continues in his American career. In an address delivered in 1942, Tillich argues: "more important than the immediate economic consequence of the monopolistic stage [of capitalism] are its psychological effects on the masses." Thus, the worst element of monopolistic capitalism is "not the economic misery connected with unemployment but the feeling of absolute meaninglessness."[50] Such cultural-spiritual concerns in Tillich's critique of capitalism would not seem to reflect Marx's influence on him. After all, the critique of the economic-material dimension of capitalism—important for the Marx of *Capital* and for "orthodox Marxists"—does not play a significant role in Tillich's critique of capitalism. However, Tillich does seem to be profoundly influenced by the young Marx of the *Economic and Philosophical Manuscripts of 1844,* which "become an important source for Tillich's interpretation of Marx as a 'secular prophet' and an 'existentialist.'"[51] In particular, he acknowledges that he borrowed from the early Marxist concepts of alienation, objectification, and dehumanization.[52] These concepts play a crucial role in Tillich's critique of the cultural-spiritual dimension of capitalism and capitalistic modernity throughout his career. In the 1930s Tillich saw religious socialism as the countermovement to the dehumanizing tendency of capitalism,[53] and in 1949 Tillich still regarded Marx's concept of dehumanization as "particularly relevant to the fundamental problems of our time."[54] Near the end of his life, he remained convinced that the struggle against dehumanization "is as valid today as it was at that time," when religious socialism fought for the human dignity of the proletariat.[55] In fact, the critique of alienation, objectification, and dehumanization in capitalistic society is a recurrent theme in Tillich's later writings,[56] especially the existential analysis, in parts 1 and 4 of *Systemic*

---

[50] "Storms of Our Times," *TPE*, 240–41.

[51] John R. Stumme, introduction to *SD*, xix.

[52] *SD*, 171 n. 8; *MW/HW* 3:52223; Paul Tillich, "Between Utopianism and Escape from History," *CRDSB* 31 (1959) 32.

[53] *SD*, 133.

[54] *MW/HW* 3:522. Tillich does not explicitly refer to capitalism, he nevertheless points out that dehumanization is present in American culture. "We are being culturally and psychologically conditioned to fit into a system dominated by monopolistic industrial and financial power. And beyond this, machine technology itself fosters trends toward standardization, impersonality, and the stifling of creative freedom" (ibid., 3:523).

[55] Tillich, "Rejoinder," *JR* 46 (1966) 191.

[56] See, for example, "Thing and Self" (1958), "The Person in a Technical Society" (1953) and "Conformity" (1957), in *SSOTS*, 111–21, 123–37, 145–50.

Theology, of problems in epistemology and of ambiguities of human life. We shall see more of this in detail in the next chapter, in which I reconstruct Tillich's critical interpretation of capitalistic modernity. We shall also see that Tillich was not alone in his focus on the cultural dimensions of capitalism. In a similar way, the leading members of the Frankfurt School, especially Horkheimer and Adorno, who were good friends of Tillich, did not follow the political-economic critique of "orthodox Marxism" but developed a critique of the cultural dimension of capitalism in Western societies.

From the above interpretation of Tillich we can draw two conclusions. First, the critique of capitalism is a persistent thread in Tillich's writings. Such continuity should be emphasized, to counter the mistaken view that the "later Tillich" discontinued the social-critical thrust of his German years. Second, Tillich sharpened the focus of his critique of the cultural dimension of capitalism. Such critiques cannot be understood apart from his theology of culture, which is the subject of the next section.

Tillich's Critical Theology of Culture

Religion as the Substance of Culture

While Tillich adopted Marx's ideas and shared some similarities with the Frankfurt School in focusing on the cultural dimension of capitalism, he differed from them in offering a critique of capitalism from a distinctive *theological* perspective. This theological perspective is Tillich's theology of culture, which forms an integral part of his religious socialism.[57] One distinctive aspect of his perspective is that he does not consider a theological critique separable from social, cultural, and other critiques, i.e., that religion is not a separate sphere of culture but is actualized in and through various spheres of culture. This points to the inseparability and interdependence of what Tillich calls "rational criticism" (confined to the realm of reason, involving concepts and ideals, and presupposing definite standards and criteria) and "prophetic criticism" (possessing no criterion at all but proceeding from that which transcends form-creation).[58] On the one hand, prophetic

---

[57] "Though he later toned down its political substance, Tillich's theology of culture was originally conceived as a project within the tradition of religious socialism" (Gary J. Dorrien, *Reconstructing the Common Good: Theology and the Social Order* [Maryknoll, N.Y.: Orbis, 1990] 51; see also *TPE*, xvii).

[58] *PE*, 14.

criticism (proceeding, for example, from the expectation of the kingdom of God) must be informed by the concreteness of rational criticism (based, for example, on ideals of economic justice and political freedom).[59] On the other hand, rational criticism requires the transcendent, unconditioned ground of prophetic criticism:[60]

> In rational criticism prophetic criticism becomes concrete. In prophetic criticism rational criticism finds both its depth and its limit: its depth through the unconditionedness of the demand, and its limit through grace.[61]

The integration of both rational and prophetic criticisms in Tillich's critique of capitalism and capitalistic modernity will become evident later in this chapter and in the next chapter. In the meantime, we shall take a closer look at how his theology of culture informs his critique of capitalism.

As is evident from his first public lecture (an address to the Kant Society at Berlin in 1919), titled "On the Idea of a Theology of Culture,"[62] the religious interpretation of culture was Tillich's lifelong preoccupation. For him, religion is the substance or depth dimension of culture, and culture is the form or expression of religious substance.[63]

> Religion as ultimate concern is the meaning-giving substance of culture, and culture is the totality of forms in which the basic concern of religion expresses itself. In abbreviation: religion is the substance of culture, culture is the form of religion.[64]

---

[59] Tillich faults dialectical theology for overlooking "the indissoluble relationship between the theological ideal and all other ideals, and therefore of theological criticism and all other rational criticism." It unintentionally relegates everything related to theology to a separate domain of prophetic criticism. Thus it weakens religious criticism of other spheres and strengthens the existing status quo (*PE*, 13–14).

[60] "Even a critical social theory cannot avoid an 'ultimate' in which its criticism is rooted because reason itself is rooted therein" (Paul Tillich, review of *Reason and Revolution: Hegel and the Rise of Revolution*, by Herbert Marcuse, *SPhilSocS* 9 [1941] 478, quoted by Gary M. Simpson, *Critical Social Theory: Prophetic Reason, Civil Society, and Christian Imagination* [Minneapolis, Minn.: Fortress, 2002] 34).

[61] *PE*, 15.

[62] "Über die Idee einer Theologie der Kultur," in *MW/HW* 2:69–86. English translations in *WR*, 155–81 and *VS*, 19–47.

[63] Religion as substance, ultimate concern, or the dimension of depth is Tillich's "larger concept of religion" (*TPE*, xvi; *MSA*, 131; see also *TC*, 7–9).

[64] *TC*, 42. See also *TPE*, 57; *OB*, 69–70. An early formulation is this: "the basic substance of culture is religion and the necessary form of religion is culture [*der tragende Gehalt der Kultur ist die Religion und die notwendige Form der Religion ist die Kultur*]" (*MW/HW* 2:110).

The task of a theology of culture is to discover the ultimate concern, the holy, the unconditional ground and depth, in all aspects of cultural expression.[65] Crucial in this conception of the relation between religion and culture is the idea that *all* aspects of human culture—not only art and literature but also politics and economics and in fact all aspects of the self-creativity of the human spirit—are expressions of a religious substance, of an ultimate concern, of something holy and unconditional, which therefore can be interpreted religiously. The reverse is also true. Not only are all aspects of human culture the expression of religion, but religion as the substance of culture can *only* express and actualize itself in various cultural forms. As Tillich writes, "The substance, representing unconditioned meaning, can be glimpsed only indirectly through the medium of the autonomous form granted by culture."[66] He asserts, "All culture is actualized religion, and all religion is actualized as culture."[67] Tillich explicates the relation between form and substance as a triad of elements that constitutes every cultural creation: content (or subject matter), form, and substance (or import): "*Substance* [Gehalt] *is grasped in a content* [Inhalt] *by means of form* [Form] *and given expression.* Content is contingent, substance is essential, and form is the mediating element."[68] Content or subject matter can be anything selected from the universe. What is decisive is the form. "The form makes a cultural creation what it is—a philosophical essay, a painting, a law, a prayer." Substance is that which gives meaning or significance to form and its content.[69]

---

[65] *TPE*, 58; *ST* 1:39.

[66] *OB*, 70.

[67] *PE*, 63.

[68] "*Der Gehalt wird an einem Inhalt mittels der Form ergriffen und zum Ausdruck gebracht.* Der Inhalt ist das Zufällige, der Gehalt das Wesentliche, die Form das Vermittelnde" (*MW/HW* 2:76 [emphasis original]; see also *ST* 3:60). In translating the two sentences, I have consulted the following translations: *VS*, 27; *WR*, 165; John P. Clayton, *The Concept of Correlation: Paul Tillich and the Possibility of a Mediating Theology* (Berlin: de Gruyter, 1980) 197; as well as a slightly revised version of the *WR* version in Paul Tillich, "Religious Style and Religious Material in the Fine Arts" in *On Art and Architecture* (ed. John Dillenberger; trans. Robert P. Scharlemann; New York: Crossroad, 1987) 51 n. 3.

[69] *ST* 3:60. In Michael Palmer's view, import or substance, for Tillich, "is the name given to the unconditioned meaning intended in religion and is presupposed in every cultural creation" (Michael Palmer, "Paul Tillich's Theology of Culture," in *MW/HW* 2:12–15 [emphasis omitted]). According to John P. Clayton, Tillich's use of the terms *Inhalt, Form,* and *Gehalt* was not so much influenced by the philosophers of idealism as by his encounter with the visual arts, especially expressionism, during the First World War (Clayton, *The Concept of Correlation*, 193–99).

Tillich's theology of culture, like other forms of theology, deals normatively with religion.[70] Yet it does not deal with religion as a special "religious" sphere alongside culture, for religion, as the substance of culture, cannot be not a special sphere within culture.[71] Theology of culture is concerned with all aspects of culture as the expressions of its religious substance. Economy, politics, and international relations do not fall outside the proper concern of theology. Social and cultural movements are religious according to their innermost being and belong to various types of "non-ecclesiastical autonomous religion" (*nichtkirchliche autonome Religion*).[72] All of these are no less religious than those generally considered properly religious (such as church, mysticism, revelation), as they are the various ways in which the religious substance expresses itself. They are the proper subjects of a theology of culture.[73] In treating them as such, Tillich carves out a proper space for the relevance of theology to the social and cultural situation.

Religious Analysis of Capitalistic Culture

A telling example of Tillich's theology of culture is his first best seller, *The Religious Situation*.[74] One might expect him to discuss various religions and religious movements. Yet his book deals first of all with science and art, then with the religious situation in the economy, politics, and in relation to social problems; it follows all that with a discussion of religious movements

[70] As Tillich defined it in his 1919 lecture, theology is the "concrete normative science of religion" (*VS*, 20).

[71] *VS*, 25. This is a theonomous view of religion and culture. However, Tillich himself cautions that "a simple identification of religion and culture can never be asserted" (*PE*, 64).

[72] These types include romantic-conservative, utopian-revolutionary, critical-skeptical, and belief-ful realism (Paul Tillich, "Nichtkirchliche Religionen" [1929], in *MW/HW* 5:137–40).

[73] "In and through every preliminary concern the ultimate concern can actualize itself. Whenever this happens, the preliminary concern becomes a possible object of theology. But theology deals with it only insofar as it is a medium, a vehicle, pointing beyond itself" (*ST* 1:13). For example, "social ideas and actions, legal projects and procedures, political programs and decisions, can become objects of theology, not from the point of view of their social, legal, and political form, but from the point of view of their power of actualizing some aspects of that which concerns us ultimately in and through their social, legal, and political forms" (*ST* 1:13–14).

[74] Paul Tillich, *Die religiöse Lage der Gegenwart* (Berlin: Ullstein, 1926). For the German text and the English translation, I will use, respectively, *MW/HW* 5:27–97 and *RS*. Tillich mentions this book as an example of his theology of culture (*ST* 1:39). For the widespread reception of that book, see Pauck and Pauck, *Tillich*, 66, 98.

outside the churches. Only in the last chapter does it deal with the churches. As Tillich explains, "A book on the religious situation of the present must deal with the whole contemporary world, for there is nothing that is not in some way the expression of the religious situation." To look at the religious situation requires looking at the society which expresses it, for the "religious situation is always at the same time the situation of a society."[75] Religion, as Tillich conceives of it, deals with the relationship of human beings to the eternal. This relationship has two sides: the temporal (human) and the eternal (divine). If one proceeds from the temporal side, one will deal with churches, sects, theologies, and religious movements. Tillich's book, in contrast, proceeds from the side of the eternal. The religious situation then becomes "a question about the situation of a period in all its relations and phenomena, about its essential meaning, about the eternal which is present in a time."[76] Religion in its conventional sense is only a part of the whole picture. Moreover, in certain periods it is even less important or less effective than other phenomena in expressing the ultimate.[77] Tillich believed that the religious situation at his time was exactly so, as social concerns and political ideologies largely took up the functions and effects that religion in the narrower sense used to have.[78] He mentions this to explain why, in *The Religious Situation*, religious issues in the narrower sense occupy less space than social and cultural issues.[79]

While Tillich takes up politics, economics, social and intellectual movements, and so on, as legitimate and indeed significant subjects in his theology of culture, he does not study them in the way a political scientist, an economist, or a sociologist would do. As a theologian of culture, Tillich looks at them as various cultural forms or spiritual phenomena that express

---

[75] *RS*, 25, 39. "An ultimate concern must express itself socially. It cannot leave out any sphere of human existence" (*TC*, 178).

[76] *RS*, 37. Tillich maintains and develops a distinction (and an inseparable relation) between the narrow and larger senses of religion in his later writings. In *Theology of Culture*, the former is called, quite counterintuitively, "public religion," while religion in the larger sense (as the state of being ultimately concerned) is called "religion of the heart" (*TC*, 177).

[77] Ibid.

[78] "Political and social concerns have absorbed the energies of religion to such a degree that for great numbers of Europeans and Americans religious and political ideals coincide. The myths of the nation and of social justice are widely replacing Christian doctrine and have had effects that can be regarded only as religious even though they appear in cultural forms" (*OB*, 70–71).

[79] Ibid.

religious substance. Among these he seeks to identify the cultural form that most expresses the religious substance of his own time: "For every spiritual phenomenon of a period expresses its eternal substance, and one of the most important characteristics of a time-situation is found by considering which one of the various aspects of the spirit [i.e., culture] is most expressive of its real substance [*Gehalt*]."[80] To identify and to take seriously the dominant or most significant cultural form of an era is important in Tillich's theology of culture, because he perceives no other way to understand the religious situation of a given period except through understanding the cultural forms. Religion as substance can only actualize itself in culture, which is its form.

What then, in more concrete terms, is the "religious situation" of a society? By "religious situation," Tillich refers to "an unconscious, self-evident faith" (similar to what he later would call "ultimate concern"):[81]

> This unconscious faith which is not assailed because it is the presupposition of life and is lived rather than thought of, this all-determining, final source of meaning constitutes the religious situation of a given period. We must attempt to penetrate through to this faith.[82]

In *The Religious Situation*, Tillich looks at various aspects of modern Western society from the point of view of someone "located in the midst of a deeply shaken mid-European society."[83] He tries to "penetrate through" these aspects (science, metaphysics, art, economy, politics, ethical problems, social movements, mysticism, eschatological movements, and churches) to discover the religious situation or the "unconscious faith" that underlies these social and cultural forms.

Tillich analyzes the religious situation or the "unconscious faith" of Western society in terms of "the spirit of bourgeois society" (*der Geist der bürgerlichen Gesellschaft*),[84] which does not differ from Max Weber's

---

[80] *MW/HW* 5:30.

[81] *RS*, 40. The analysis of ultimate concern in culture is for Tillich the task of theology of culture, which he defines as "the attempt to analyze the theology behind all cultural expressions, to discover the ultimate concern in the ground of a philosophy, a political system, an artistic style, a set of ethical or social principles" (*ST* 1:39).

[82] Ibid.

[83] *RS*, 40.

[84] H. Richard Niebuhr, in most cases, translates *bürgerlich* as "capitalist" (see, for example, *RS*, 27, 219). It seems that "bourgeois" renders more faithfully the broader meaning of *bürgerlich*, which can refer to the capitalist class as well as the rationality, attitude, and

notion of "the spirit of capitalism."[85] It is not the spirit of a class or party but is rather "a symbol for an ultimate, fundamental attitude toward the world" and is thus wider than the bourgeois society in which it is most concretely visible and from which it gets its name.[86] The characteristic of such a spirit is "self-sufficient finitude" (*in sich ruhenden Endlichkeit*),[87] which is especially seen in the three spiritually powerful and representative products of the nineteenth century: mathematical natural science, technology, and the capitalist economy.[88] For Tillich, the unconditional domination of the capitalist economy most distinctly characterizes the spirit of capitalist society, and capitalism with all its consequences "determine[s] the religious situation of the present more than almost anything else."[89] Nevertheless, the spirit of bourgeois society was, in Tillich's view, being shaken and revolted against in every sphere of society and culture after the First World War.[90] He makes it clear in the preface that the purpose of *The Religious Situation* is to bear

---

practice of, or anything else pertaining to, that class that has become dominant in modern society. Moreover, the term "bourgeois society" coheres well with the crucial term "bourgeois principle" in *SD*. But the difference in translation should not obscure the fact that a bourgeois society is no doubt a capitalist society. Also, Tillich in at least one place uses "*der Geist des Kapitalismus*" instead of "*der Geist der bürgerlichen Gesellschaft*" for the same meaning (*MW/HW* 5:58).

[85] Mary Ann Stenger and Ronald H. Stone, *Dialogues of Paul Tillich* (Macon, Ga.: Mercer University Press, 2002) 152. See also Ronald H. Stone, *Paul Tillich's Radical Social Thought* (Atlanta, Ga.: John Knox, 1980) 55. Weber did not clearly define "the spirit of capitalism." The phrase seems to refer to an ethos of industrious and rational organization of conduct for profit seeking, which is regarded as morally desirable. For Weber, the spirit of capitalism had an elective affinity with the this-worldly asceticism of Puritan Protestants (working hard in a worldly calling in order to ascertain the sign of their divine election, while shunning the spontaneous enjoyment of life), and its origin in Europe can be traced to the unintended—in fact unwished—consequence of the latter. See Max Weber, *The Protestant Ethic and the Spirit of Capitalism* (trans. Talcott Parsons; intro. Anthony Giddens; New York: Routledge, 1992).

[86] *MW/HW* 5:27.

[87] I will explicate this concept in the next chapter. Put simply, "self-sufficient finitude" refers to an attitude characteristic of modern culture that shuts out the eternal while endlessly seeking this-worldly pursuits in the finite.

[88] *MW/HW* 5: 96, 32, 34, 36 = *RS*, 218, 42, 47, 52. The German original only has *die Wirtschaft* without specifying it to be "capitalist," as the English translation does. However, the economy in nineteenth-century European society was indeed capitalist. Also, the economic order analyzed in the book is nothing other than capitalism.

[89] *MW/HW* 5:53, 56 = *RS*, 105, 111.

[90] *MW/HW* 5:27, 96 = *RS*, 27, 52, 218–19. In particular, Tillich was certain that the capitalist economic and social order was being "shaken to its foundations" (*RS*, 116).

"effective testimony to the shaking of this spirit and hence to the shaking of our time by eternity."[91] He concludes the book by saying that all of his observations "can have meaning only for those who are themselves engaged in the movement" against the spirit of bourgeois society. Such people are not allowed to be nonparticipating observers but should speak about the contemporary religious situation "with unconditioned, active responsibility."[92] In other words, Tillich, in a spirit similar to that of Marx's eleventh thesis on Feuerbach,[93] regards his theology of culture, which *The Religious Situation* exemplifies, as oriented to social praxis and aims at the transformation of the spirit of bourgeois society.[94]

Tillich's Critique of Capitalism as Demonic

The previous section has given a general overview of Tillich's theology of culture and briefly mentioned Tillich's interpretation of the spirit of bourgeois society (or the spirit of capitalism) as the unconscious faith of Western society. This next section focuses on his religious critique of capitalism as demonic.

Tillich's theology of culture rests upon the idea that religion is the substance of culture and that culture is the form of religion. Religion should not be considered a separated sphere alongside culture.[95] However, the unity of religious substance and cultural form is only completely actualized in theonomy.[96] In the existing, hence fallen, world, religion and secular culture lie side by side as a duality.[97] That is because the kingdom of God has not

---

[91] *RS*, 27.

[92] *MW/HW* 5:97 = *RS*, 219.

[93] "The philosophers have only *interpreted* the world, in various ways; the point, however, is to *change* it" (Karl Marx, "Theses on Feuerbach," in *The Marx-Engels Reader* [ed. Robert C. Tucker; 2d ed; New York: Norton, 1978] 145).

[94] As a commentator points out, "Paul Tillich never forgot Marx's eleventh thesis on Feuerbach" and he wanted both to interpret and to change the world. "He sought relentlessly to probe the structures and dynamics of contemporary civilization, to question its purposes, to redirect it" (Roger L. Shinn, "Tillich as Interpreter and Disturber of Contemporary Civilization," in *The Thought of Paul Tillich*, 44).

[95] See page 27 above.

[96] Tillich's concept of theonomy is explicated in the next chapter.

[97] In Tillich's view, creation coincides with the Fall, which is the transition from essence to existence (*ST* 2:29–44). Tillich attributes the existence of "religion in the narrower and

yet come, and God is not yet all in all.[98] Moreover, in the existing world, the demonic, which means the embodiment of forms that contradict the divine and are therefore destructive and self-destroying, is always present.[99]

> In every culture, we find divine and demonic forms intermingled. Consequently, a simple identification of religion and culture can never be asserted. Religion always has a dual relation to culture. It contains within itself a No, a *reservatum religiosum*, and a Yes, an *obligatum religiosum*.[100]

The essential unity and the existential separation of religion and culture are, therefore, the basic premise of Tillich's critical and prophetic theology of culture. In order to struggle for a theonomous society, which is the goal of religious socialism,[101] his theology of culture aims to struggle against the demonic forms in culture and society. For him, the most decisive demonic power in modern society is capitalism.[102]

Tillich finds capitalism demonic in two primary aspects. First, it subjects all other spheres of human life to itself, deprives things of their intrinsic independent meaning, and leads to mass disintegration. Second, it causes class struggle and other destructive divisions in society.[103]

As the exemplar of "the spirit of self-sufficient finitude," capitalism is an autonomous economic system subject only to its own laws. It actualizes itself in the free market and in the unlimited possibilities of accumulating capital.[104] The rational attitude of capitalism removes the intrinsic qualities

---

customary sense" to the "tragic estrangement" of human spiritual life from its own ground and depth (*TC*, 8).

[98] *TPE*, 57, 59. That is, Tillich's synthesis of religion and culture is an "eschatological statement" (Terence Thomas, *Paul Tillich and World Religions* [Cardiff, U.K.: Cardiff Academic Press, 1999] 52).

[99] *PE*, 63.

[100] *PE*, 64.

[101] *PE*, 66.

[102] *IH*, 119 = *PTC*, 88. Tillich saw capitalism as "the central demonization founded upon Christian humanism and upon bourgeois society that represents it" and that has "decisive significance for the present situation" (*PE*, 50–51). The other influential demonic power is nationalism, which, in Tillich's view, is a reaction against capitalism (*MW/HW* 5:121 = *IH*, 119 = *PTC*, 88).

[103] *TP*, 48. Tillich notes that the problems of industrial capitalism have two aspects: the relationship between a person and things, as well as the relations of persons to each other. He remarks that the first aspect has been neglected in most economic theories (*PE*, 76).

[104] *RS*, 105–6.

of things and turns them into commodities. "The more a thing becomes a mere commodity, the less it exists in an *eros*-relation to the possessor and the less intrinsic power it possesses."[105] Things then become the object of the subjective will to power. The "desire for pleasure" and the "infinite desire for domination" take possession of things.[106] Thus, in the capitalistic economy, the attitude toward things is loveless (*eroslos*), without community (*gemeinschaftlos*), and dominating (*herrschaftlich*).[107] The loveless attitude toward things impoverishes personality through consumerism and leads to a mix of both constructiveness and destructiveness, and this mixture of the two contrasting aspects is a characteristic of the demonic. On the one hand, capitalism emancipates human beings from "finite holy things, which claim for themselves the holiness of the eternal," from "a sanctified bondage to things," from "the bonds of animal existence and from the merely fortuitous satisfaction of its needs."[108] On the other hand, it impoverishes personality by "pressing it into endless service in the rule over impoverished things," which, having lost their meaning, do not satisfy. Without a definitely directed love, the impoverished personality is driven "to engage in unending, ever-increasing, life-consuming activity in the service of unlimited wants. [Capitalism] means the domination of the economic function over all the other functions of life; its consequence is bondage to time and hence also the lack of time for attention to the eternal."[109] Also demonic in capitalism is the fact that it produces the mechanized masses in the service of a rational management of things.[110]

The demonic impact of capitalism on social relationships is, for Tillich, even more significant. He writes, "The infinite drive to dominate things, supported by the subjective eros of every individual, leads to an endless conflict of all against all."[111] In his view, the free market is "the manifestation of the conflict of interests, of the war of all against all, accepted as a principle,

---

[105] *PE*, 74.

[106] *PE*, 74. Even the subject will to power loses its intrinsic import and becomes a thing "in the oppressive process of a limitless economy" (*PE*, 74–75).

[107] *MW/HW* 5:54.

[108] *RS*, 107–8.

[109] *MW/HW* 5:54–55 = *RS*, 107–9.

[110] *MW/HW* 5:55–56 = *RS*, 109–111. Tillich also mentions other consequences of the domination of the capitalistic economy: Nation-states are drawn into the service of the imperialist will of the bourgeois class. Bonds of community are broken. Even ethical ideals become subservient to the economic end, with economic efficiency and impersonal charity, for example, being upheld as virtues (*RS*, 43–44).

[111] *PE*, 77.

hence of an activity motivated always by an impulse to seek one's own interests at the expense of others."[112] Such society-wide conflict is demonic in that the conflict is necessary to the maintenance of the capitalist economic system itself. Following Marx, Tillich sees the most important conflict generated by capitalism as the conflict between those who own the means of production and those who do not. It destroys human solidarity before the eternal.[113] Inasmuch as class struggle is a defense against injustice, it should be affirmed. He still considers class struggle demonic, however, as it "compels every individual to share in the destructive tendency of the system." Moral demands, such as the demand that one should renounce or minimize it, are ridiculous or "perhaps even a weapon in the class struggle."[114] Since class struggle is inherent in the structure of capitalism, capitalism itself is demonic.[115]

The Idea of the Demonic

We have been examining Tillich's critique of capitalism as demonic. The demonic (together with *kairos* and theonomy) is one of the most important concepts in Tillich's theology of culture and interpretation of history.[116] As early as the 1920s, he used the concept in many of his works, up to and including his last public lecture, "The Significance of the History of Religion for the Systematic Theologian,"[117] delivered ten days before his death.[118] He presents the classical formulation of the idea of the demonic in a long essay, "The Demonic: A Contribution to the Interpretation of History,"[119] published in 1926, the same year as *The Religious Situation* was published. Most of

---

[112] *MW/HW* 5:55 = *RS*, 109.

[113] *MW/HW* 5:55–56 = *RS*, 109–10.

[114] "The Class Struggle and Religious Socialism," *PTC*, 105.

[115] *PTC*, 105; *MW/HW* 5:55–56 = *RS*, 109–111.

[116] Tillich himself acknowledges this (*TPE*, xix).

[117] First published in Paul Tillich et al., *The Future of Religions* (ed. Jerald C. Brauer; New York: Harper & Row, 1966) 80–94; repr., Paul Tillich, *Christianity and the Encounter of World Religions* (foreword by Krister Stendahl; Minneapolis, Minn.: Fortress, 1994) 63–79.

[118] Pauck and Pauck, *Tillich*, 282–83.

[119] Paul Tillich, *Das Dämonische. Ein Beitrag zur Sinndeutung der Geschichte* (Tübingen: Mohr, 1926). I use the edition in *MW/HW* 5:99–123. There are two English translations: "The Demonic: A Contribution to the Interpretation of History" (trans. Elsa L. Talmey) in *IH*, 77–122, and "The Demonic: A Study in the Interpretation of History" (trans. Garrett E. Paul) in *PTC*, 63–91.

its content is historical and theoretical. Only in the final section does he talk concretely about the demonic forces of the present. However, like that of *The Religious Situation*, the aim of the essay is also socially-critical and prophetic, seeking to name, unmask, and resist the demonic forces of his time. In his preface to the essay, he points out that it is dangerous for the nonprophet to call the demon by name, but naming the demon can "strengthen the prophetic spirit of our time." That is why, he explains, he includes the final section on present demons, such as intellectualism and aestheticism in the theoretical sphere and capitalism and nationalism in the practical sphere.[120]

The Origins of Tillich's Idea of the Demonic

The idea of "the demonic" (*das Dämonische*)[121] was not an innovation of Tillich's, whose contribution lies in his retrieval and synthesis of the thought of various thinkers and traditions, which he made relevant for social and cultural critique in the twentieth century. He was most influenced by Jacob Boehme and Friedrich Schelling for the idea of the demonic, although Rudolf Otto was also influential.[122] Yet one should not overlook the German intellectual tradition as the general background for Tillich's view of the demonic.

The idea of the demonic can be traced to early Greek thinking, in which the word δαίμων (*daímōn*) was used to denote gods and divine powers. Until the fifth century the word could be used interchangeably with θεός (*theós*). Influenced by Greek popular religion, which saw the demon as a capricious supernatural being at work in terrifying events, Greek philosophy later incorporated demons into its system as intermediary beings.[123] As the *TDNT*

---

[120] *MW/HW* 5:99; *PTC*, 63. The other English translation in *IH* does not have the preface. "The preface to the essay, in the way that it portrays the risk connected with any effort to do battle with demonic powers, is a paragraph of almost singular personal intensity in Tillich's writings" (Robert Scharlemann, "Tillich's Religious Writings," *MW/HW* 5:11).

[121] The term "the demonic" (*das Dämonische* in German, το δαιμόνιον in Greek), as the neuter substantive of the adjective "demonic," conveys a twofold tendency: "its tendency away from mythology and superstition coupled with a romantic trend toward preserving the existential, though not ontic, reality of the demons" (Wolfgang M. Zucker, "The Demonic: From Aeschylus to Tillich," *TT* 26 [1969] 36).

[122] Tillich's biographers name Schelling as the source of Tillich's idea of the demonic: "It was in Schelling's thought that he first stumbled upon the idea of the demonic as the irrational potential in God, and to the Schellingian interpretation he remained faithful" (Pauck and Pauck, *Tillich*, 108).

[123] *Theological Dictionary of the New Testament* (ed. Gerhard Kittel; trans. Geoffrey W.

puts it, "Fundamentally, the whole Greek and Hellenistic view of demons is marked by the fact that everything demonic is brought into conjunction with the divine."[124] The Greek divinization of the demons was consistently resisted by New Testament writings, which portrayed the evil spirits as acting in fulfillment of the will of Satan by attacking the spiritual and physical life of the human being.[125]

In the Enlightenment the belief in the demonic became perceived as a superstition,[126] then Romanticism,[127] as a reaction to the Enlightenment, rejuvenated the idea of the demonic. The rediscovery of the demonic as a creative, as well as a destructive, potency of human beings and as a force that transcends moral categories of good and evil was ushered in by the cult of genius at the end of the eighteenth century. The artist, as an extraordinary person, was seen as being possessed by a supernatural power, that is, a "genius," which determined one's fate and drove one to greatness or despair—thus the demon became a genius.[128] This identification of genius and demon was, according to Zucker, "the root of the modern use of the concept of 'the demonic,' " which "appears to have been coined in the Jena circle of the early romantics to which men like [Friedrich] Schleiermacher, [Ludwig] Tieck , Novalis [the pseudonym of Friedrich von Hardenberg], and Friedrich Schlegel belonged."[129] Tillich, on the other hand, located the rediscovery of the demonic in the second period of Romanticism during the 1820s. While in the first period of Romanticism "the presence of the infinite in the finite" developed into a dominant theme, the second period of Romanticism showed a strong awareness of "the presence of the demonic in the finite."[130] At a time

---

Bromiley) s.v. "δαίμων, δαιμόνιον"; Zucker, "The Demonic," 35.

[124] *Theological Dictionary of the New Testament*, s.v. "δαίμων, δαιμόνιον."

[125] Ibid. In New Testament the much more common word for demon is δαιμόνιον. Also common is πνευμα ακάθαρτον (ibid.).

[126] *Religion in Geschichte und Gegenwart. Handwörterbuch für Theologie und Religionswissenschaft* (4th ed.; Tübingen: Mohr Siebeck, 1998–2005), s.v. "Dämonische, Das."

[127] "Romanticism emphasized the individual, the subjective, the irrational, the imaginative, the personal, the spontaneous, the emotional, the visionary, and the transcendental." *Encyclopædia Britannica Online*, s.v. "Romanticism," http://search.eb.com/eb/article-9083836 (accessed 23 June 2006).

[128] *Religion in Geschichte und Gegenwart*, s.v. "Dämonische, Das"; Zucker, "The Demonic," 41–42.

[129] Zucker, "The Demonic," 42.

[130] *HCT*, 383–84; *CTB*, 122.

when the Romantic movement had already faded out, Goethe repeatedly discussed the subject of the demonic with fascination.[131] His discussion on the demonic was appropriated by Otto, who then influenced Tillich.

In "Philosophical Background of My Theology,"[132] Tillich traces the origin of the idea of the demonic to a development of Augustine's idea of the divine will by the Franciscan School of medieval philosophy and particularly by Duns Scotus. According to this line of thought, the will of God appeared increasingly irrational, incalculable, inscrutable, and capricious. This idea, Tillich remarks, received substantial development by Jacob Boehme: "In the depths of the divine, there is both a divine and a demonic; there is something irrational which nobody can understand."[133] Schelling, who influenced Kierkegaard, further developed the idea, and it came to full development in Nietzsche, who in turn influenced the existentialist philosophers.[134]

What Tillich referred to as the demonic element in the depth of the divine was what Boehme called the *Ungrund* or abyss. From the abyss in God comes forth the will to self-manifestation and self-actualization, which stands in contrast to the abyss. The divine life is thus seen as a dialectical, theogonic process spurred on by opposing elements within it.[135] Boehme greatly influenced Schelling's ideas about the inner life of God,[136] and Schelling distinguishes three "potencies," principles, or atemporal moments in the divine life. The first is the abyss, which he calls the meontic nonbeing, the primordial form-negating principle, or the irrational or unconscious will to personal existence. The second is the rational will of love, and the third is the spiritual unity of the two. The first two principles, which are indissoluble in God, are dissoluble in human beings. This provides the possibility of good and evil.[137] As we can see below, Tillich's explication of the demonic follows a

---

[131] Zucker, "The Demonic," 43. For Tillich, Goethe was similar to Schelling in that he "in some way" also synthesized Kant's critical epistemology and Spinoza's mystical ontology (*HCT*, 438).

[132] *HW/MW* 1:411–20.

[133] *MW/HW* 1:415. Tillich could have mentioned the influence of Luther, who emphasized the reality of the demonic powers and saw the devil as closely related to, if not indistinguishable from, divine wrath (*HCT*, 246). Boehme was Lutheran.

[134] *MW/HW* 1:415.

[135] H. Frederick Reisz, Jr., "The Demonic as a Principle in Tillich's Doctrine of God: Tillich and Beyond," in *Theonomy and Autonomy: Studies in Paul Tillich's Engagement with Modern Culture* (ed. John J. Carey; Macon, Ga.: Mercer University Press, 1984) 138–39.

[136] *HCT*, 490.

[137] Reisz, "The Demonic, 139–43; Frederick Copleston, S.J., *Modern Philosophy: From*

line of thought quite similar to that of Schelling:[138] the ontological possibility of the demonic has its root in the dialectics of divine life.

Otto was also influential on Tillich's thought on the demonic.[139] His concept of the demonic was closely related to the concept of the numinous,[140] the holy that is experienced in human consciousness as *mysterium tremendum*, a mysterious, non-rational experience that is both awful (daunting) and fascinating (wonderful). For Otto, the feeling of "daemonic dread," which is the primordial experience of the numinous, lies at the root of the entire development of religion. From this root emerge "daemons" and "gods."[141] Otto refers to Goethe's emphasis on the ambiguity, irrationality, and incomprehensibility of the demonic: "It was not divine, for it seemed unreasonable; not human, for it lacked understanding; not devilish, for it was beneficent; not angelic, for it often displayed malicious joy. It was like chance, for it pointed to no consequence; it resembled providence, for it indicated connexion and unity."[142] For Otto, Goethe's account of the demonic shows features similar to his own description of the numinous: "the wholly non-rational, incomprehensible by concepts, the elements of mystery, fascination, awefulness, and energy."[143] Tillich's appropriation of Otto can be seen, for example, in his view of the demonic as not distinguished from the divine in the original, undifferentiated conception of the holy.[144]

---

the Post-Kantian Idealists to Marx, Kierkegaard, and Nietzsche (vol. 7 of *A History of Philosophy*; New York: Image Books, 1994) 131–33; *HCT*, 444–45.

[138] Schelling's influence on Tillich cannot be overestimated. Tillich himself said: "For what I learned from Schelling became determinative of my own philosophical and theological development" (*HCT*, 438).

[139] According to Tillich's biographers, Otto and Tillich discussed the demonic and "Otto either supported or inspired Tillich's ideas on the subject" (Pauck and Pauck, *Tillich*, 98).

[140] *Religion in Geschichte und Gegenwart*, s.v. "Dämonische, Das."

[141] Rudolf Otto, *The Idea of the Holy: An Enquiry into the Non-Rational Factor in the Idea of the Divine and Its Relation to the Rational* (trans. John W. Harvey; 2d. ed.; London: Oxford University Press, 1958) 6–7, 12–15, 31–32.

[142] Goethe, *Dichtung und Wahrheit* (bk 20) in *Sämtliche Werke* (ed. Cotta; vol. 25) 124, quoted in Otto, *The Idea of the Holy*, 152–53.

[143] Otto, *The Idea of the Holy*, 151.

[144] *WR*, 85–87. "The less developed a religion, the less it will distinguish the demonic from the anti-demonic, i.e., the divine. The sacred will be viewed as both divine and demonic" (*PTC*, 77).

Summary of Tillich's Idea of the Demonic

Having reviewed the origins of the idea of the demonic, we are now ready to examine in detail Tillich's own idea of the demonic. This is indispensable for understanding Tillich's critique of capitalism as demonic.

What is the demonic?[145] Tillich gives the following characterization:

> The demonic is a power in personal and social life that is creative and destructive at the same time. In the New Testament, men possessed by demons are said to know more about Jesus than those who are normal, but they know it as a condemnation of themselves because they are divided against themselves. The early church called the Roman Empire demonic because it made itself equal to God, and yet the church prayed for the emperor and gave thanks for the civic peace he assured. Similarly, religious socialism tries to show that capitalism and nationalism are demonic powers, insofar as they are simultaneously destructive and creative, and attribute divinity to their system of values. The course of European nationalism and Russian communism and their quasi-religious self-justification has fully confirmed this diagnosis.[146]

This paragraph highlights the basic characteristics of Tillich's conception of the demonic. To call capitalism demonic does not mean that it is simply evil. It means that capitalism 1) is a structure of evil which is both creative and destructive; 2) assumes the quality of holiness and demands religious commitment but is antidivine; 3) involves the claim of something finite to ultimacy, thus causing split and antagonism; 4) has the character of possession, which cannot be overcome by acts of goodwill or moral action but only by the structure of grace. An adequate understanding of this last aspect is crucial for correct social praxis.

The Demonic as an Ambiguous Structure

First, to call capitalism demonic means that it is a structure of evil characterized by the ambiguous unity of creative and destructive powers. Tillich stresses that the demonic is no individual act of evil based on the free decision of personality. Rather, it is "a 'structure of evil' beyond the moral

---

[145] Besides the essay "Das Dämonische," the following explication is based on "Der Begriff des Dämonischen und seine Bedeutung für die systematische Theologie" in *GW* 8:285–91; "The Philosophy of Religion," in *WR*, 27–121; and *ST*.

[146] *OB*, 79–80.

power of good will, which produces social and individual tragedy precisely through the inseparable mixture of good and evil in every human act."[147] In another instance, he specifies the demonic as "that destructive, blind, chaotic element which is implied in all powerful creating [sic] movements and drives them toward final dissolution."[148] As a union or intertwining of creative and destructive powers, the demonic is therefore both ambiguous and the source of ambiguity of everything that exists.[149] The demonic is not unambiguously destructive; in such a case, it would be satanic, which is the abstraction of a purely negative principle that cannot exist in itself but has reality only in the demonic, while the demonic still participates in the creative power of the divine.[150] As Tillich writes, "The demonic is ambiguous; it is both creative and destructive. So the demonic is the ground of everything creative but which, in the way in which it appears, becomes destructive."[151] Tillich reminds us that whenever one hears about a demonic power, one must always ask about the creative element before speaking about the destructive element.[152] He points out that capitalism, with its autonomous economics and the free market, is the most successful means that has ever existed for producing goods, for balancing supply and demand, and for increasing both want and satisfaction. The capitalist economy no doubt has the sustaining, creative, and transformative character of the demonic; yet its destructive power on society is also sweeping.[153] Thus, he explains, social demonic powers (which include capitalism), creative and destructive at the same time, are not to be found in weak social structures or in chaos. Rather, they are to be found in

---

[147] *TPE*, xx–xxi.

[148] *TP*, 35.

[149] Paul Tillich, *Dogmatik. Marburger Vorlesung von 1925* (ed. Werner Schüssler; Düsseldorf: Patmos, 1986) 214, cited in Uwe C. Scharf, "Dogmatics between the Poles of the Sacred and the Profane: An Essay in Theological Methodology," *Enc* 55 (1994) 277. Tillich describes the demonic as "the ambiguous ground of the creative" (*CTB*, 122).

[150] *TP*, 35; *PTC*, 65; Scharf, "Dogmatics between the Poles of the Sacred and the Profane," 278.

[151] "The Demonic in Arts," in *OAA*, 107.

[152] Ibid.

[153] *PTC*, 88–89. I have already mentioned Tillich's examples of the creativeness and destructiveness of capitalism on p. 23 above.

the most elevated, most powerful symbols of an era.[154] Thus the demonic carries a certain tragic quality.[155]

The Demonic as Antidivine Religion

Second, to call capitalism demonic means that it has the quality of the holy. Tillich perceives a polarity of the demonic and the divine in the holy, as he writes, "The demonic is the Holy (or the sacred) with a minus sign before it, the sacred antidivine [*das heilig Gegengöttliche*]."[156] It is still holy, but its holiness is antidivine.[157] It can assume the quality of the holy, for it is a breakthrough (*Durchbrechung*) from the same abyss from which the positive manifestation of the holy (divine grace) bursts forth.[158] Thus, the demonic is, in certain ways, similar to the divine to which is opposed:

> The demonic is the contradiction of the unconditioned form, an eruption of the irrational ground of any realization of form that is individual and creative. The irrational can contradict unconditioned form only when it clothes itself in forms and opposes these to unconditioned form. The demonic is never formless. In this respect it is like the divine. It is also like it in the fact that it is not reduced to form (that is, is not exhausted in it) but, rather, filled with import, it bursts form open. The demonic, like the divine, is perceptible in the ecstatic, the overwhelming, and the dreadful. But whereas the ecstatic element of

[154] *MW/HW* 5:107 = *PTC*, 72. Goethe holds a similar view. He includes Napoleon as an exemplar of the demonic, while excluding Mephistopheles (the devilish figure in *Faust*) because the latter is too negative. "The daemonic manifests itself in a downright positive and active power." (Johann Peter Eckermann, *Gespräche mit Goethe* [ed. A. v. d. Linden; part 2] 140ff., quoted in Otto, *The Idea of the Holy*, 152). We cannot be sure whether Tillich indeed borrowed from Goethe.

[155] "A situation is tragic in which the very elements which are most valuable by their very value drive it to self-destruction. This is the case with the humanistic elements contained in capitalism, as well as with the purpose of reintegration which is contained in nationalism, and with the expectation of justice which is contained in Bolshevism. All three in a tragic fate contradict their own original intention and are driving society as a whole, in the Christian West, toward self-destruction" (*TP*, 52). However, Tillich in his later writing makes a fine distinction between the tragic and the demonic (*ST* 3:102–3).

[156] *MW/HW* 4:148 = *WR*, 85. In the *Dogmatik* of 1925, Tillich describes the demonic as the "divine anti-divine" (Scharf, "Dogmatics between the Poles of the Sacred and the Profane," 278).

[157] *ST* 1:216.

[158] *MW/HW* 4:149 = *WR*, 86.

the divine affirms the unconditioned form and therefore creates forms, the ecstatic element of the demonic destroys form.[159]

Moreover, demonic forces are "not simply the negation of the divine but participate in a distorted way in the power and holiness of the divine."[160] In fact, the union of the form-creative and form-destructive power in the demonic—which accounts for its ambiguity—is actually rooted in the dialectic of the divine life, the depth of being, which is both the ground of being (*Seinsgrund*) and the inexhaustible abyss (*Abgrund*).[161] Influenced by Boehme and Schelling, Tillich sees the divine life as a dialectical process. The pairs of terms he uses vary. Adrian Thatcher finds in Tillich "the dialectic between being and non-being as it works out itself in three other areas of the ontology—between the ground and abyss of being, between the divine and the demonic, and between dynamics and form."[162] In affirming that God is living, Tillich asserts, one must posit an element of nonbeing in God's being, which establishes otherness.[163] The divine life would then be "the eternal process in which separation is posited and is overcome by reunion."[164] An alternative form of this dialectic is the dialectic between the abyss and the ground of being (which for Tillich constitutes the double symbol of the holy) or, using

---

[159] *PE*, 66. "The demonic has all the forms of expression that obtain for the sacred, but it has them with the mark of opposition to the unconditional form, and with the intention of destruction. The holy negativity of the abyss becomes demonic negativity through the loss of the unconditional form" (*WR*, 86).

[160] *ST* 3:102.

[161] *MW/HW* 5: 103 = *PTC*, 67. See also *GW* 8:286.

[162] Adrian Thatcher, *The Ontology of Paul Tillich* (Oxford: Oxford University Press, 1978) 49. Peter Slater offers a similar interpretation: "As is well known to Tillich scholars, Schelling, in opposition to Hegel, conceived of the ground and abyss in such a way as to affirm the dialectical movement of divine power without assuming that in history this always works out for the best. The divine ground is dipolar, divine-demonic, so that every subsequent stage in living development has its obverse side, affirmative-negative or negative-affirmative" ("Dynamic Religion, Formative Culture, and the Demonic in History," *HTR* 92 [1999] 95–110).

[163] *ST* 3:284. "Nonbeing belongs to being, it cannot be separated from it. . . . being must be thought [of] as the negation of the negation of being" (*CTB*, 179).

[164] *ST* 1:242. "Being has nonbeing 'within' itself as that which is eternally present and eternally overcome in the process of the divine life" (*CTB*, 34). "Nonbeing makes God a living God. Without the No he has to overcome in himself and in his creature, the divine Yes to himself would be lifeless" (*CTB*, 180).

another set of polar elements, the dialectic between depth and form.[165] The dialectical tension between the polar elements is the root of the possibility of the demonic:

> The possibility of the demonic is based on the fact that the holy is always at the same time the unconditioned support and the unconditioned claim, that it is at the same time depth and form, ground and abyss; and that in the creature these elements can separate; that the creature wants to drag into itself the inexhaustibility of the divine depth, to have it for its own, and thus the creative potency becomes destructive. For creation is where abyss and form are united in one entity, and destruction is where the abyss elevates itself and shatters the form.[166]

The nuanced position that Tillich articulates is this: The possibility of the demonic has the same root as the possibility of divine creation. "The demonic, the anti-divine principle . . . nevertheless participates in the power of the divine."[167] Even so, it remains a mere potentiality. The possibility of the demonic only becomes actual when the unity of abyss and ground (or depth and form) is broken. This occurs in the creature, when it intends to seize the infinity of the divine depth; thus the abyss (or depth) turns destructive and shatters the form. We may then understand the relation between the divine and the demonic in this way: the divine consists of the polar elements in essential unity, while the demonic consists of the polar elements in existential separation.

---

[165] *WR*, 82. For Tillich, abyss and ground correspond respectively to Otto's *tremendum* and *fascinosum*. *ST* 1:216; Thatcher, *Ontology of Paul Tillich,* 55, 57–58. "Abyss" and "ground" can be found in Tillich's account of the first trinitarian principle, which he calls "the abyss of the divine," "the divine depth," "the inexhaustible ground of being," and "the power of being infinitely resisting nonbeing, giving the power of being to everything that is" (*ST* 1:250–51). For Tillich, without the second principle, which he describes as "the fullness of the divine," "the divine *logos*," and "the principle of meaning and structure," the first principle is "chaos, burning fire" and "is demonic, is characterized by absolute seclusion, is the 'naked absolute' (Luther)" (ibid.).

[166] *GW* 8:286 [translation mine]. I have consulted the translation of James Luther Adams, *Paul Tillich's Philosophy of Culture, Science, and Religion* (New York: Harper & Row, 1965) 230. "The power of the demonic is therefore divine power. There is no power at all outside or other than the power of God, but the manner of the manifestation of demonic power within existence is what makes it perverse and destructive" (Thatcher, *Ontology of Paul Tillich,* 63).

[167] *CTB*, 34.

The form of being [*Seinsgestalt*] and the inexhaustibility of being [*Seinsunerschöpflichkeit*] belong together. Their unity as depth of essence as such is divine; their separation in existence, the relatively independent breaking forth of the "abyss" in things, is demonic. . . . In the demonic, on the other hand, the divine, the unity of ground and abyss, of form and the consuming of form, is still contained; therefore, the demonic can come to existence, admittedly in the tension of both elements. The tension is actually in the thing, in which the demonic is borne.[168]

Everything contains both the drive to realize its form and the drive to break through the limit of form to realize the inexhaustible abyss in itself. Demonic distortion results from the formless breaking forth out of the will-to-infinity (*des Unendlichkeitswillens*).[169] "Demonry is the form-opposing breaking forth of the creative ground in things."[170]

The holy, ecstatic quality of the demonic, its intricate relation with the divine, and its will to infinity give the demonic, including capitalism, a religious or quasi-religious character. In fact, the demonic is "antidivine religion."[171] "Wherever the demonic appears, it shows religious traits, even if the appearance is moral or cultural."[172] He mentions a few examples of "distorted self-transcendence," such as the unconditional demands for commitment by states, the cultural domination of scientific absolutism, the self-idolization of individuals, and the historical Roman empire.[173]

The Demonic as Self-Elevation to Infinity

Third, to call capitalism demonic means that it has a claim to infinity or ultimacy. This claim causes social division and class struggle. The self-elevating claim to ultimacy or infinity or divinity by something finite is, in Tillich's later writings, the definition of the demonic.[174] This development is

---

[168] *MW/HW* 5:103 [translation mine]. As one scholar puts it, "the demonic can come into being only as a creaturely existence comes into being" (Vernon R. Mallow, *The Demonic: A Selected Theological Study: An Examination into the Theology of Edwin Lewis, Karl Barth, and Paul Tillich* [Lanham, Md.: University Press of America, 1983] 115).

[169] *MW/HW* 5:103.

[170] *MW/HW* 5:103 [translation mine; emphasis omitted].

[171] *PE*, 66.

[172] *ST* 3:103.

[173] *ST* 3:103.

[174] *ST* 3:102, 344. According to Tillich's earlier definition, the demonic is an antidivine structure of evil with an ambiguous mixture of creative and destructive elements, and the

related to his understanding of holy objects: "Holy objects are not holy in and of themselves. They are holy only by negating themselves in pointing to the divine of which they are the mediums. If they establish themselves as holy, they become demonic."[175] In such a case, the symbols or mediums of one's ultimate concern become one's ultimate concern. Considered inherently holy, they become idols.[176] The demonic is then a distortion of self-transcendence (religion) by identifying a particular, finite medium of holiness with the holy itself.[177] The ambiguous is deified.

> The demonic is a negative absolute. It is the elevation of something relative and ambiguous (something in which the negative and the positive are united) to absoluteness. The ambiguous, in which positive and negative, creative and destructive elements are mingled, is considered sacred in itself, is deified.[178]

Unlike his earlier writings where the demonic is a destructive breakthrough from the inexhaustible abyss of being, here the accent falls on the act or change of the object by which it becomes demonic, rather than the ontological origin of that act or change.[179] Nevertheless, the later view is implicit in the earlier one, since there is in everything an ontological will-to-infinity seeking to break through the limit of form.[180]

In capitalism, according to Tillich, the claim or drive to infinity takes a particular form, which might be called "infinite finitude."[181] As we have seen in *The Religion Situation*, Tillich characterizes the spirit of capitalism as "self-sufficient finitude," which means something always restless, never self-transcendent, and characterized by a limitless drive to acquire things,

---

destructive element breaks through. His later definition highlights the aspects of the will-to-infinity, self-elevation, self-deification, and self-destructiveness in the demonic. Such highlighting entails a shift in focus rather than a substantial change in meaning.

[175] *ST* 1:216.

[176] *ST* 1:216.

[177] *ST* 3:102.

[178] *MSA*, 132–33.

[179] Tillich's ambiguous notion of the demonic is succinctly expressed by an author: "On the one hand the demonic seems to be a breakthrough of the divine creativity gone awry. On the other hand it seems to be the elevation of the finite to the infinite, so that it is hard to distinguish the demonic from idolatry." Jerome A. Stone, "Tillich and Schelling's Later Philosophy," in *Kairos and Logos: Studies in the Roots and Implications of Tillich's Theology* (ed. John J. Carey; Macon, Ga.: Mercer University Press, 1984) 28.

[180] *MW/HW* 5:103.

[181] Tillich actually uses the term "infinite finitude" in *RS*, 107.

as exemplified in people engaging in unceasing and ever-increasing activity to satisfy their unlimited wants.[182] In volume 3 of his *Systematic Theology,* Tillich also alludes to the "infinite finitude" of capitalism in pointing out the need for a theonomous solution to "the indeterminate freedom of producing means for ends which in turns become means, and so on without limit"; he mentions as an example the gearing of a whole economy to the production of the "gadget."[183] This self-elevation of the finite to infinity is demonic.

Even more important in Tillich's critique of the demonic character of capitalism is its inevitable causing of class conflict, which has to do with the claim of its finitude to infinity. Tillich argues that "a main characteristic of the demonic is the state of being split."[184] He explains:

> This is easily understandable on the basis of the demonic's claim to divinity on a finite basis: the elevation of one element of finitude to infinite power and meaning necessarily produces the reaction from other elements of finitude, which deny such a claim or make it for themselves. The demonic self-elevation of one nation over against all the others in the name of her God or system of values produces the reaction from other nations in the name of *their* God.[185]

The paragraph from *Systematic Theology* quoted here does not mention as an example the formation of class struggle due to the self-elevation of the bourgeois class to infinite power and meaning in capitalism,[186] but the idea is already found in *The Religious Situation* where Tillich talks about the development of class conflict in capitalist society as an expression of its demonic character: "The component elements of the self-sufficient finite world regard themselves as absolute, each in its own right, instead of seeing themselves as complementary pointers toward the eternal."[187] Conflict between the bourgeoisie and the proletariat is perhaps the most important aspect of the society-wide conflict produced by capitalism. Like the specific case of class antagonism, such universal conflict also originates in the drive to infinity in capitalist society. "The infinite drive to dominate things,

---

[182] *RS*, 108–9.

[183] *ST* 3:259.

[184] *ST* 3:103.

[185] *ST* 3:103.

[186] Tillich's omission of class struggle in his *Systematic Theology* might be due to his apprehension about the potential harm of using Marxist ideas in the United States at his time. See p. 9 above.

[187] *RS*, 110.

supported by the subjective eros of every individual, leads to an endless conflict of all against all."[188]

Before we go to the next point, it is appropriate here to take up one remark made by Tillich in his critique of the demonic character of capitalism. He maintains that one should not reduce the demonic element in capitalism to the level of general sinfulness by invoking religious-moral categories such as the "service of mammon." Sinfulness is indeed the general presupposition of every demonic power: "But the genuinely demonic—if this word is to have a specific meaning—is found only where this general sinfulness is combined with a positive, sustaining, creative-destructive form."[189] It is tempting to interpret Tillich's definition of the demonic in later writings—the self-elevation of something finite to infinity—simply as idolatry.[190] To be sure, the idolatrous element is present in the demonic, in its claim to ultimacy or divinity, yet Tillich's emphasis falls on the "split" it produces.[191] In other words, he is concerned not so much with the "vertical" dimension of the demonic as with the "horizontal." More important, "idolatry" suggests a moral failure (sinfulness) on the part of the human individual or community, the solution to which is repentance, that is, changing one's attitudes and behaviors. Thus, we hear the prophetic message in the Bible calling for the people of God to repent, to renounce idolatry, and to worship the true God. However, the solution to the demonic is not repentance and moral improvement. Tillich underscores the inevitability and surpassing power of the demonic, "in the face of which all moralizing is doomed to impotence."[192] Tillich repeatedly stresses exactly the structural, superhuman, and overwhelming nature of the demonic. In his view, a correct understanding of such nature is important

---

[188] *PE*, 77.

[189] *PTC*, 89.

[190] Cf. Tillich's definition of idolatry: "Idolatry is the elevation of a preliminary concern to ultimacy. Something essentially conditioned is taken as unconditional, something essentially partial is boosted into universality, and something essentially finite is given infinite significance (the best example is the contemporary idolatry of religious nationalism)" (*ST* 1:13).

[191] See *ST* 3:103. Talking in 1956 about the demonic nature of the cold war, Tillich also stressed the "split" consciousness that the demonic structure of the cold war produces: "One of the most conspicuous demonic structures in history is the present cold war. We are in a continual social neurosis by the split consciousness and possession which is implied in this inescapable structure, in which everything which is done is, either in reality or by suspicion of the other, that which strengthens the destruction of mankind" (*OAA*, 107).

[192] *IH*, 120.

for a correct social praxis that will not fall into optimism or pessimism. This will become clear in the next point.

The Demonic as Possession

Fourth, to call capitalism demonic means that it has the character of possession. We have already seen in the first point above that the demonic is a structure of evil with both creative and destructive powers. In using the term "structure," Tillich means that it is inescapable, inevitable, limiting of individual freedom, and going beyond the moral power of goodwill.[193] As he emphasizes, the demonic is metaphysical perversion, not ethical defect. It does not lie in personal decision. It has the character of a superpersonal power and, indeed, a "possession."[194] It destroys the unity and freedom at the center of personality and takes away personal autonomy.[195] Likewise, social demonic powers have effects similar to those of possession. They shatter the spiritual autonomy of the personality.[196] World-transforming action is no solution for social demonic powers, for their power can put "the good will" into their service against its will.[197] That is how Tillich can say: "Demonic structures in the personal and communal life cannot be broken by acts of freedom and good will. They are strengthened by such acts—except when the changing power is a divine structure, that is, a structure of grace."[198] Only a structure of grace alone is able to overcome the possession of the demonic, which is a structure of evil. He continues: "If evil has demonic or structural character limiting individual freedom, its conquest can come only by the opposite, the divine structure, that is, by what we have called a structure or 'Gestalt' of grace."[199]

---

[193] *TPE*, xx–xxi.

[194] Tillich's word is *überpersönlicher*, meaning "beyond the personal."

[195] *GW* 8:287.

[196] *IH*, 92 = *PTC*, 72.

[197] *GW* 8:288.

[198] *ST* 3:103. For Tillich, the "latent church" (or what he calls the "Spiritual Community" in *ST*) is a structure of grace (*TPE*, xxi, 206–21).

[199] *TPE*, xxi. For Tillich, demonic possession and grace are structurally similar, corresponding states. Both elevate the spirit above autonomous isolation and use the same powers. Their only difference is that while grace unites these powers to the highest form, thereby giving the subject both form and meaning, possession uses these powers to contradict the highest form, destroying meaning and form (*IH*, 87–88 = *PTC*, 70).

Tillich believed that the effect of capitalism on society and on every individual resembles that of demonic possession.[200] Everyone is inevitably drawn into the limitless and unceasing processes of the capitalist system. The most important process is class struggle, which results from the demonic structure of capitalism:

> No men in our time, regardless of whether they belong to the bourgeois or the proletarian group, can escape the permanent and essential contradictions of the capitalist system. The most obvious and basic of these contradictions is the class struggle that is going on at every moment, both from above and from below. No one can avoid having a part in it, since in capitalism it necessarily produces the struggle for existence. This does not mean that anyone should or could accept the class struggle as desirable. It is the symptom of a disease, or, symbolically speaking, it is the symptom of a demonic possession in the grip of which modern society lives.[201]

Contributions of Tillich's Idea of the Demonic

Tillich's idea of the demonic enables a more nuanced theoretical critique of capitalism and a more realistic praxis in response to capitalism. Tillich is convinced that recognizing the demonic qualities of capitalism (among other social demonic powers) is crucial for a correct attitude to social praxis. He laments that people are least conscious about demonic powers in the social sphere. One might see problems, needs, even sinfulness, but not the unique dialectic of the great powers in society. Without understanding the social demonic powers, one is left with two alternate responses to capitalism that are both, in Tillich's estimation, socially and ethically impotent. The first possible response is to believe that the defects and meaninglessness of the society can be improved or overcome by progressive reform. This belief does not recognize the demonic in society; it is thus somehow utopian in outlook and will be disappointed by the destructive outbreak of major social demonic powers. The second possible response to capitalism is resignation or religious indifference over the shortcomings of the power relations in society; it is the

---

[200] *PE*, 50.

[201] *TPE*, 168. Tillich did not have the benefit of looking back on the fading of the discourse of class struggle in capitalist societies due to the development of the welfare state, the appeal of economic neoliberalism, or the ever-changing situation and configuration of the working class as a result of the globalization of labor and capital. Yet, if he had lived up to now, he would still identify the demonic in the ubiquity and apparent inescapability of the market, competition, and consumerism.

insistence on conservative preservation. One sees the facts of the demonic with perspicacity but does not recognize them religiously as demonic; one sees them as profane realities that one can only feel sorry about, believing that this resignation is the only viable religious position with respect to the hope of an otherworldly consummation.[202] However, the religious concept of the demonic goes beyond the impasse of these two views towards a more realistic and religiously informed social praxis beyond optimism and pessimism:

> The knowledge of the dialectic of the demonic leads beyond these opposing views. It leads to the recognition of an anti-positive that is overcome not through progress, nor through mere revolution, but through creation and grace. At the same time it leads one to take account of the particular demonries of every social situation so as to identify and fight against them. The struggle against the demonries of an era becomes an unavoidable religious-political duty. Politics gets the depth of a religious action. Religion gets the concreteness of a struggle with the "principalities and powers."[203]

As he says further, "the church authorities are obliged to challenge demonries in mental, social, and political life, from the point of view of the coming of the kingdom of God. The anti-demonic struggle of the Church is to be considered the continuation of the victory of Christ over the demonic powers."[204]

However, Tillich is quick to caution that no way can be devised to overcome cultural and social demonic powers: "The question about ways and means is the question of intellectualism. Thus it is already a question originated from the demonic situation. Every answer to it strengthens the demon. *Demonry breaks only before the divine, possession before grace, the destructive before the redeeming destiny.*"[205] We are unconditionally demanded, he says, to unmask the demonic, using every possible weapon of resistance, but we can expect no certainty about the results.[206]

> The only thing that is certain is that the demonic is overcome in eternity, that it is united with the clarity of the divine in the eternal

---

[202] *GW* 8:290–291; *IH*, 115–116 = *PTC*, 86–87.

[203] *MW/HW* 5:120 [translation mine; emphasis in original].

[204] "The Church and Communism," *RelLife* 6 (1937) 347–57.

[205] *MW/HW* 5:123 [translation mine; emphasis in original]. For Tillich, intellectualism does not mean an excess of the intellect and rationality. Rather, it means the violation of the whole of reality by the rational subject (*HW/MW* 5:121 = *PTC*, 87).

[206] Ibid. He expresses a similar idea as he rejects the progressive view of history; see "The Decline and the Validity of the Idea of Progress," in *SSOTS*, 94–95.

depths of the divine. It is only with a view to the eternal that we may speak of overcoming the demonic, and not in reference to any specific time, whether in the past or the future. But—that we can even glimpse the eternal, that we need not grant the demonic the same right as the divine. . . . That is what, in the final analysis, breaks the dominion of the demonic in the world.[207]

From what we have seen above, Tillich's religious critique of capitalism as demonic avoids several pitfalls in the theological critique of capitalism. First, by stressing the demonic as the union of both destructive and creative powers, Tillich avoids the pitfall of seeing capitalism as entirely bad, for instance, as the worst form of evil or as the "beast" in the Book of Revelation,[208] thereby assigning it a place in the apocalyptic struggle between Christ and Anti-Christ. From Tillich's perspective, such a view fails to recognize the profound ambiguity of capitalism. Also, such a view can easily become a self-elevation and absolutization of communities and movements that are fighting against capitalism, which may themselves thus succumb to the demonic. Second, by stressing the structural and superpersonal character of the demonic, Tillich avoids the pitfall of judging capitalism moralistically in terms of the idolatry of wealth or the market.[209] To be sure, we perceive a strong idolatrous element in the claim of the market to infinity or ultimacy. The concepts of idolatry and the demonic nevertheless differ in connotation and focus. The former underscores the aspect of "freedom," stressing the fact that idolatry is, in the final analysis, created and sustained by human beings

---

[207] *HW/MW* 5:123 = *PTC*, 90.

[208] One statement issued by the Ecumenical Association of Third-World Theologians has the following words on capitalism: "Like a huge idol, like the Beast in the Apocalypse (Rev 13), the present economic system covers the earth with its open sewer of unemployment and homelessness, hunger and nakedness, despair and death. . . . In its insatiable greed for prosperity, it offers people themselves as sacrifice in a bloody holocaust, pre-eminently in the Third World but increasingly in the First World too. The Beast has become a ravening monster, armed to the teeth with tanks and guns, atomic bombs . . . ." (*Herausgefordert durch die Armen. Dokument der Ökumenischen Vereinigung von Dritte-Welt Theologen 1976–1986* [Freiburg, 1990] 156–57, quoted in Jürgen Moltmann, *The Coming of God: Christian Eschatology* [trans. Margaret Kohl; Minneapolis, Minn.: Fortress, 1996] 216).

[209] On the idolatry of wealth, see John Cobb Jr., "Liberation Theology and the Global Economy," in *Liberating the Future: God, Mammon, and Theology* (ed. Joerg Rieger; Minneapolis, Minn.: Fortress, 1998) 32. On the idolatry of the market, see Jung Mo Sung, "Hunger for God, Hunger for Bread, Hunger for Humanity: A Southern Perspective," in *Hope and Justice for All in the Americas: Discerning God's Mission* (ed. Oscar L. Bolioli; New York: Friendship, 1998) 40.

and thus is a moral problem. The second underscores the aspect of "destiny," stressing the fact that human beings are "thrown" into the givenness of such idolatrous situation and are not so free to think or to do otherwise.[210] The nature of capitalism seems to fit better with the latter.[211] Third, stressing that the demonic can only be overcome by a divine structure of grace, Tillich rejects the certainty that capitalism as demonic can be defeated or transformed by human effort and thus avoids the pitfall of utopian fanaticism in social praxis, which easily turns into disillusioned cynicism and despair if human efforts turn out to be in vain.

Nevertheless, the use of Tillich's concept of the demonic in the critique of capitalism is not without problems. There is a tension between criticizing the demonic *character* of capitalism and the demonic *elements* of capitalism. Regarding religious socialism, Tillich believes that "its most decisive religious task in behalf of the present society is to participate in exposing and combating a demonic capitalism."[212] In calling for struggle against capitalism, he does not entertain any possibility of reforming capitalism.[213] This seems to imply the first position, that is, the criticizing of the demonic character of capitalism. His position is actually more nuanced, however, as he identifies the "demonic element" in bourgeois society and emphasizes that in every culture one finds "divine and demonic forms intermingled."[214] Even more significant are the remarks that follow his statement that "the struggle against the demonries of an era becomes an unavoidable religious-political duty":[215]

> Certainly this cannot mean that one phenomenon could be designated simply as demonic and another simply as divine. The conflict of the two principles penetrates every person and every phenomenon. Any institution or community that wanted to withdraw from this judgment would degenerate into pharisaic demonry. But perhaps it is necessary to look at demonic symbols in the particular forms which a society

[210] Freedom and destiny constitute one pair of the ontological polarities in Tillich's systematic theology (*ST* 1:182–184).

[211] Not all social systems have such a strong "givenness" as capitalism. A contemporary human being can hardly choose to stay out of the globalized system of capitalism, while choosing to stay out of the education system or the political system is relatively less difficult.

[212] *PE*, 50.

[213] "From the beginning, Tillich stood on the critical left wing of democratic socialism, searching for a third way beyond Marxism-Leninism and mere reformism" (John R. Stumme, introduction *SD*, xv).

[214] For example, *RS*, 109; *PE*, 64.

[215] *MW/HW* 5:120.

carries, and to open the fight with the characterization of these symbols against the demonries of an era. There is no other way at all, since all that points to the unconditioned has a symbolic character and can never really be grasped empirically. In this way and only in this way shall the demonries of the present to be spoken of as follows.[216]

What he says implies that one should not simply label capitalism as demonic, for both demonic and divine elements are intermingled in it. Yet one can regard capitalism as a symbolic form of the demonic and struggle against it as an instance of the demonic. This theoretically more nuanced position poses difficulties in praxis. As his religious socialism advocates, struggling against capitalism as a symbolic form of the demonic requires a radical solution such as a transformation to socialism, instead of reforming capitalism. As we can infer from his position described above, however, capitalism, like any other social phenomenon, involves an intermingling of divine and demonic elements. So one should say both yes and no to capitalism at the same time.[217] Although this does not necessarily result in weakening concrete calls for action, as one author has suggested,[218] it is still difficult to work out a practical strategy while taking seriously the dialectical position that demonic and divine elements intermingle in capitalism.

Capitalism as Quasi-Religion?

The above-mentioned problems do no serious harm to Tillich's major theoretical contributions to the theological critique of capitalism. His critical-prophetic theology of culture and his theological concept of the demonic open up a new horizon for the critical interpretation of capitalism and other social phenomena as *religious* phenomena. Capitalism (or its spirit) is the "unconscious faith" or religious substance of bourgeois society and has the holy and ecstatic qualities that give it a religious character. Thus, capitalism not only *can* be analyzed by theology; it *should* be analyzed by theology, because it has an important religious dimension that other academic disciplines are not primarily equipped to understand, interpret, and criticize adequately.

---

[216] *MW/HW* 5:120 [translation mine].
[217] See page 32 above.
[218] Slater, "Dynamic Religion, Formative Culture, and the Demonic in History," 109.

In addition to his theology of culture and concept of the demonic, Tillich's notion of "quasi-religion" is also crucial for developing a religious critique of capitalism. Unlike the concept of the demonic, the notion of quasi-religion became an important concept in Tillich's thought rather late in his life, when he showed an increasing interest in the encounter of world religions.[219] Tillich was preoccupied with the encounter with non-Christian religions during the last five years of his life—as testified by his last public lecture, "The Significance of the History of Religions for the Systematic Theologian."[220] Yet what is most significant for Tillich is not the encounter of Christianity with other world religions but the encounter of world religions with secular quasi-religions.[221]

For Tillich, quasi-religions, as the prefix implies, are not religions in the conventional sense, nor are they intended to be deceptively similar to traditional religions—in that case they would be "pseudo-religions." Quasi-religions have a structural similarity and points of identity with religions in the conventional sense, and such similarities are not intended.[222]

Tillich uses the term "quasi-religions" to analyze major political, social, and ideological systems in the world.[223] It can describe ideologies,[224] "systems of life,"[225] or "systems of secular thought and life."[226] Tillich

---

[219] It should be noted that Tillich had already used the term "quasi-religion" in the 1940s (*TPE*, 57, 248).

[220] Krister Stendahl, foreword to *Christianity and the Encounter of World Religions*, ix.

[221] *ST* 3:6; *CEWR*, 4. "In light of [Tillich's own definition of quasi-religion] I dare to make the seemingly paradoxical statement, that the main characteristic of the present encounter of the world religions is their encounter with the quasi-religions of our time. Even the mutual relations of the religions proper are decisively influenced by the encounter of each of them with secularism, and one or more of the quasi-religions which are based upon secularism" (*CEWR*, 4).

[222] *ERQR*, 61; *CEWR*, 4.

[223] See *CEWR*, 4–16, 29–32; *ERQR*, 31–36, 61–63. The term "quasi-religions" appears at two points in an unpublished eleven-point note handwritten by Tillich titled "Theology of Politics." See "Theology of Politics," MS, n.d., box 408:022, Paul Tillich Archives, Andover-Harvard Theological Library, Harvard University, Cambridge, Mass.

[224] Tillich regards quasi-religions as "ideologies, such as nationalism and socialism, which claim the loyalty or veneration of their followers with the intensity sometimes of their theistic religions" (*UC*, 4).

[225] "Like traditional religions, [quasi-religions] elevate their basic dogmas beyond question and make them refer to all areas of man's life. . . . The result is systems of life with an all-pervasive absolute, under an authority that is absolute, and generating absolutes in all parts of ourselves" (*MSA*, 134–35).

[226] *ERQR*, 9.

mentions several major quasi-religions of his time: nationalism, socialism, and liberal humanism, as well as their radicalization, fascism, communism, and scientism.[227] In his view, quasi-religions have developed from the soil of secularism, which destroys old religious and cultural traditions through the invasion of technology. However, there are religious elements in the depth of the secular mind, such as "the desire for liberation from authoritarian bondage, passion for justice, scientific honesty, striving for a more fully developed humanity, and hope in a progressive transformation of society in a positive direction"[228] Quasi-religions arise out of these religious elements and provide new answers to the meaning of life.[229] Thus, to label these ideologies or systems of life and thought "quasi-religions" is not just to employ a term that looks familiar to theologians. In fact, interpreting them theologically as quasi-religions is vital to understanding them. "Neither their nature nor their success can be explained without the analogy of religion."[230]

How can such systems of secular thought and life be counted as religions? That has to do with his broad definition of religion, that is, religion as ultimate concern:

> Religion is the state of being grasped by an ultimate concern, a concern which qualifies all other concerns as preliminary and which itself contains the answer to the question of the meaning of our life. Therefore the concern is unconditionally serious and shows a willingness to sacrifice any finite concern which is in conflict with it. . . . In secular quasi-religions the ultimate concern is directed towards objects like nation, science, a particular form or stage of society, or a highest ideal of humanity, which are then considered divine.[231]

With this definition of religion, Tillich is able to say that if one does not profess a religion in the conventional sense, one nevertheless may belong to a quasi-religion.[232]

Tillich does not use the term "quasi-religion" to describe capitalism. This is understandable, as the quasi-religions he mentions are political-ideological systems (even though socialism refers more to economy than to politics),

---

[227] *CEWR*, 17; *ERQR*, 9; *UC*, 23. Tillich did not have a consistent list of quasi-religions. "Scientisim" is only found in *UC*.

[228] *CEWR*, 9.

[229] Ibid..

[230] *ERQR*, 9.

[231] *CEWR*, 3.

[232] Ibid., 2.

while capitalism is not generally considered a political ideology, but there is no reason why economic-ideological systems cannot be counted as "quasi-religions." After all, "quasi-religions" are "systems of secular thought and life,"[233] and capitalism is arguably the most influential system of secular thought and life in the contemporary world. Moreover, "all religions are related to something which they consider to be holy."[234] There are a number of elements in capitalism that are often considered holy or sacred. They are to be venerated and their validity is not subject to question. Unlimited growth, free trade, and the "invisible hand" of the market are some examples.

We have seen that Tillich's prophetic theology of culture seeks to find out the "unconscious, self-evident faith" of a culture.[235] We have also seen how capitalism is seen by him as demonic. Now the concept of "quasi-religion" is able to bring these two together. Quasi-religion is included in Tillich's broader definition of religion in terms of ultimate concern. This shares considerable similarities with his notion of "unconscious, self-evident faith" in society. Also, Tillich seems to imply that quasi-religion is similar to the demonic at least in terms of its oppressiveness.[236] It is thus possible for Tillich to work out a critique of capitalism as a quasi-religion using his own ideas. Nevertheless, the concept of quasi-religion remains underdeveloped. In particular, Tillich does not work out the full implications of his understanding of quasi-religions as "systems of secular thought and life." In chapter 4, I shall attempt to develop Tillich's notion of "quasi-religion" into a more adequate interpretation and critique of capitalism.

---

[233] *ERQR*, 9.

[234] *ERQR*, 10.

[235] *RS*, 79.

[236] "The secular that is right in fighting against domination by the Holy becomes empty and becomes victim of what I call 'quasi-religions.' And these 'quasi-religions' imply an oppressiveness like that of the demonic elements of the religions. But they are worse, as we have seen in our century, because they are without the depths and richness of the genuine religious traditions" (*ERQR*, 74).

Conclusion

The purpose of this chapter is not just descriptive or analytical. What I have just examined also constitutes the first step toward the construction of a religious critique of global capitalistic modernity. The first section provides a framework for interpreting Tillich; this framework supports the critique of capitalism and its cultural dimension as a persistent thread throughout his writings. Thus we draw upon the thought of this prophetic theologian for our critical purpose. The second section is the key to understanding the theological presuppositions, which inform Tillich's critical interpretation of capitalism and capitalistic culture. It also lays the theoretical groundwork for my constructive proposal (to be put forward in chapter 4) to interpret the relation between capitalism and capitalistic modernity as the relation between religious substance and cultural forms. Tillich's profound idea of the demonic as an ambiguous structure of evil and the use of this idea in the critique of capitalism, which are introduced and analyzed in the third section, remain relevant to the critique of contemporary global capitalism. The same is true for the concept of quasi-religion, which will be developed and incorporated into my constructive proposal in chapter 4 for the critique of capitalism.

CHAPTER TWO

Tillich's Critique of Capitalist Modernity

The previous chapter introduced Tillich's theology of culture and briefly mentioned his critique of the cultural dimension of capitalism. The present chapter takes up that critique in detail. In the first section, I shall argue that Tillich's theological interpretation and critique of the cultural dimension of capitalism are the same as his critique of cultural modernity. That section also introduces Tillich's concept of theonomy, which, as a critical and constructive ideal, is a key to his interpretation of the pathologies of autonomous, capitalistic modernity. The second section is an overview of Tillich's interpretation of modernity and the historical development of bourgeois society. The third section contains a thematic reconstruction and examination of Tillich's critical interpretation of various aspects of cultural modernity including autonomy, self-sufficient finitude, technical reason, controlling knowledge, objectification, and conformity. The fourth and last section highlights the distinctive characteristics of Tillich's critical interpretation of modernity: 1) that he treats problems of modernity as the manifestations of a universal human predicament; 2) that theonomy is the critical and constructive ideal in response to modernity; and 3) that the ideal of theonomy provides theological hope that goes beyond the pessimism of Weber and of the Frankfurt School.

Preliminary Remarks: Capitalism and Modernity

By the time Tillich was active, during and in the immediate aftermath of the First World War, the term "modernity" and its equivalents in European languages had been in use for centuries. The use of the English word "modernity," in the sense of "the quality or condition of being modern," can be traced back to a time as early as 1627.[1] The Latin term *modernus* was first used in the fifth century to distinguish the Christian present from the pagan past.[2] As Habermas writes, "With a different content in each case, the expression 'modernity' repeatedly articulates the consciousness of an era that refers back to the past of a transition from the old to the new. . . . The French Enlightenment's ideal of perfection and the idea, inspired by modern science, of the infinite progress of knowledge and the advance towards social and moral development" enabled the early moderns to be free from the normativeness of the classical works of antiquity.[3] According to Habermas, Romanticism in the nineteenth century "produced a radicalized consciousness of modernity that detached itself from all previous historical connection and understood itself solely in abstract opposition to tradition and history as a whole."[4] In the European languages, as he notices, "the adjective 'modern' only came to be used in a substantive form, not in a chronological sense, in the middle of the nineteenth century," at first in the realm of the fine arts.[5] Baudelaire, for example, defines modernity in this way: "Modernity is the transient, the fleeting, the contingent; it is one-half of art, the other being the eternal and immovable."[6]

The use of the word "modernity" has become popular in recent decades. This is due in part to the discourse of "postmodernity," which looks back, as it were, to modernity as already exhausted.[7] Whether or not one accepts the postmodern position, modernity is now usually understood as the societal and cultural conditions that originally began in European societies from this

---

[1] *Oxford English Dictionary,* 2d ed., s.v. "modernity."

[2] David Lyon, *Postmodernity* (Minneapolis, Minn.: University of Minnesota Press, 1994) 19; Jürgen Habermas, "Modernity: An Unfinished Project," in *Habermas and the Unfinished Project of Modernity: Critical Essays on "The Philosophical Discourse of Modernity"* (ed. Maurizio Passerin d'Entrèves and Seyla Benhabib; Cambridge, Mass.: MIT Press, 1997) 39.

[3] Habermas, "Modernity: An Unfinished Project," 39.

[4] Ibid., 39.

[5] Jürgen Habermas, *Philosophical Discourse of Modernity: Twelve Lectures* (trans. Frederick G. Lawrence; Cambridge, Mass.: MIT Press, 1987) 8.

[6] Charles Baudelaire, "The Painter of Modern Life," in *Selected Writings on Art and Artists* (New York: Harmondsworth, 1972) 403, quoted in Habermas, *Philosophical Discourse of Modernity,* 8.

[7] "Modernity, though a relative newcomer on the conceptual scene, has actually been around for a long time, under other names. But the arrival of 'postmodernity' forces us to ask, well, what is or was modernity?" (Lyon, *Postmodernity,* 19).

specific historical epoch, although the questions about when that epoch began and what constitutes modernity are still subjects of debate.

The word *Modernität* or "modernity" appears only occasionally in Tillich's works. But he uses a cluster of interrelated terms that belong to what is commonly regarded as "modernity" in contemporary academic discussions: "modern society" (*die moderne Gesellschaft*), "modern age" (*die Moderne*), "bourgeois society" (*die bürgerliche Gesellschaft*), or even "the present" (*die Gegenwart*). Thus, while it may appear anachronistic to talk of Tillich's understanding of the *term* "modernity," one can still talk of his understanding of the *idea* of modernity.

In fact, Tillich's works can be seen as the interpretation and critique of, as well as response to, capitalistic modernity and its pathologies. Tillich's numerous writings on culture and politics, including his exposition of religious socialism, contain his perceptive analysis of modern Western society, his diagnosis and prophetic critique of its problems and crises, and the "therapy" that he offers for those problems. His three-volume *Systematic Theology* does not just contain an analysis of modern culture[8] but also comprises a conscious theological response to modernity. As he states at the beginning of the work, a theological system must satisfy two basic needs: the statement of the Christian message as well as the interpretation of the message for every new generation.[9] For him, the persistent question of theology for more than two centuries has been: "Can the Christian message be adapted to the *modern* mind without losing its essential and unique character?"[10] His own systematic theology is an attempt to interpret the Christian message in response to the cultural dimension of capitalistic modernity.

As we saw in the previous chapter, Tillich has a holistic perspective on capitalism. For him the economic sphere is interdependent with other social and cultural factors. He writes, "The economic sphere is itself a complex sphere, to which all other spheres essentially contribute, so that they cannot

---

[8] In *Systematic Theology,* Tillich constructs his theological system according to the "method of correlation," which "makes an analysis of the human situation out of which the existential questions arise" and "demonstrates that the symbols used in the Christian message are the answers to these questions" (*ST* 1:64). Constitutive of each part of his system (reason and revelation, being and God, existence and the Christ, life and the Spirit, and history and the kingdom of God) is an analysis of the human situation, often with specific reference to modern culture.

[9] *ST* 1:3.

[10] *ST* 1:7 [emphasis mine].

be derived from it, although they can never be separated from it."[11] Capitalism as an economically established system of domination is embedded in an all-encompassing system of life.[12] Thus modern society and culture are as much constitutive of capitalism as they are shaped by it. Despite their theoretical differences, both Marx and Weber—two theorists of capitalistic modernity to whom Tillich was indebted[13]—would agree on this wider understanding of capitalism and its inseparable relation to modernity.[14] They both regard capitalism as the most significant force shaping the modern world. However, as the sociologist Derek Sayer observes, neither Weber nor even Marx understand it in the sense of economic determinism. "Each comprehends capitalism, rather, as what Marx calls a 'mode of life.'"[15] Capitalism lies at the center of a "nexus of relationship" where social and cultural phenomena constitute the economy. Sayer writes, "Bound up with capitalism are novel and distinctive forms of sociation, and embedded in these are new kinds of individual subjectivity. Wherever these may have originated historically, they form an essential part of what *bürgerliche Gesellschaft*—that German term which translates both as 'bourgeois society' and 'civil society'—comes to be."[16] Capitalism as a "mode of life" or "nexus of relation" is inseparable from and intertwined with modern society and its culture. This lends support to my view that Tillich's critique of the cultural dimension of capitalism is the same as his critique of cultural modernity.

---

[11] *TPE*, 258; *MW/HW* 3:481.

[12] *MW/HW* 3:199.

[13] As I mentioned in the previous chapter, Tillich was indebted to Marx throughout his career, especially for his analysis of capitalist society, and for the concepts of alienation, objectification, and dehumanization. Weber's influence on Tillich can be seen in his focus on the spirit of bourgeois society and his analysis of technical reason (to be discussed in the present chapter).

[14] For the significance of capitalism in modernity and their close connection according to Marx and Weber, see Derek Sayer, *Capitalism and Modernity: An Excursus on Marx and Weber* (London: Routledge, 1991). For the affinity between Marx and Weber on capitalism and modernity, see Karl Löwith, *Max Weber and Karl Marx* (ed. Tom Bottomore and William Outhwaite; new preface by Bryan S. Turner; London: Routledge, 1993).

[15] Sayer, *Capitalism and Modernity*, 1–2.

[16] Ibid., 2. According to Sayer, Marx insists, "what makes modernity modern is, first and foremost, capitalism itself" (ibid., 12).

Theonomy, Autonomy, and Modernity

As we shall see below, the concept of autonomy is the key to Tillich's interpretation of cultural modernity. Kant's idea of the Enlightenment as representing the free and independent use of one's own self-legislating reason lies behind Tillich's conception of autonomy,[17] but Tillich goes beyond Kant by interpreting autonomy from a theological perspective. What he means by autonomy cannot be understood apart from his other two concepts: heteronomy and theonomy.[18] He uses these three concepts as a typology to analyze different states or types of culture in history. They differ in how they understand the nature of the νομος, the "law," in personal and social life. Tillich writes:

> Autonomy asserts that man as the bearer of universal reason is the source and measure of culture and religion—that he is his own law. Heteronomy asserts that man, being unable to act according to universal reason, must be subjected to a law, strange and superior to him. Theonomy asserts that the superior law is, at the same time, the innermost law of man himself, rooted in the divine ground which is man's own ground: the law of life transcends man, although it is, at the same time, his own.[19]

The term "universal reason" in Tillich's definition of autonomy is important. It does not mean that human beings follow a subjective notion of reason out of arbitrary willfulness.[20] The law of reason, which human individuals in

---

[17] *HCT*, 320–21. For a discussion of Kant's conception of autonomy and the extent to which twentieth-century philosophers differ from him, see Lewis Hinchman, "Autonomy, Individuality, and Self-Determination," in *What is Enlightenment? Eighteenth-Century Answers and Twentieth-Century Questions* (ed. James Schmidt; Berkeley, Calif.: University of California Press, 1996) 488–516.

[18] Clayton notices that Tillich "would seem to operate with two different and potentially conflicting models" of the dialectic relation between autonomy and theonomy. In one model (which in his view "may well derive from Kant"), theonomy is considered a type of autonomy, that is, a self-transcending autonomy. In the other model (which, for him, "shows rather greater affinities to Schelling"), both autonomy and heteronomy are moments within theonomy (John P. Clayton, "Introducing Paul Tillich's Writings in the Philosophy of Religion," in *MW/HW* 4:25–26). However, Clayton also concedes: "There may well be ways of construing these two models so that they are made to be compatible with one another (and Tillich himself sometimes conflated them), but in their natural state they would seem to be at odds with one another—as much at odds as Kant and Schelling" (ibid., 26). The conflation of the two models, with the result that they are not mutually incompatible, is what I argue that Tillich has achieved.

[19] *TPE*, 56–57.

[20] *HCT*, 289, 321.

the condition of autonomy obey, is "the law of subjective-objective reason," which is implied in "the *logos* structure of mind and reality."[21] Thus autonomy should be distinguished from individualism and subjectivism.

Tillich goes on to elaborate the implication of these different understandings of *nomos* to the relationship between culture and religion:

> Applying these concepts to the relation between religion and culture, we called an autonomous culture the attempt to create the forms of personal and social life without any reference to something ultimate and unconditional, following only the demands of theoretical and practical rationality. A heteronomous culture, on the other hand, subjects the forms and laws of thinking and acting to authoritative criteria of an ecclesiastical religion or a political quasi-religion, even at the price of destroying the structures of rationality. A theonomous culture expresses in its creations an ultimate concern and a transcending meaning not as something strange but as its own spiritual ground. "Religion is the substance of culture and culture the form of religion." This was the most precise statement of theonomy.[22]

The difference among the three concepts lies mainly in the role of reason in culture. In autonomy, culture adheres only to reason and nothing beyond reason; the religious dimension is excluded. In heteronomy, culture submits to something religious or quasi-religious that imposes on and overrides reason. In theonomy, culture follows reason that is united with and expresses its own inexhaustible depth and ground.[23] In other words, reason in theonomy is, unlike the case of autonomy, still connected with the religious dimension; yet, unlike the case of heteronomy, the religious dimension is not an alien authority suppressing the free use of reason.

Theonomy, autonomy, and heteronomy are interrelated. Theonomy is both the origin and reunion of autonomy and heteronomy and is in constant struggle against both. Tillich writes: "Theonomy is prior to both; they are elements within it. But theonomy, at the same time, is posterior to both; they

---

[21] *ST* 1:84. According to Tillich, "from the time of Parmenides it has been a common assumption of all philosophers that the *logos*, the word which grasps and shapes reality, can do so only because reality itself has a *logos* character" (*ST* 1:75). Subjective reason and objective reason refer respectively to "the rational structure of the mind and the rational structure of reality" (ibid.).

[22] *TPE*, 57.

[23] See *ST* 1:79, 85.

tend to be reunited in the theonomy from which they came. Theonomy both precedes and follows the contrasting elements it contains."[24]

Tillich considers both autonomy and heteronomy problematic.[25] But they are not equally problematic. Tillich certainly prefers autonomy to heteronomy. For him, autonomy is inadequate, while heteronomy borders on the demonic.[26] Heteronomy should be rejected outright, while the basic thrust of autonomy should be retained, even though autonomy should be transformed (into theonomy). In fact, autonomy and theonomy are closely related, even mutually dependent.[27] Moreover, Tillich often defines theonomy in terms of autonomy. Theonomy is a "self-transcending autonomy,"[28] "an autonomy informed by a religious substance,"[29] or "autonomy, which is aware of its divine ground."[30] It means, "autonomous reason united with its own depth."[31] Lying behind these descriptions are both Tillich's assumption of the essential relatedness of religion and culture, as expressed in the axiom that "religion is the substance of culture and culture the form of religion," as well as his affirmation of the principle of autonomy in rejection of the

---

[24] *ST* 3:251. Tillich describes the process in this way: "The original theonomous union is left behind by the rise of autonomous trends which necessarily lead to a reaction of the heteronomous element" (ibid.).

[25] "Autonomy and heteronomy are rooted in theonomy, and each goes astray when their theonomous unity is broken" (*ST* 1:85).

[26] See *OB*, 36–45. Tillich characterizes the demonic as "something finite and limited which has been invested with the stature of the infinite" (*OB*, 40). Heteronomy comes close to being demonic because it elevates certain finite authorities to unconditioned validity, subjecting human reason to its domination.

[27] In an early formulation, Tillich regards theonomy and autonomy as two different directions of the same function of meaning: "Theonomy is a turning toward the Unconditioned for the sake of the Unconditioned. The autonomous spiritual attitude is directed toward the conditioned, and toward the Unconditioned only in order to support the conditioned; theonomy employs conditioned forms in order to grasp the Unconditioned in them. . . . All meaning-fulfillment is possible only in the unity of theonomy and autonomy: autonomy alone drives toward empty form without import, and theonomy alone drives toward import without form. But both options are impossible" (*The System of Sciences according to Objects and Methods* [trans. Paul Wiebe; London: Associated University Press, 1981] 203). In another formulation, autonomy is regarded as a critical and dynamic principle of history, while theonomy is "the substance and meaning of history" (*TPE*, 45).

[28] *TPE*, xvi.

[29] *OB*, 38.

[30] *HCT*, 323.

[31] *ST* 1:85.

heteronomy that was on the rise in his days.[32] Theonomy affirms rather than rejects the autonomous forms of cultural creativity; when autonomous elements are rejected, theonomy becomes heteronomy.[33] Yet autonomy, inasmuch as it excludes the depth of reason and the religious substance of culture, is problematic. Thus, for Tillich, the problem of autonomy is not what it is, but what it *lacks*. Just as one should not reject reason for what it is, one should not reject autonomy; and just as reason alone is inadequate (so we need revelation),[34] autonomy alone is also inadequate (so we need theonomy).[35] This informs his interpretation of modern culture.

Tillich's idea of the relation between autonomy and theonomy expresses a theological view of modernity that is dialectical (with both yes and no). Theonomy, in his view, entails a self-transcending human culture (pointing beyond itself to the unconditioned or the religious substance) with an eros-relation of human beings to things and to other human beings. Autonomous reason, rationalization, and even secularization (insofar as it emancipates human culture from religious heteronomy) in modernity are to be affirmed. However, insofar as rationalization and secularization cut off modern culture from its meaning-giving religious substance and produce meaninglessness, they must be critiqued and transformed. Technical reason and controlling knowledge are not bad in themselves, but insofar as they squeeze out ontological reason (which determines the ends) and existential knowledge (knowing with participation), resulting in objectification and dehumanization, they too must be critiqued and transformed.[36]

---

[32] Tillich insisted, against Karl Barth, that a constant struggle against the Grand Inquisitor (heteronomy) was still necessary (*OB*, 40–41).

[33] *ST* 3:251.

[34] See Part 1, "Reason and Revelation," of Tillich's *Systematic Theology*. (*ST* 1:71–159.)

[35] Tillich's position here is similar to the Thomist position of mediaeval Roman Catholic theology. Reason, philosophy, and nature are affirmed, but they are inadequate without revelation, theology, and grace as their fulfillment.

[36] These ideas will be discussed later in this chapter.

Tillich and the Frankfurt School

In this chapter I shall make occasional comparisons of Tillich with the Frankfurt School. Tillich not only had a close relation with the leading members of the Institute for Social Research at the University of Frankfurt[37] but also shared with them a similar intellectual heritage. Both Tillich and the Frankfurt School theorists synthesized the intellectual traditions of Marx, Weber, and Freud. In particular, they were all heavily influenced by the more humanistic "Young Marx." Unlike traditional Marxism, their Marxism, which might be called neo-Marxism (or Western Marxism), was more concerned with the cultural dimension of capitalist society. They were influenced by Weber's interpretation of modern society in terms of rationalization and tended to see the pathologies of capitalist society in terms of the domination of a calculating, instrumental rationality. They also accepted Freud's psychoanalytic theory as a paradigm to unmask the processes through which social domination became internalized.[38]

---

[37] Tillich was professor of philosophy at the University of Frankfurt from 1929 until his suspension shortly after Hitler's rise to power in 1933. Tillich helped Max Horkheimer become the director of the institute, examined the *Habilitationsschrift* of Theodor W. Adorno, and taught courses with them. He shared good friendship with Horkheimer, Leo Löwenthal, and Friedrich Pollock, as well as with other key members of the Frankfurt School, who together formed a *Kränzchen* "coffee circle" and held regular discussions. For the many aspects of their relations and Tillich's time at Frankfurt in general, see Jean-Paul Gabus, "Paul Tillich et l'école de Francfort. Bilan d'une recherche," *RHPR* 78 (1998) 313–31; Rolf Wiggershaus, *The Frankfurt School: Its History, Theories, and Political Significance* (trans. Michael Robertson; Cambridge, Mass.: MIT Press, 1994) 37, 91, 93, 111, 116; Martin Jay, *The Dialectical Imagination: A History of the Frankfurt School and the Institute of Social Research, 1923–1950* (Berkeley, Calif.: University of California Press, 1996) 24–25, 30, 307 n. 87; Pauck and Pauck, *Paul Tillich: His Life and Thought*, 110–20, 288.

[38] See Ronald Stone, *Paul Tillich's Radical Social Thought* (Atlanta, Ga.: John Knox, 1980) 63–72; Mary Ann Stenger and Ronald H. Stone, *Dialogues of Paul Tillich* (Macon, Ga.: Mercer University Press, 2002) 174–84; Guy B. Hammond, "Tillich and the Frankfurt School on Protestantism and the Bourgeois Spirit," in *Religion et Culture* (ed. Michel Despland, Jean-Claude Petit, and Jean Richard; Laval, Québec: Les Presses de l'Université Laval, 1987) 327–37; Terence O'Keeffe, "Paul Tillich and the Frankfurt School," in *Theonomy and Autonomy: Studies in Paul Tillich's Engagement with Modern Culture* (ed. John J. Carey; Macon, Ga.: Mercer University Press, 1984) 67–87; James W. Champion, "Tillich and the Frankfurt School: Parallels and Differences in Prophetic Criticism," *Soundings* 69 (1986) 512–30; John W. Murphy, "Paul Tillich and Western Marxism," *AJTP* 5 (1984) 13–24; Gabus, "Paul Tillich et l'École de Francfort," 321–29.

Such shared intellectual heritage led to similarities in their critical interpretation of cultural modernity.[39] Pointing to domination as a characteristic of bourgeois society in *The Religious Situation*, Tillich "was already alluding to a theme that would gain a central place in Critical Theory [of the Frankfurt School]."[40] Tillich's critique of controlling knowledge, objectification, and dehumanization in *Systematic Theology* and other works continues the critique of domination and echoes similar themes in the works of Horkheimer and Adorno. In analyzing how the rise of technical reason and controlling knowledge has eventually led to dehumanization, Tillich offers a version of the dialectic of enlightenment that is not substantially different from the version of Horkheimer and Adorno. Moreover, Tillich's critique of technical reason (in Part 1 of *Systematic Theology*) borrows from Horkheimer's critical discussion of the subjective, formalized, and instrumentalized concept of reason, which echoes Weber's concept of instrumentally rational social action.[41] In this respect, one may say that

[39] It is a subject of debate as to whether such similarities show the mutual influence between Tillich and the Frankfurt School or whether these were parallel and independent developments. O'Keeffe ("Paul Tillich and the Frankfurt School") argues for the "parallel development" position. This is challenged by Champion ("Tillich and the Frankfurt School"), who argues for the "mutual influence" position. For a discussion about these two positions, see Gary M. Simpson, *Critical Social Theory: Prophetic Reason, Civil Society, and Christian Imagination* (Minneapolis, Minn.: Fortress, 2002) 27–33.

[40] Hammond, "Tillich and the Frankfurt School on Protestantism and the Bourgeois Spirit," 328. On the theme of domination, Hammond refers to *RS* 75–77, 107, 161.

[41] Weber classifies social action in a fourfold typology: instrumentally rational (*zweckrational*), value-rational (*wertrational*), affectual (*affektuell*), and traditional (*traditional*) types. Instrumentally rational action takes into account the end, the means, and the secondary results. Choice of action is determined by the rational weighing of alternative means for the achievement of rationally considered ends. In his discussion of rational economic action, Weber distinguishes between substantial rationality and formal rationality. See Max Weber, *Wirtshaft und Gesellschaft. Grundriss der verstehenden Soziologie* (ed. Johannes Winckelmann; 5th ed.; Tubingen: Mohr, 1985) 12–13, 44–45 = *Economy and Society: An Outline of Interpretative Sociology* (ed. Guenther Roth and Claus Wittich; trans. Ephraim Fischoff et al.; Berkeley, Calif.: University of California Press, 1978) 1:24–26, 85–86. Horkheimer remarked that his distinction between subjective reason (concerned with the choice of means for ends that are taken for granted) and objective reason (reason as corresponding to the objective structure of reality) resembles Weber's distinction between "functional" (*sic*) rationality and "substantive" rationality. See Max Horkheimer, "Means and Ends," *Eclipse of Reason* (New York: Continuum, 1974) 3–57. He did not explicitly mention that his concept of subjective reason was similar to Weber's concept of instrumental rationality, although this is not hard to see throughout the whole chapter. Tillich cites Horkheimer's

Tillich's interpretation of modernity follows a particular Weberian version as developed by the Frankfurt School in dialogue with Marxism. Tillich and the Frankfurt School theorists also share an insistence on the importance of religion for social critique, but they take quite different paths. For Tillich, the social relevance of religion and theology is both critical and constructive. Religious thought, such as the concept of theonomy, offers a critique of society and culture; it also provides a constructive orientation for the transformation of society and culture. For the Frankfurt School theorists, who share a Jewish background, religion (especially the belief in an absolutely transcendent God) is crucial for critique (as relativization) and for keeping alive the hope of justice.[42] As Horkheimer said on the occasion of Tillich's death: "I believe that there is no philosophy to which I could assent which did not contain a theological moment, for it relates indeed to the recognition of how much the world in which we live is to be interpreted as relative."[43] To quote him again: "Without God one will try in vain to preserve absolute meaning. . . . Without reference to something divine, a good deed like the rescue of a man who is being persecuted unjustly loses all its glory. . . . The death of God is also the death of eternal truth."[44] Yet he would not go so far as Tillich to make positive symbolic statements about God. He can only speak of a yearning (*Sehnsucht*) that the foundation (*Grund*) of this world is all-loving and all-powerful and that the terror of this world is not the last word.[45]

Eclipse of Reason in *ST* 1:72 and discusses "Subjective and Objective Reason" (without citing Horkheimer) in *ST* 1:75–79.

[42] See Eduardo Mendieta's introduction to *Religion and Rationality: Essays on Reason, God, and Modernity,* by Jürgen Habermas (ed. Eduardo Mendieta; Cambridge, Mass.: MIT Press, 2002) 7.

[43] Max Horkheimer, *Vorträge und Aufzeichnungen, 1949–1973* (ed. Alfred Schmidt and Gunzelin Schmid Noerr; vol. 7 of *Gesammelte Schriften*; Frankfurt am Main: S. Fischer, 1985) 276, quoted in Mendieta, introduction to *Religion and Rationality,* 6–7.

[44] Max Horkheimer, *Critique of Instrumental Reason* (trans. Matthew J. O'Connell et al.; New York: Continuum, 1996; repr., New York: Seabury, 1974) 47–48.

[45] Max Horkheimer, "Meine Begegnung mit Paul Tillich. Eine Antwort in Form eines Briefes," in *GW* 13:568–69.

Tillich's View of Modernity: Bourgeois Society and Its History

The most crucial concept in Tillich's interpretation of modernity is "the spirit of bourgeois society" (*der Geist der bürgerlichen Gesellschaft,* used frequently in *The Religious Situation*). He uses it interchangeably with "the spirit of capitalism"[46] and "the bourgeois principle" (used in *The Socialist Decision*). Tillich emphasizes that this is not the spirit of a class or party but is rather "a symbol for an ultimate, fundamental attitude toward the world" and is thus wider than the bourgeois society in which it is most concretely visible and from which it gets its name.[47] In other words, Tillich understands modernity as historically originating from and concretely expressed in the bourgeois society that first emerged in modern Europe, although its principle or spirit is not bound to a specific historical and cultural context. Before going on to examine the spirit of bourgeois society in greater detail, I present a brief synopsis of Tillich's understanding of bourgeois society and its history.

Bourgeois Society and Modernity: An Introduction

Bourgeois society is, for Tillich, the most representative group of modern times.[48] What then are its unique features? Tillich has given several summary accounts of bourgeois society, which have different yet overlapping foci and main themes. We shall look at some of the accounts and try to distill the major elements.

Principal Characteristics of Bourgeois Society

In *The Religious Situation,*[49] originally published in German in 1926, Tillich describes bourgeois society (*die bürgerliche Gesellschaft*) as the carrier of the three most powerful and representative products of modernity: mathematical

---

[46] *MW/HW* 5:58 = *RS*, 116. Although Tillich does not mention Max Weber, he has certainly drawn from him. "Max Weber haunts the socialist writing of Paul Tillich. Basic concepts are taken over, utilized, and usually not acknowledged" (Mary Ann Stenger and Ronald Stone, *Dialogues of Paul Tillich* [Macon, Ga.: Mercer University Press, 2002] 152).

[47] *MW/HW* 5:27–28 = *RS*, 27.

[48] "Das Christentum und die Moderne, " in *GW* 13:114.

[49] Paul Tillich, *Die religiöse Lage der Gegenwart* (Berlin: Ullstein, 1926). I use *MW/HW* 5:27–97 for the German text and *RS* for the English translation. Tillich says that the bourgeois principle is fully dealt with in *The Religious Situation* (*SD*, 170 n. 1).

natural science, technology, and the capitalist economy.[50] These three belong together. Natural science serves technology, and technology makes possible the development of a worldwide economic system.[51] Thus, the capitalist economy is the most important and culminating factor of bourgeois society. In fact, it is the "unconditioned dominance" of the capitalist economy that most decisively characterizes the bourgeois spirit.[52] Everything else is put into service of the capitalist economy. In political life the powers of the nation state are used by the capitalist class to control the proletarian masses in domestic affairs and to further its imperialist will in foreign relations. In social life bourgeois society is a group of radically separate individuals held together by economic purposes and needs. Even the ethical ideal serves the economic end: economic efficiency for the leaders, submissive acceptance of their economic role for the masses, obedient subjection to bourgeois conventions for all, and impersonal charity to support the economically helpless.[53]

Technology and Modern Society

Besides "bourgeois society," Tillich often uses the terms "industrial society" and "technical society." In the handwritten notes for the lecture entitled "The Spiritual Situation in Our Technical Society,"[54] Tillich identifies the "determining structures and decisive trends" of modern society as those of an "industrially determined society" in which human destiny is to be determined by the "methods and organization of industry." We live in a society ordered for the production of means, as he writes, a "world of tools above the given world."[55] Such analysis points to the predominance of modern technology

---

[50] *RS*, 42. Tillich describes these three elements—mathematical science, technology, and the capitalist economy—as the products of the closing decades of nineteenth century. The adjective "capitalist" is not found in the original German text (*MW/HW* 5:32), but the idea is implied.

[51] *RS*, 42.

[52] *RS*, 105.

[53] *RS*, 43–44.

[54] "The Spiritual Situation in Our Technical Society," manuscript, [1954], box 408:039, Paul Tillich Archives, Andover-Harvard Theological Library, Harvard University, Cambridge, Mass. According to one Tillich scholar, the handwritten notes are "from a lecture delivered at the Wesley Foundation at the University of Mississippi during his visit, 3–4 April 1954." J. Mark Thomas, "Ambiguity in Our Technical Society," in *Religion in the New Millennium: Theology in the Spirit of Paul Tillich* (ed. Raymond F. Bulman and Frederick J. Parrella; Macon, Ga.: Mercer University Press, 2001) 337 n. 1.

[55] Tillich, "Spiritual Situation in Our Technical Society," 3. See also Thomas, "Ambiguity in Our Technical Society," 338.

for industrial production, and increasingly for other aspects, in capitalist society. As Tillich says, "The incentive of technology is production. Every technology is driven by economic necessity. . . . Ordinarily it is embedded in economic impulses. And no economy has ever given such impulses as has the capitalist one. It gave technology the possibility of subduing the earth."[56] In Tillich's view, however, technology and capitalism are not always good friends. To protect the interest of power groups, capitalism hinders technology by preventing technological innovation. It prevents the machine from freeing human beings from mechanical labor. It also uses the boundless possibilities of the machine to produce goods that "artificially generate needs for the sake of profits."[57]

From this we can see that Tillich does not have a negative stance toward modern technology. He considers technology neutral and ambiguous. Technology can hardly be avoided, for it is the use of means for an end.[58] Tillich recognizes the liberating effects of technology. For him, technology can liberate human beings from the burden of mechanical labor, from the pains and dangers of natural processes, from the spatial-temporal limits to human community, and from the fear of the demonic in things.[59] On the other hand, technology is emptied. In technology, with the pressure of capitalism, power replaces *eros*; rationality becomes dominating, and its boundless possibility is temptation.[60]

Globalization of the Bourgeois Principle

For Tillich, the bourgeois principle is not limited to the West. The bourgeois principle, through the spread of industrial capitalism throughout the world, has undergone a process of globalization.

> Western bourgeois society, viewed from the standpoint of universal history, is an attack on the myth of origin and the bond of origin everywhere on earth. It is the proclamation and realization of an autonomous this-worldliness even for the most remote, most mythbound human groups. Through the triumphant spread of its principle it has established a world dominion which no one on earth can completely elude. Wherever

---

[56] *SSOTS*, 58.

[57] *SSOTS*, 58.

[58] "To employ technology is to enlist means to an end. For this reason technology is present as an element whenever purposes are realized. Thus technology is universal" (*SSOTS*, 51).

[59] *SSOTS*, 59–60.

[60] *SSOTS*, 60.

technology and capital are at work, the spirit of Western bourgeois society is active.[61]

In Tillich's view, the bourgeois principle dissolves "all conditions, bonds, and forms related to the origin into elements that are to be rationally mastered."[62] The bourgeoisie subjects the "arbitrary powers of existence" to its own ends by objectification, which involves the analysis and mastery of both nature and society. As he writes, "The spirit of bourgeois society is the spirit of a human group that, after cutting every bond of origin, subjugates an objectified world to its own purposes."[63]

Historical Background of Bourgeois Society

Double Break with the Myth of Origins

The emergence of bourgeois society and the bourgeois spirit in the West was the result of a complex constellation of socioeconomic and cultural trends. Tillich identifies two historical movements as most significant: the Reformation and the Enlightenment. They realize respectively two different ideas or principles: prophetism and autonomy. Both principles were crucial in the breakdown of what he called the "myth of origin" characteristic of traditional societies, which hold myths about human ties to soil, blood, and social group.[64] "Western bourgeois society is the product of a double break with the bond of origin: the prophetic and the humanistic."[65] Protestantism (especially Calvinism), which inherits prophetism, enables Western consciousness to be free from "the medieval bonds of origin" guarded by the priesthood. Likewise, the Enlightenment, which realizes autonomy, sets Western consciousness free from the heteronomy of religious and political absolutism. The result is the Western bourgeois society and its spirit that is unique in history.[66]

---

[61] *SD*, 47–48 [emphasis omitted].
[62] *SD*, 48 [emphasis omitted].
[63] *SD*, 48.
[64] For myths of origin, see *SD*, 14–18.
[65] *SD*, 47.
[66] *SD*, 47.

Protestant Reformation

Like Weber and Ernst Troeltsch, Tillich underscores the significance of Protestantism for the emergence of modern bourgeois society.[67] According to Tillich, Christianity "has permeated all the institutions and customs of modern society." Thus, no one living in the modern world can free himself or herself from Christianity.[68] As he writes, "Christianity is the background of modern society in its religious substance—Christianity in general and Protestant Christianity in particular."[69] For example, "the faith of the Renaissance in the earth as a place of meaningful creative activity" and the utopian themes of that age come from Christianity.[70] Not all Christian traditions, however, were equally well received in the modern age. Tillich points out that when mystical ideas, carried by Catholic mysticism and pietistic Protestantism, tried to advance, as particularly in romanticism, they were eliminated, deprived of power, or transformed by the superior power of the bourgeois spirit. In his view, it is not what he calls the medieval, pervasively mystical and organic-cultic form of Christianity (as expressed in Roman Catholicism) but what he calls the critical-intellectual and ethical-active form (as expressed in orthodox Protestantism, especially Calvinism) that stands behind modernity.[71] He writes, "The active, world-shaping Protestantism is the background of bourgeois society and thus the modern age."[72] Tillich identifies several characteristics for which modernity is influenced by Protestantism: the ideal of individual personality with conscience and responsibility that breaks down any sacramental and hierarchical religion; the sanctification of daily life and the daily practice of an active ethic of obedience; the work ethic that lingers in the economic process; the will to subject all reality to the ideals of the

---

[67] See Max Weber, *The Protestant Ethic and the Spirit of Capitalism* (trans. Talcott Parsons; introduction by Anthony Giddens; London: Routledge, 1992); Ernst Troeltsch, *Protestantism and Progress: The Significance of Protestantism for the Rise of the Modern World* (trans. W. Montgomery; Philadelphia: Fortress, 1986; repr., *Protestantism and Progress: A Historical Study of the Relation of Protestantism to the Modern World*; New York: G. P. Putnam, 1912). It should be noted that neither Weber, Troeltsch, nor Tillich sees the link between Protestantism and modern society as a direct causation.

[68] *PE*, 1.

[69] *PE*, 2. For Tillich's discussion of the Protestant roots of capitalistic modernity, see, for example, *RS*, 49, 198–200.

[70] *PE*, 3.

[71] *GW* 13:115.

[72] "Der aktive, weltgestaltende Protestantismus ist der Hintergrund der bürgerlichen Gesellschaft und damit der Moderne" (*GW* 13:115).

Kingdom of God, which gives passion and not just ideology to British and American imperialism; the freedom and inviolability of every person that underlies the ideal of democracy; and immanence as inner infinity, that is, the presence of the infinite at every point of finitude, which gives great cultural creations transcendence and mystery.[73]

Nevertheless, Tillich warns against a simplistic view of how Protestantism is related to modern society. To be sure, he recognizes that the history of Protestantism "has proceeded in very close connection" with the history of the bourgeois spirit. He writes, "Indeed, the popular exaggeration of Max Weber's thesis about the significance of Calvinism for the rise of the capitalist spirit often makes it appear as though Protestantism itself were nothing but the capitalist spirit."[74] Yet Tillich points out that original Protestantism was "the sharpest protest it is possible to think of against the spirit of self-sufficient finitude," that is, the spirit of bourgeois society.[75] However, Protestantism has an intrinsic dilemma: "that it must protest against every religious or cultural realization which seeks to be intrinsically valid, but that it needs such realization if it is to be able to make its protest in any meaningful way."[76] Eventually, Lutheranism became more and more dependent on the state, while Calvinism depended on the society. This made it difficult for either movement to revolt against the spirit of bourgeois society.[77]

European Enlightenment

Besides the Protestant Reformation, which inherits prophetism, the other historical movement that has contributed to the breaking away of modern bourgeois society from the myths of origin is the Enlightenment, which realizes autonomy. While both have contributed to the rise of modern society by shattering the myth of origin, they differ, in Tillich's view, in one important aspect. The prophetism that lies behind Protestantism retains its connection with the father symbol, who represents both the bond of origin and the bearer of primal demand; it is the latter aspect which makes possible the break with the myth of origin. The autonomous consciousness of the Enlightenment, on the other hand, breaks away from every bond of origin, including every

---

[73] *PE*, 3; *GW* 13:115–16.
[74] *RS*, 191–92.
[75] *RS*, 192.
[76] *RS*, 192.
[77] *RS*, 193–201.

kind of tie to the father symbol.[78] The dimension of origin is suppressed in various aspects by the autonomous consciousness. The soil is to be dealt with technically as a means for the production of goods. With new technologies of transportation which created an overarching spatial unity, people are no longer tied to particular pieces of land. Reason, rational education for all, and the rational structuring of existence shatter the status structure, disregard the divine election of the nobility, break up traditions, and challenge religious authorities.[79] The "break" with the bond of origin entails not just the break with the past but also the break with all kinds of community as well as with the religious substance. Tillich would agree with the depiction in the *Communist Manifesto* of the sweeping transformations—vividly captured by the saying "All that is solid melts into the air, all that is holy is profaned"—that modern bourgeois society has brought to the world.[80] Although breaking away from

---

[78] *SD*, 15, 20–24. According to Tillich, the human tie to father and mother lies behind all myths of origin: "The myth of origin envisions the beginning of humankind in elemental, superhuman figures of various kinds. Common to them all is the fact that they are expressions of the human tie to father and mother, and that by the power of this tie they want to hold consciousness fast, not allowing it to escape from their dominion" (*SD*, 13). In his view, the mother symbol is more commonly associated with the origin of soil and blood, while the father symbol predominates in the myths of origin of social groups. Both supportive and demanding aspects are present in the father. It is the demanding aspect of father symbols that enables the break with the tie to the origin. See *SD*, 13–15. Tillich's stress on the human tie to father and mother as the background of myths of origin shows the influence of Freud. (Freud is mentioned three times in the note to the paragraph quoted above. See *SD*, 166 n. 1). Yet his "distinction between the father as origin and the father as liberating demand reflects Tillich's effort to come to grips with Freud's analysis of the primal father (and the repressive superego) while at the same time affirming a potentially more positive role for a father figure" (Guy B. Hammond, "Tillich and the Frankfurt Debates about Patriarchy and the Family," *Theonomy and Autonomy: Studies in Paul Tillich's Engagement with Modern Culture* [ed. John J. Carey; Macon, Ga.: Mercer University Press, 1984] 97–98). Tillich's position is similar to that of Horkheimer and Adorno, and unlike that of Fromm and Marcuse (ibid., 99–101). For Tillich, Jewish prophetism, which was itself based on "a powerful social myth of origin," was significant in shattering the myth of origin, especially the human tie to the soil, by radicalizing the social imperative. God is free from the soil "precisely because he has led foreign conquerors into his own land in order to punish the 'people of his inheritance' and to subject them to an unconditional demand" (*SD*, 20). In Tillich's view, Protestantism—in which "Western consciousness freed itself from the medieval bonds of origin supported and protected by the priesthood" (*SD*, 47)—has inherited the prophetic tradition.

[79] *SD*, 23–24.

[80] See *SD*, 47. Marx and Engels, "Manifesto of the Communist Party," in *The Marx-Engels Reader* (ed. Robert C. Tucker; 2d ed.; New York: Norton, 1978) 476. For an analysis of Marx's view of modernity, see Marshall Berman, *All That Is Solid Melts into the Air: The Experience of Modernity* (New York: Penguin, 1988) 87–129.

the myths of origin, the Protestant Reformation retains its tie to its religious substance. The Enlightenment, however, quickly lost its religious substance and became in some expressions completely secular.[81]

That is, even the Enlightenment has a Christian background. The Enlightenment is for Tillich an example of revolutionary humanism, which is one of the three forms of Christian humanism.[82] Tillich defines humanism as "humankind's attempt to rely upon itself, to find the fullness of its meaning in its own being."[83] It struggles against demonic religion and guards the integrity of human nature. In Tillich's view, such a struggle has reached its victory in Christianity.[84] "Post-Christian humanism is therefore a stage in the development of Christianity."[85] The present life of Western Christian people is dominated by Christian humanism as a "developed form of Christianity."[86]

Development of Bourgeois Society

In "The World Situation," an essay published in 1945, Tillich outlines the historical development of bourgeois society, which has shaped the modern world. He writes, "The present world situation is the outcome—directly in the West and indirectly elsewhere—of the rise, the triumph, and the crisis of what we may term 'bourgeois society.'"[87] Like Weber and the Frankfurt School (which integrates insights of Marx, Weber, and Freud), Tillich regards the historical change in the type of reason as a key to understanding modernity. He divides the history of bourgeois society into three overlapping phases. The first phase is the period of political, economic, and cultural revolutions in Western Europe and America, during which the bourgeois way of life became "the determining though not the only influential factor" in Western culture. The guiding principle was a belief in reason as the principal means of achieving justice and of arriving at the truth. The basis of the struggle

---

[81] *TPE*, 58.

[82] *PTC*, 100. The other two forms of Christian humanism are classical humanism and romantic humanism.

[83] *PTC*, 99 [emphasis omitted]. The human being, according to humanism, remains in himself (*bleibt das menschliche Sein in sich selbst*) (*MW/HW* 3:174). This is the basis of "self-sufficient finitude" (to be examined later in this chapter), which characterizes modernity.

[84] "Insofar as this struggle against demonic religion has, in Christianity, reached its zenith and—in principle—also its victory, it must be said that humanism rests upon a Christian background" (*PTC*, 99).

[85] *PTC*, 99.

[86] *PTC*, 100.

[87] *TP*, 112.

against feudalism and authoritarianism was the acknowledgement of every human being as rational and capable of autonomy. The "principle of automatic harmony"—the belief that the free use of reason in every person would lead to harmony between individuals and society—was the main presupposition behind the economy, politics, and even religion. Thus the "laws of the market" and democracy based upon political judgment of individual citizens would lead to the common good, and personal interpretation of the Bible and religious experience would be uniform enough to maintain the church. The achievements of mathematical science, the development of national states, and the establishment of natural laws in ethics vindicated the Enlightenment belief in reason and harmony.[88]

The second phase in the history of bourgeois society, the nineteenth century, is what Tillich called "the period of the victorious bourgeoisie." When the bourgeoisie became the ruling class, revolutionary reason was replaced by "technical reason," which "provides for means for ends but offers no guidance in the determination of ends." Human beings became more and more able to control nature. With the tools of technical reason the worldwide system of industrial capitalism took shape as a kind of "second nature," over which human beings then increasingly lost control. Human life gradually became subordinated to the demands of the worldwide economy, which produced the profit of the few and poverty of the many, and which might raise the living standard of the working masses today and throw them into the misery of chronic unemployment tomorrow. The all-embracing mechanism of capitalism has become a new face of "the Leviathan."[89] "The decisive feature of the period of the victorious bourgeoisie is the loss of control by human reason over man's historical existence."[90]

The third phase in the history of bourgeois society, the first half of the twentieth century and thus when Tillich was writing "The World Situation," is characterized by crisis. The foundation of bourgeois society—"the conviction of automatic harmony between individual interest and general interest"—had broken down; the totalitarian systems of fascism and communism had attempted to replace laissez-faire liberalism by planned economy; technical reason had given way to "planning reason." These totalitarian attempts were ambiguous. While they tried to bring the incalculable mechanism of capitalism

---

[88] *TP*, 112–14.
[89] *TP*, 114–16, 119.
[90] *TP*, 115.

back under human control, they also "aggravate[d] the self-destructive forces generated by the second stage of bourgeois society."[91]

This account of the historical development of bourgeois society resembles the historical process that Horkheimer and Adorno interpret as the "dialectic of enlightenment."[92] As they maintain, the process of enlightenment, once emancipating, has turned oppressive and self-destructive, as industrial capitalism has developed. Economic development, which is supposed to liberate humankind from nature and to create more favorable conditions for economic justice, has brought increasing domination over nature and people.[93] Thus, according to Horkheimer and Adorno, "humanity, instead of entering a truly human state, is sinking into a new kind of barbarism."[94]

Interim Observations

From the above accounts of Tillich's view of bourgeois society and its spirit, we may make some preliminary observations about Tillich's understanding of modernity: 1) Modernity has emerged from the Reformation and the Enlightenment, both of which have a Christian background. 2) Societal modernity consists primarily in capitalism, which dominates all aspects of bourgeois society. 3) Technology plays an important role in societal modernity, and it has various and ambiguous effects on culture. 4) Modernity, considered especially in its technological and capitalistic aspects, has been spreading throughout the world. 5) Cultural modernity is characterized primarily by the principle of autonomy, which involves the victory of reason. 6) A "dialectic of

---

[91] *TP*, 116–18.

[92] Max Horkheimer and Theodor W. Adorno, *Dialectic of Enlightenment: Philosophical Fragments* (ed. Gunzelin Schmid Noerr; trans. Edmund Jephcott; Stanford, Calif.: Stanford University Press, 2002).

[93] In the preface to the *Dialectic of Enlightenment*, Horkheimer and Adorno describe vividly the ironic character of progress in capitalistic modernity: "The enslavement to nature of people today cannot be separated from social progress. The increase in economic productivity which creates the conditions for a more just world also afford the technical apparatus and the social groups controlling it a disproportionate advantage over the rest of the population. The individual is entirely nullified in face of the economic powers. These powers are taking society's domination over nature to unimagined heights. While individuals as such are vanishing before the apparatus they serve, they are provided for by that apparatus and better than ever before. In the unjust state of society the powerlessness and pliability of the masses increase with the quantity of goods allocated to them" (Horkheimer and Adorno, *Dialectic of Enlightenment*, xvii).

[94] Horkheimer and Adorno, *Dialectic of Enlightenment*, xiv.

enlightenment" has taken place. Reason, once liberating, becomes dominating in the form of technical reason and has brought destructive effects such as the objectification of nature and human society. 7) The belief in harmony, once important for the emergence and maintenance of bourgeois society, has been shattered.

Tillich's Critique of Modernity and the Spirit of Bourgeois Society

Given the preceding survey of Tillich's understanding of the basic features of bourgeois society (or modernity) and its historical development, I will now go on to highlight and examine the major principles and cultural features of bourgeois society as analyzed by Tillich. These principles or features constitute what Tillich calls the spirit of bourgeois society. His analysis of this spirit reveals his critical interpretation of cultural modernity.

Spirit of Bourgeois Society: A General Analysis

"The spirit of bourgeois society" refers to a set of different yet interrelated cultural features of modern society. Tillich also groups these features under the label of "the spirit of industrial society,"[95] which I will use here as a convenient introduction to the various features of modernity to be examined later.

Modern industrial society, according to Tillich, is characterized by the concentration of human activities "upon the methodological investigation and technical transformation of this world" (human beings also being objects of such activities), "and the consequent loss of the dimension of depth" in the human encounter with reality. "Reality has lost its inner transcendence," and the universe as a system of finite relations has become "self-sufficient," calculable, and manageable. From the eighteenth century onward, "God has been removed" from the field of human activities and has become superfluous. Human beings disregard the conflict between their essential and existential state, that is, their self-estrangement. Sin and universal sinfulness, the bondage of the will, the demonic powers, the structures of destruction in persons and communities—all these are ignored or denied. Instead, the picture of human beings is one of optimism about the progressive fulfillment of their potentialities.[96]

---

[95] *TC*, 43.
[96] *TC*, 43–44.

Tillich deals with a number of "pathologies" of modern society. In the lecture manuscript "The Spiritual Situation in Our Technical Society," he names three spiritual problems in technical society. The first is the "disproportion between means and ends." Tillich talks about "the concentration on means and the perversion of making means into ends. . . . [The] question of the ultimate end disappears from the center of consciousness." This situation produces emptiness.[97] This is essentially the problem of technical reason, which we shall examine below. The second spiritual problem in technical society is the "transformation of reality into objects." The industrial domination of the world is the controlling principle, expressed in the "cognitive transformation of things into their elements, in order to compose them for purposes." Truth becomes identified with "scientific, manageable truth." Artistic, ethical, and religious realms, which disclose the inner quality of things, are relegated to emotion. This circumstance increases the experience of emptiness, which either is cynically rejected or is to be covered by seeking pleasure from the world.[98] The third spiritual problem in technical society is the "transformation of the person into a thing." The "seemingly contradictory trends" of competition and conformity contribute to this problem.[99] The latter two spiritual problems correspond to the objectification of things and persons which we will examine below. Before that, however, I will look at Tillich's idea of autonomy and the problem of technical reason.

Autonomy and Self-Sufficient Finitude

At the beginning of this chapter, I introduced Tillich's idea of autonomy and its relation to theonomy. Here I will examine the way in which he uses the idea of autonomy, together with the closely related idea of "self-sufficient finitude," in his critical interpretation of cultural modernity.

Autonomy as the Main Principle of Modernity

In an article published in 1928, "Das Christentum und die Moderne," Tillich describes the social, intellectual, and religious aspects of modernity. In his view, bourgeois society is characterized socially by economic liberalism and political democracy, intellectually by empirical-rational outlook of the world and technical-rational organization of the world, and religiously

[97] Tillich, "Spiritual Situation in Our Technical Society," 4–5.
[98] Ibid., 5–6.
[99] Ibid., 7.

by consciousness of immanence and autonomy. Above all, however, it is autonomy, as a cultural-spiritual principle, that Tillich considers the most crucial: "The most important characteristic in principle, from which the rest can be understood, is autonomy, the spirit that is itself closed in itself, and follows its own rational necessity."[100] This sentence expresses in a nutshell Tillich's understanding of the spirit of bourgeois society and cultural modernity.

Although autonomy was also present in other periods, such as pre-Socratic Greek philosophy (as Tillich claims), it is in the eighteenth and the nineteenth centuries that "autonomy won an almost complete victory."[101] Even antiautonomous movements, such as the attacks on the freedom and rationality of the personal center characteristic of depth psychology and of the philosophy of life, as well as the fascist and Bolshevist struggles against democracy, are themselves creations of autonomy.[102]

Problems of Autonomy

What does autonomy lack? For Tillich, this is almost the same as asking, "What is the main problem of the spirit of bourgeois society?" A preliminary answer to this question is already implied in Tillich's definitions of theonomy in terms of autonomy: Theonomy is autonomy united with the religious substance or dimension of depth.[103] What autonomy lacks is precisely such union. Lacking the religious dimension of depth, autonomy is confined to the realm of the finite. The difference between autonomy and theonomy is that "in an autonomous culture the cultural forms appear only in their finite relationship, while in a theonomous culture they appear in their relation to the unconditional."[104] While theonomy is a culture in which "the ultimate meaning of existence shines through all finite forms of thought and action, . . . self-complacent autonomy cuts the ties of a civilization with its ultimate

---

[100] "Das prinzipiell wichtigste Merkmal, von dem her die übrigen begriffen werden können, ist die Autonomie, der in sich selbst geschlossene, seiner eignen rationalen Notwendigkeit folgende Geist" (*GW* 13:114).

[101] *ST* 1:86.

[102] *GW* 13:117–18. For example, depth psychology in its original form carries the mechanistic-psychological tendencies of the nineteenth century, and Bolshevism is based on the radically autonomous philosophy of Marxism (ibid.).

[103] For Tillich, religion not a special function of the human spirit but is "the dimension of depth" in all the functions (moral, cognitive, aesthetic) of human spiritual life (*TC*, 6–7).

[104] *TPE*, 45.

ground and aim," thus becoming empty and exhausted.[105] Autonomy is not secularization merely in a sociological sense, i.e., "the process by which sectors of society and culture are removed from the domination of religious institutions and symbols."[106] Rather, autonomy is primarily the fact that society and culture are no longer self-transcendent, that finite realities are no longer the vehicles of the unconditional or of ultimate concern, that persons and things have lost the qualities of holiness and mystery.

Theonomous culture, according to Tillich, is oriented toward the ultimate in being and meaning. The style of cultural creation "expresses the ultimacy of meaning even in the most limited vehicles of meaning—a painted flower, a family habit, a technical tool, a form of social intercourse." These things are experienced as consecrated.[107] In other words, in theonomy, "the consciousness of the presence of the unconditional permeates and guides all cultural functions and forms."[108] The holy inflames and imbues all reality, and nothing is profane. Nor is there any separation of subject and object; the relation of things is "not that of technical manipulation but that of immediate spiritual communion." The purpose of the knowledge of things is not control over them but the finding of their inner meaning and divine significance. Individuals are surrounded by the all-penetrating spiritual substance. Merely individual culture and individual economic interests are impossible.[109]

The "always present, always driving, always restless" principle of autonomy has destroyed such a theonomous situation:

> [Autonomy] replaces mystical nature with rational nature; it puts in the place of mythical events historical happenings, and in the place of the magical sense of communion it sets up technical control. It constitutes communities on the basis of purpose, and morality on the basis of individual perfection. It analyzes everything in order to put it together rationally. It makes religion a matter of personal decision and makes the inner life of the individual dependent upon itself. It releases also the forces of an autonomous political and economic activity.[110]

[105] *TPE*, xvi.

[106] See Peter L. Berger, *The Sacred Canopy: Elements of a Sociological Theory of Religion* (New York: Doubleday, Anchor Books, 1990; repr., Garden City, N.Y.: Doubleday, 1967) 107. I offer this quotation from Peter Berger only for illustration, without intending to suggest that this is the only or the best sociological definition of secularization.

[107] *ST* 3:249, 250.

[108] *TPE*, 43.

[109] *TPE*, 43–44.

[110] *TPE*, 44.

Yet for Tillich the significance of autonomy is more than the cultural and societal rationalization described in the above quotation.[111] According to his theological perspective, autonomy also signifies the destruction of the primordial theonomous unity of religion and culture, the breaking away of society and culture from their religious substance or ultimate meaning, the exclusion of the dimension of depth or transcendence from the finite world.

> The *autonomous consciousness* suppresses the dimension of the origin, the depth dimension of existence, so to speak. Finite forms in their finitude become the objects of knowledge and manipulation. Also the goal of such manipulation remains in the realm of finitude; it can always be stretched out further, indeed indefinitely, but it does not break through the limits of finitude. Such expectation directs itself to progress, not to the really "new."[112]

This is vividly depicted by Tillich's symbol of the horizontal line, which he describes as being "so typical for modernity."[113] In his view, the root symbol for the world of classical antiquity is the circle, which symbolizes the fulfillment of life within the cosmos and the returning of time to itself. In late antiquity and the middle ages, the archetypal symbol became the vertical line, which tried to go beyond the cosmos to the divine, to reach the ultimate itself in being and meaning. In the Renaissance and the Enlightenment, the horizontal line prevailed. Subsequent developments continued to use the horizontal line, which symbolized "going ahead in time and space endlessly" and "going ahead in this world indefinitely, without termination."[114] As Tillich writes, "In the eighteenth century the belief in progress, and in the nineteenth century belief in universal evolution, supported the industrial, social, and political revolutions which shaped the modern world."[115] The vertical dimension, the dimension of depth or of ultimate concern, was lost.[116] The horizontal line can extend toward infinity, but even so it is still an

---

[111] See Jürgen Habermas, *Reason and Rationalization of Society* (trans. Thomas McCarthy; vol. 1 of *The Theory of Communicative Action*; Boston: Beacon, 1984) 143–271.

[112] *SD*, 23 (emphasis original).

[113] *IRCM*, 29.

[114] *IRCM*, 24.

[115] *IRCM*, 27–30.

[116] For Tillich's discussion of the loss of the dimension of depth and the dimension of religion as ultimate concern in industrial society, see "The Lost Dimension of Religion," in *SSOTS*, 41–48.

infinity within the realm of finitude. One might call it "infinite finitude."[117] It represents a thorough this-worldliness that never goes beyond the finite realm. Tillich frequently invokes technological production as an example. The production of goods, as well as technological advancement, are unceasing and limitless activities; however, the question "production for what?" is never adequately answered, for the dimension of ultimate meaning is lost. Such is the state and the predicament of autonomy, and this is why autonomy is described by Tillich as the spirit that is closed in itself and follows its own rational necessity.[118]

Self-Sufficient Finitude

The understanding of autonomy as the self-enclosed spirit that follows its own rationality shares almost the same meaning as the spirit of "self-sufficient finitude" (*in sich ruhenden Endlichkeit*), which Tillich uses to characterize the spirit of bourgeois society.[119] To say that the spirit is closed in itself or self-sufficient is to imply forms of life from which the eternal is being shut out. Existence is directed to itself and complacent with this-worldly pursuits.[120] This is the secularization which is intrinsic to the nature of humanism. As Tillich writes, "Humanity has become self-sufficient. One seeks the fulfillment of one's meaning in oneself."[121] In this light, so Tillich says, we can understand the characteristic attitude of the West, such as the endless attempt to find unconditional meaning in the finite.[122]

For Tillich, the spirit of self-sufficient finitude is most clearly seen in the three representative products of modernity: natural science, technology, and capitalist economy.[123] Natural science aims to show that "reality is governed wholly by its own laws and is rationally intelligible." World-ruling technology conquers time, space, and nature for the sake of human beings. More important,

---

[117] Tillich actually uses "unendlichen Endlichkeit" (infinite finitude) in *MW/HW* 5:54 = *RS*, 107.

[118] *GW* 13:114.

[119] "Der Geist der in sich ruhenden Endlichkeit ist für unsere Zeit der Geist der bürgerlichen Gesellschaft [The spirit of self-sufficient finitude is for our time the spirit of bourgeois society]" (*MW/HW* 5:53). See also *MW/HW* 5:47, 58, 63, 69, 72, 73, 78, 79, 92, 96. The expression "in sich ruhenden Endlichkeit" can be translated as "finitude resting in itself" or "self-relying finitude."

[120] See *MW/HW* 5:35 = *RS*, 50.

[121] *PTC*, 101.

[122] Ibid.

[123] *RS*, 42.

the capitalist economy "seeks to arouse and to satisfy ever increasing demands without raising the question as to the meaning of the process which claims the service of all the spiritual and physical human abilities."[124] For Tillich, the "technologically based, scientifically implemented and politically organized economic system of Western capitalism" is the most striking expression of the self-sufficient finitude of humanism.

> Capitalism is the perfect symbol of secularized humanism. It is by nature a limitless, all-engrossing activity, a ceaseless unrest that partakes of no larger peace. Human life in this system constantly alternates between tension and release, and no relaxation can be permitted under these conditions.[125]

Nevertheless, Tillich is quick to add that even these manifestations of the spirit of self-sufficient finitude are the results of "past devotion to the eternal."[126] The mathematical natural science of Johannes Kepler, Galileo Galilei, and Issac Newton emerged from the desire to know the laws of God's creation. Technology originally had the purpose of emancipating human beings from the demonic powers in natural things. Liberal economy and the bourgeois society were based upon the high evaluation of the individual, whose emancipation proceeded from the recognition of the sacredness of personality. Only once the emancipated person in the capitalist economy had acquired an unlimited desire for economic power and free competition had forced most sectors of society towards infinite profit seeking did there come a turning away from the eternal.[127] In other words, these embodiments of self-sufficient finitude were the result of the secularization of activities that were originally theonomous. Autonomous modernity originated from a theonomous background from which it broke away. Modern society, Tillich maintains, is the secularization of religious heritage. As "self-sufficient finitude," its concerns are this-worldly: "The sanctification of daily life has been replaced by the commonplace. The acceptance of creation and the world has become worldliness, and the will to religious transformation of the world has become

---

[124] *RS*, 47–48.
[125] *PTC*, 101 = *MW/HW* 3:176. See also Walter Benjamin, "Capitalism as Religion," in *Walter Benjamin: Selected Writings 1913–1926* (ed. Marcus Bullock and Michael W. Jennings; vol. 1; Cambridge, Mass.: Harvard University Press, 1996]) 288–89.
[126] *RS*, 48.
[127] *MW/HW* 5:35 = *RS*, 48–50.

autonomous politics, economics, and technology. . . . Modern society is the autonomous and secular phase of Protestant Christian society."[128]

Problems of Self-Sufficient Finitude

Capitalism is self-sufficient finitude *par excellence*. As Weber points out, modern capitalism, born from the spirit of Protestant asceticism, has emerged victorious as an irresistible force, and no longer needs the support of its religious foundation.[129] Secularization is complete in an autonomous economic system that is subject only to its own laws. The effects of capitalism on human relations to things and to community bear the marks of what Tillich describes as autonomy in contrast to theonomy:

> In the free market economy the relation to things becomes loveless [*eroslos*], without community [*gemeinschaftlos*], and dominating [*herrschaftlich*]. Things become commodities, i.e., objects whose meaning is to make profit through buying and selling, but not to expand the compass of personal life. They are purchased and sold in a way of domination, not community moderation. Hence their acquisition does not have any limit. Free economy drives necessarily toward the in itself infinite commercial imperialism. It is infinite—but in relation to finitude. Just because of this its infinity is the most complete expression of the finitude which is self-sufficient, always restless, but never transcends itself.[130]

Just as autonomy is ambiguous, so is self-sufficient finitude. On the one hand, the dominating and loveless relation to things as characteristic of capitalism emancipates human beings from finite holiness and exalts personality above the whole realm of things. On the other hand, it impoverishes personality through the infinite service to the domination of things and the devotion to the finite. Human beings have no possibility of finding real satisfaction in things that have lost their inner meaning. Without a definitely directed love, the impoverished personality is driven "to engage in unending, ever-increasing, life-consuming activity in the service of unlimited wants. [Autonomy] means the domination of the economic function over all the other functions of life; its consequence is bondage to time and hence also the lack of time for attention to the eternal."[131] This is the major problem of the spirit of self-sufficient finitude: Human beings are confined to the endless pursuit of things within

---

[128] *PE*, 4.
[129] Weber, *Protestant Ethic and the Spirit of Capitalism*, 180–82.
[130] *MW/HW* 5:54.
[131] *MW/HW* 5:54–55 = *RS*, 107–9.

the realm of finitude and thereby alienate themselves from the eternal, from the ultimate meaning of life.

> In all this one finds no self-transcendence, no hallowing of existence. The forms of the life-process became completely independent of the depth of life. They are self-sufficient and establish a self-sufficient presence.[132]

Technical Reason

Tillich's idea of autonomy and self-sufficient finitude describes a state or a type of culture that is cut off from the religious depth and follows reason as its own law.[133] The prevalence of self-sufficient reason is a crucial feature of autonomy and modernity and is also the origin of the pathologies of modernity that will be examined in the rest of this chapter.

From Ontological to Technical Reason

As we have seen in Tillich's account of the development of bourgeois society in "The World Situation," the rise and victory of reason were decisive for the emergence and establishment of modernity.[134] It is not precise enough, however, to talk about reason in general. Tillich identifies different kinds of reason, making a distinction primarily between "ontological reason" and "technical reason"; elsewhere, however, he distinguishes four kinds of reason: universal reason, critical reason, intuitive reason, and technical reason.[135] In the fight of the bourgeois society against feudalism and absolutism, it was critical reason (which Tillich also calls "revolutionary reason") as the principle of truth and justice that played an indispensable role. It is a passionate and revolutionary emphasis on the essential goodness of human beings in the name of justice. Critical reason displays a "passionate belief in the logos structure of reality" and in the ability of the human mind to reestablish this structure by social transformation.[136] As it involves a passion for the logos in mind and in reality, it presupposes what Tillich calls "ontological reason"

---

[132] *MW/HW* 5:34 = *RS*, 48 [translation modified].

[133] *GW* 13:114.

[134] *TP*, 112–18.

[135] For the distinction between ontological reason and technical reason, see *ST* 1:72–74. For the four concepts of reason, see *HCT*, 326–30.

[136] See *HCT*, 328. For the "logos structure" of mind and reality, see page 64 above.

or "universal reason."[137] Ontological reason, which predominates in the classical tradition of Western philosophy, is understood as "the structure of mind which enables the mind to grasp and to transform reality." It operates not just in the cognitive and technical functions of the human mind but in the emotional, aesthetic, and practical realms as well.[138]

After the success of the bourgeois revolutions, a major change in the predominant type of reason took place, which corresponded to the development of a worldwide economy of industrial capitalism. The preceding types of reason—"ontological reason" and "revolutionary reason"—were replaced by "technical reason," which has become "the instrument of a new system of production and exchange." It "became decisive throughout the world as far as the dominance of Western influences reaches."[139] According to Tillich, "technical reason" is a partial and reductive form of reason. Once it prevails, it reduces the classical, ontological concept of reason to the capacity for "reasoning," for cognitive acts that "deal with the discovery of means for ends."[140] Technical reason as "reasoning" does not pose any problem for Tillich as long as it accompanies ontological reason, which determines the ends. In the middle of the nineteenth century, however, "reasoning" began to separate from reason, and technical reason began to part company from ontological reason.[141] As the concept of reason is severely narrowed, the ends—that is, purposes, values, and norms—become excluded from the former realm of reason. The result is devastating and dehumanizing.

> The consequence is that the ends are provided by nonrational forces, either by positive traditions or by arbitrary decisions serving the will to power. Critical reason has ceased to exercise its controlling function over norms and ends. At the same time the noncognitive sides of reason have been consigned to the irrelevance of pure subjectivity. In some forms of logical positivism the philosopher even refuses to "understand" anything that transcends technical reason, thus making his philosophy completely irrelevant for questions of existential concern. Technical reason, however refined in logical and methodological

---

[137] *HCT*, 326. "The logos is the principle through which God creates the world. . . . Reality and mind have a logos structure. As a structure of reality and mind, logos includes our power of knowledge, our ethical awareness or conscience, and our aesthetic intuition. They are all expression of the logos in us" (ibid.).

[138] *ST* 1:72.

[139] *ST* 1:72; *TP*, 114–15, 140.

[140] *ST* 1:72–73. This kind of reason is also called "calculating reason" (*SSOTS*, 79).

[141] *ST* 1:73.

respects, dehumanizes man if it is separated from ontological reason. And, beyond this, technical reason itself is impoverished and corrupted if it is not continually nourished by ontological reason.[142]

Tillich's critique of technical reason echoes the critique of instrumental reason by the Frankfurt School. In fact, he cites Horkheimer's *Eclipse of Reason* when he makes the distinction between ontological reason and technical reason.[143] Horkheimer does not use the terms "ontological reason" and "technical reason" but rather "objective" and "subjective" reason.[144] Their ideas are similar, however, and each illuminates the other. According to Horkheimer, objective reason is a principle or structure inherent in reality that calls for corresponding behaviors or attitudes.[145] It is used for understanding and determining the ends.[146] Subjective reason, by contrast, is formal and instrumental. It is concerned with the adequacy of means or procedures for ends or purposes that are more or less taken for granted and cannot determine the desirability of any end in itself.[147] Horkheimer writes, "It attaches little importance to the question whether the purposes as such are reasonable. If it concerns itself at all with ends, it takes for granted that they too are reasonable in the subjective sense, i.e., that they serve the subject's interest in relation to self-preservation."[148] Because of the dissolution of objective reason, ideas such as justice, equality, and happiness lack any confirmation by reason. Moreover, subjective reason lends itself easily to ideological manipulation.[149]

The grave implications of technical (or subjective) reason that cannot determine the desirability of ends are not difficult to imagine. For example, Auschwitz (and the entire system of deportation and extermination camps) was apparently regarded by the Nazis as the most efficient method, calculated

---

[142] *ST* 1:73.

[143] See *ST* 1:72. Tillich also notes Weber's critique of technical reason: "One of the greatest scholars of the 19th century, Max Weber, described the tragic self-destruction of life once technical reason has come into control" (*CTB*, 136).

[144] See Max Horkheimer, *Eclipse of Reason* (New York: Continuum, 1974) 3–5. Tillich himself talks about objective and subjective reason in *ST* 1:75–78.

[145] Horkheimer, *Eclipse of Reason*, 9–11.

[146] Ibid., 10.

[147] Ibid., 3, 21.

[148] Ibid., 3–4. The value of subjective reason lies in the domination of human beings and nature, serving the social process, i.e., the status quo (ibid., 21).

[149] Ibid., 23–24.

by technical reason, for carrying out the mass extermination of Jews and other non-Aryans, an end which the Nazis considered justified in the interest of the German nation. This is one of the most extreme cases of the dehumanizing results of technical reason that concerns itself only with means and leaves the ends to what Tillich calls "nonrational forces," such as the "will to power" or "instincts and will."[150] As Tillich says, technical reason "can be used for any purposes dictated by the will, including those which deny reason in the sense of truth and justice."[151]

Problem of Means and Ends

Though we can conceive of less extreme examples of the consequences of the reduction of reason to technical reason, such consequences or problems are intrinsic to technical reason itself. Tillich writes, "Technical reason provides means for ends but offers no guidance in the determination of ends."[152] It chooses the most effective means for an end but leaves the end unquestioned or ignored. Thus, in reality, technical reason "became concerned with means to stabilize the existing order." This is why, in Tillich's view, technical reason is "conservative with respect to ends and revolutionary with respect to means."[153] The conservative orientation of technical reason implies that the ends are taken for granted and eventually disregarded, faded out, forgotten, and lost. The problems associated with this loss can be seen clearly in the realm of capitalistic production, where technical reason is paramount. Industrial capitalism engages in the endless invention of means. For Tillich, this endless production of means accords with the definition of the telos (the inner aim of life) of human beings in modernity as the subjection and transformation of nature and human being. Tillich considers this telos to be problematic, as its end is not really an end: "All means are by definition means for an end. But what is the end, if the production of means is the inner aim of man's being?" While some people might regard happiness as the end, he argues that happiness might accompany the fulfillment of a telos but does not constitute it. The human subjection of nature and human

---

[150] ST 1:73; TP, 140. I use the example of Auschwitz for illustration. The example is not used by Tillich.

[151] TP, 115.

[152] TP, 114.

[153] TP, 115.

beings is thus "a telos that negates a telos."[154] The inner aim of human life is lost in modernity. Tillich describes an "inner contradiction of an end that is the endless production of means without an end."[155] Economic production in industrial capitalism, facilitated by technical reason, becomes a "vicious circle of production of means as ends which in turn become means without any ultimate end."[156]

Tillich calls this "the ambiguity of means and ends" in technical production. Technical freedom is limitless. The question of "for what?" exposes the problem when, after the satisfaction of basic needs, "new needs are endlessly engendered and satisfied and—in a dynamic economy—engendered to be satisfied." In such a situation, technical possibility becomes a temptation, and, as Tillich says, this leads to cultural emptiness. "The production of means—of gadgets—becomes an end in itself, since no superior end is visible. This ambiguity is largely responsible for the emptiness of contemporary life."[157] Tillich notes that the domination of technical reason results in emptiness, meaninglessness, and anxiety as expressed in existentialist art, literature, and philosophy.[158]

Tillich describes such a situation in *The Courage to Be* as the third period of anxiety in the history of Western civilization. He characterizes this period, which takes place "at the end of the modern period," as that in which "the anxiety of emptiness and meaninglessness is dominant."[159]

---

[154] *SSOTS*, 79–80. According to Tillich, Western thought has given three different answers to the question about the telos of human beings. The classical-humanist definition views the inner aim of the human being as the "actualization of [one's] potentialities" and the overcoming of distortions of one's nature caused by error and passions. The transcendental-religious definition of human telos in late antiquity and early Christianity is "the elevation from the universe of finitude and guilt to the reunion with ultimate reality." The scientific-technical definition of telos, prevalent since the Renaissance and the Reformation, is "the active subjection and transformation of nature and man" (*SSOTS*, 78–79).

[155] *SSOTS*, 80.

[156] *TP*, 132. "There is no end in the chain of means and ends except the person. And if the person himself becomes a means, an endless chain of means-and-ends-and-means is established that crushes purpose, meaning, and person" (*SSOTS*, 133–34).

[157] *ST* 3:74.

[158] *SSOTS*, 80.

[159] *CTB*, 57, 61.

Objectification and Dehumanization

Controlling Knowledge

Modern capitalism requires technical reason to determine the best means, by calculation and analysis, for a desirable economic end. Such calculation and analysis obtain knowledge of the processes of production and consumption in order to control them, and the same cognitive attitude applies to other aspects of modern society. Borrowing from Max Scheler, Tillich calls such knowledge "controlling knowledge"[160] in contrast with "existential knowledge."[161] In the act of knowing, the former tends toward detachment and the latter toward participation. In Tillich's view, however, controlling knowledge still contains an element of participation because complete detachment is ontologically impossible. Every act of knowing is a "union through separation." This is the ontological structure of knowledge.[162] Controlling knowledge is not bad in itself. In fact it is "an essential element in every cognitive act." What Tillich finds problematic is "its attempt to monopolize the whole cognitive function" and to deny other ways of knowledge.[163]

Objectification

Controlling knowledge, which is "the outstanding, though not the only, example of technical reason,"[164] tends toward objectification, that is, toward the reduction of the object of knowledge to a "thing":[165]

> [Controlling knowledge] unites subject and object for the sake of the control of the object by the subject. It transforms the object into a

---

[160] *ST* 1:97; Tillich, "Participation and Knowledge: Problem of an Ontology of Cognition," in *MW/HW* 1:381–89, at 385 = *SSOTS*, 65–74, at 69. The essay was originally published in 1955 in *Aufsätze, Max Horkheimer zum sechzigsten Geburtstag gewidmet* (ed. Theodor W. Adorno and Walter Dirks; vol. 1 of *Sociologica*; Frankfurter Beiträge zur Soziologie 1; Frankfurt am Main: Europäische Verlagsanstalt) 201–9. "Controlling knowledge" is Tillich's own translation of Scheler's term *Herrschaftswissen*.

[161] *MW/HW* 1:385. Another term for the opposite pole of "controlling knowledge" is "receiving knowledge" in which there is no means-ends relationship. The object, including the emotional element, is taken into union with the subject (*ST* 1:98).

[162] *MW/HW* 1:385; *ST* 1:94–95.

[163] *ST* 1:89–90.

[164] *ST* 1:97.

[165] For Tillich, a thing is something that is completely conditioned without any subjectivity. Even a mechanical tool is not completely a "thing," as it still has some unique structures and forms to express its purpose. See *ST* 1:173; *SSOTS*, 113.

completely conditioned and calculable "thing." It deprives it of any
subjective quality. Controlling knowledge looks upon its object as
something which cannot return its look. Certainly, in every type of
knowledge subject and object are logically distinguished. There is
always an object, even in our knowledge of God. But controlling
knowledge "objectifies" not only logically (which is unavoidable) but
also ontologically and ethically.[166]

For Tillich, objectification is fundamental to the spirit of bourgeois
society, that is, to modernity. Nature and human society are involved in
an objectification[167] that corresponds to the increasing control of each by
technology in the service of capitalistic production. Objectification occurs
both at the theoretical and the practical levels. At the theoretical level,
objectification is exemplified by the philosophy of Descartes, which reduces
the human being to a knowing subject.[168] Tillich writes, "Isolated subjectivity
appears in idealistic epistemologies which reduce man to a cognitive subject
(*ens cogitans*), who perceives, analyzes, and controls reality." The subject
does not have any participation in the object. Between the subject and
the object, Tillich sees no eros[169] but rather only calculation, control, and
domination. The objective analysis of nature, for example, leads to "the
utilization of functionally calculable elements in the service of technical
and economic goals."[170] Likewise, the objective analysis of society "leads to
the factoring out of individual persons, driven by instinct and choice." The
social processes can then be rationally mastered by manipulating the drive
mechanisms of individuals and the masses.[171] Thus, theoretical objectification,
sustained by controlling knowledge, leads to objectification in the practical
sphere. Practical objectification is also brought about by industrial capitalism
through commodification. The intrinsic power of things is taken away and
they become "rational economic instruments." Tillich writes, "The more a
thing becomes a mere commodity, the less it exists in an eros relation to the
possessor and the less intrinsic power it possesses. In this inner emptiness,
however, the thing becomes the object of the subjective eros and of the
subjective will to power." The subjective will to power in turn "becomes a

[166] *ST* 1:97.
[167] *SD*, 48.
[168] *SSOTS*, 101–2.
[169] *ST* 2:66.
[170] *SD*, 48.
[171] *SD*, 48.

thing in the oppressive process of a limitless industrial economy."[172] Thus, the most significant aspect of this objectification in the practical sphere is the objectification of human beings. Controlling knowledge objectifies the world, and each human that is part of it "becomes a mere object among objects," which are thoroughly calculable. Behaviorism serves as just one example, among others, of what happens when "a theoretical objectivation is carried through which can be and is used for the practical dealing with [human beings] as though they were mere objects."[173]

Dehumanization and Dialectic of Enlightenment

Controlling knowledge and its objectifying effects are ubiquitous in modern society. As Tillich notes, "Life, spirit, personality, community, meanings, values, even one's ultimate concern, should be treated in terms of detachment, analysis, calculation, technical use. The power behind this claim is the preciseness, verifiability, the public approachability of controlling knowledge, and, above all, the tremendous success of its application to certain levels of reality." This situation holds the public mind captive. The result is "a rapid decay of spiritual (not only of the Spiritual) life, an estrangement from nature, and, most dangerous of all, a dealing with human beings as with things."[174]

> Man actually has become what controlling knowledge considers him to be, a thing among things, a cog in the dominating machine of production and consumption, a dehumanized object of tyranny or a normalized object of public communication. Cognitive dehumanization has produced actual dehumanization.[175]

Thus, a "dialectic of enlightenment" has occurred. Through the "technical control of nature," the "psychological control of the person," and the "organizational control of society," modern society, which had been devised

---

[172] *PE*, 74–75.

[173] *ST* 2:66; *SSOTS*, 81–82.

[174] *ST* 1:99.

[175] *ST* 1:99. See also *SSOTS*, 100–1. Besides objectification, Tillich also talks about the emotional, irrational reactions that controlling knowledge has triggered. Controlling knowledge is formalism in the cognitive realm (*ST* 1:89). Emotionalism reacts against formalism, but emotion without rational structure becomes irrationalism, which is destructive. For example, the "empty irrationalism of the German youth group movement" was the "fertile soil for the rational irrationalism of the Nazis" (*ST* 1:93). "If reason sacrifices its formal structure, and with them its critical power, the result is not an empty sentimentality but the demonic rise of antirational forces, which often are supported by all the tools of technical reason" (*ST* 1:94).

for human liberation, "fell under the objects it itself had created." The human being becomes objectified and alienated: "man, for whom all this was invented as a means, becomes a means himself in the service of means."[176] Tillich calls this the "ambiguity of self and thing." In transforming natural objects into things by the technical act, human beings destroy their natural structures and relations, but as one does this, one becomes "a thing among things." One's own self becomes lost among objects with which there is no communicating. Tillich writes, "He becomes a part of the technical product and loses his character as an independent self. The liberation given to man by technical possibilities turns into enslavement to technical actuality."[177]

Conformity

Another manifestation of objectification and dehumanization in modernity is conformity. While conformity is unavoidable, it becomes negative when "the individual form that gives uniqueness and dignity to a person is subdued by collective form."[178] Conformity is not confined to collectivistic societies such as the Soviet Union and other communist countries. In fact, Tillich regards the society of the United States as characterized by "democratic conformism."[179] The mechanization of consumption in America has produced standardized human beings conditioned for a "subpersonal conformity to this immense process."[180] Conformity results from objectification in industrial capitalism. As Tillich says, "The technical form of monopolistic production, not only of material but also of spiritual goods, has made the individual, both in his production and in his consumption, a part of an all-embracing machine moved by anonymous forces."[181] The human being is reduced in theory to "a bundle of conditioned reflexes without a determining center" and in practice to "a commodity, a cog in the big machine of production and consumption, an object among objects, to be tested, calculated, and managed.

---

[176] *CTB*, 138. "In order to establish control of reality for mechanical ends, humanity lost itself. This self-estrangement was the price paid for modern science and economy" (*TP*, 140).

[177] *ST* 3:74. In the production of objects, not only self and subjectivity are lost but also the self's unity (*SSOTS*, 112).

[178] *SSOTS*, 145. Tillich suggests that another word for conformity is "patternization" (ibid.).

[179] *CTB*, 103–12.

[180] *TPE*, 263–64.

[181] *TPE*, 263.

. . . Even those who determine are determined by the structure of the society they control."[182]

Moreover, conformity is caused by the "intentional imposition of patterns on the masses by interested groups."[183] Political and economic manipulations and various mechanisms of adjustment serve as examples of such impositions. In fact, "Western technical society has produced methods of adjusting persons to its demands in production and consumption that are less brutal, but in the long run, more effective than totalitarian suppression. They depersonalize not by commanding but by providing; providing, namely, what makes individual creativity superfluous."[184] The education of "adjustment," Tillich notices, "produces conformity just by allowing for more spontaneity of the child," but "the definite frame within which this spontaneity is quietly kept leads to a spontaneous adjustment that is more dangerous for creative freedom than an openly deterministic influence."[185] Then the various mass media adapt themselves to the taste of the masses, omnipresent advertising exploits the hidden desires of people, and mass culture turns cultural creations of the past and present into standardized cultural commodities for consumption.[186] All this echoes the powerful critique, by Horkheimer and Adorno in the *Dialectic of Enlightenment,* of the culture industry and of the conformity and sameness that it produces.[187]

Unsuccessful Challenges to Objectification

Controlling knowledge and its effects of objectification, which prevail in modernity, have been challenged from all sides. Tillich points out that "widespread resistance against the objectifying tendencies in industrial society, first in its capitalistic and then in its totalitarian forms," however unsuccessful in the end, did take place.[188] For example, Tillich regards Nietzsche's philosophy as a critique of bourgeois society. He observes that, for Nietzsche, the greatest obstacle to "life," which takes the place of Tillich's idea of God, "is the 'objectivating' nature of bourgeois thinking and acting."

---

[182] *SSOTS*, 146.

[183] *SSOTS*, 146.

[184] *SSOTS*, 134.

[185] *SSOTS*, 135.

[186] *SSOTS*, 134–35, 147–48. Tillich finds that even some methods for producing a religious revival resemble those used in the marketing of mass culture (*SSOTS*, 148).

[187] See Horkheimer and Adorno, *Dialectic of Enlightenment*, 94–136.

[188] *ST* 1:173.

Thus Nietzsche fought with prophetic wrath against the bourgeois spirit in the name of creative life.[189] Nietzsche, in Tillich's view, was fighting against an enemy that he could not conquer even within himself: "This foe was the world created by the victorious bourgeoisie, the world in which means replaced ends, and everything, man included, had become an object of analysis and control. But it was just analysis and control that Nietzsche applied in his attempt to overcome the world based on them." The "tragic implications" of this contradiction, Tillich remarks, are manifest in such twentieth century phenomena as fascism.[190] Like Nietzsche, other intellectuals who tried to resist "the tidal wave of controlling knowledge" had instantaneous success but were also unsuccessful in the long run. Tillich mentions Hegel's romanticism, Bergson's philosophy of life, and existentialism.[191] His remarks about existentialism are worth noting: "Existentialism is the most desperate attempt to escape the power of controlling knowledge and of the objectified world which technical reason has produced. It says 'No' to this world, but, in order to say 'Yes' to something else, it has either to use controlling knowledge or to turn to revelation."[192] This implies that, for Tillich, the real solution to the problems of modernity is theological. Existentialism or other philosophies may offer perceptive analyses of the human situation, but they are unable to provide an answer, for "human existence itself *is* the question."[193]

Theological Responses: A Snapshot

We have discussed the way that autonomy, which is the decisive principle of modernity, is characterized by the exclusion of the dimension of depth, religious substance, and ultimate meaning. Technical reason combined with autonomy produces meaninglessness and despair, which in turn provoke the reaction of a destructive heteronomy. For Tillich, theonomy is the response.

---

[189] Paul Tillich, "Nietzsche and the Bourgeois Spirit," *JHI* 6 (1945) 307–9, at 308.

[190] Tillich, "Nietzsche and the Bourgeois Spirit," 309.

[191] *ST* 1:99–100.

[192] *ST* 1:100.

[193] *ST* 1:65. Tillich stresses that the Christian message "provides the answers to the questions implied in human existence." Such answers "cannot be derived from the questions." "They are 'spoken' *to* human existence from beyond it. Otherwise they would not be answers, for the question is human existence itself" (*ST* 1:64). This is the basic conviction of his method of correlation.

> Under the guidance of technical reason autonomy conquered all reactions but completely lost the dimension of depth. It became shallow, empty, without ultimate meaning, and produced conscious or unconscious despair. In this situation powerful heteronomies of a quasi-political character entered the vacuum created by an autonomy which lacked the dimension of depth. The double fight against an empty autonomy and a destructive heteronomy makes the quest for a new theonomy as urgent today as it was at the end of the ancient world. The catastrophe of autonomous reason is complete. Neither autonomy nor heteronomy, isolated and in conflict, can give the answer.[194]

Moreover, theonomy is a solution to the problem of "producing means for ends which in turn become means, and so on without limit."[195] For Tillich, theonomous culture involves self-limitation in technical production, which can be brought about by the Spiritual Presence: "The divine Spirit, cutting out of the vertical direction to resist an unlimited running-ahead in the horizontal line, drives toward a technical production that is subjected to the ultimate end of all processes—Eternal Life."[196]

Tillich's theology offers two responses to objectification in modern society. The first is an approach of partial withdrawal for the purposes of resistance and critique. The New Reality (or what he later calls the New Being) provides the space for such a withdrawal:

> The person as person can preserve himself only by a *partial nonparticipation in* the objectifying structures of technical society. But he can withdraw even partially only if he has a place to withdraw. And this place is the New Reality to which the Christian message points, which transcends Christianity as well as non-Christianity, which is anticipated everywhere in history, and which has found its criterion in the picture of Jesus as the Christ. But the space of the withdrawal is, at the same time, the starting point for the attack on technical society and its power of depersonalization.[197]

[194] *ST* 1:86.

[195] *ST* 3:259.

[196] *ST* 3:259.

[197] *SSOTS*, 135–36 [emphasis in original]. While Tillich does not expound the meaning of the "New Reality," it seems almost identical with the concept of the "New Being," which he discusses in detail in *Systematic Theology*. The Christian message is understood as "the message of the 'New Being'" (*ST* 1:49). Tillich describes the "New Being" as "a reality in which the self-estrangement of our existence is overcome, a reality of reconciliation and reunion, of creativity, meaning, and hope" (*ST* 1:49). "New Being is essential being under the conditions of existence, conquering the gap between essence and existence. For the same idea Paul uses the term 'new creature,' calling those who are 'in' Christ 'new creatures'"

The second theological response is the transformation effected by theonomy. More specifically, Tillich asserts that theonomy is the solution to the problems of "the production of means for ends which themselves become means without an ultimate end" and "the technical transformation of parts of nature into things which are only things, i.e., technical objects."[198] These problems are expressions of a general ambiguity of culture—the ambiguity of the split between subject and object. Theonomy, brought about by the Spiritual Presence, can overcome the subject-object split in the realm of "complete objectivation," that is, the realm of technical activity, "by producing objects which can be imbued with subjective qualities; by determining all means toward an ultimate end and, by so doing, limiting man's unlimited freedom to go beyond the given."[199] Even technical objects and processes can become theonomous under the Spiritual Presence, when there is an eros toward the technical objects that is not corrupted by commercial interests.[200]

Critique of Cultural Modernity as the Critique of the Cultural Dimension of Capitalism

At the beginning of this chapter, I claimed that Tillich's critique of cultural modernity is basically his critique of the cultural dimension of capitalism. This claim has now been borne out by our examination of Tillich's critique of the crucial elements in the spirit of bourgeois society. Capitalism, which follows its own rational laws and is devoted only to the limitless pursuit of finite things, is for Tillich the paradigm of autonomy and self-sufficient finitude. The critique of autonomy and self-sufficient finitude is therefore a critique of the culture in which capitalism dominates all aspects of life. Capitalism relies on the methodical calculation of the best means toward economic ends, such as the efficient deployment of the most effective technology for industrial production and commercial operation. This involves the use of technical reason, which Tillich critiques. Capitalism employs controlling knowledge in the domination of nature, the rational organization of production, and even the manipulation of consumption. The result is that not only natural objects but also human beings are treated as things. This is the dehumanization that

---

(*ST* 2:118–19). The New Being is manifest in Jesus the Christ, "who brings the new eon, new reality" (*ST* 1:49; see *ST* 2:118–38 for details).

[198] *ST* 3:258.

[199] *ST* 3:258.

[200] *ST* 3:258–59.

Tillich so strongly criticizes and laments. Therefore, we can reasonably claim that Tillich's critique of cultural modernity in both his earlier works (such as *The Religious Situation*) and his later works (such as *Systematic Theology*) is a critique of the cultural dimension of capitalism.

The Distinctiveness of Tillich's Critique of Modernity

We have just become acquainted with Tillich's critical interpretation of modernity by exploring his analysis of the historical development and main features of bourgeois society, and by examining in greater detail several crucial elements of the spirit of bourgeois society, which he interprets and critiques. We are now ready to step back a little to consider the question: Is there anything distinctive in Tillich's critical interpretation of modernity? Other philosophers, social theorists, and cultural critics have offered various interpretations and critiques of modernity. Does Tillich, as a *theologian*, say anything substantially different from them?

Modernity as Manifestation of Universal Human Predicament

Tillich as a theologian is distinctive in seeing the problems and pathologies of modernity as the historically specific manifestations of the universal predicament of human existence. This theological perspective sets Tillich's works apart not only from social-theoretical and philosophical approaches to the pathologies of modernity, but also from theological approaches that respond specifically to certain social or existential problems of modernity (such as oppression, alienation, dehumanization) as the primary human predicament which theology must address and seek to transform. For Tillich, these problems of modernity are theologically significant insofar as they clearly disclose the existential situation of human beings.

> It is true that special situations reveal more sharply special elements in man's existential situation. They reveal them, but they do not create them. The danger of depersonalization or "objectivization" (becoming a thing) is most outspoken in Western industrial society. But there are dangers of the same character in all societies; for the separation of individualization from participation is a mark of estrangement generally.[201]

---

[201] *ST* 2:65–66.

Thus, he rejects the view (held by some social theorists and philosophers) that changing the structure of modern society would change the existential predicament of human beings. For him, such a view leads to utopianism.

> There are many sociological and existential analyses of man in industrial society which point to self-loss and world-loss, to mechanization and objectification, to loneliness and surrender to the collective, to the experience of emptiness and meaninglessness. These analyses are true as far as they go, but they are fallacious if in our period of history they derive the evil of man's predicament from the structure of industrial society. Such a derivation implies the belief that changes in the structure of our society would, as such, change man's existential predicament. All utopianism has this character; its main mistake is in not distinguishing man's existential situation from its manifestation in different historical periods.[202]

Therefore, instead of responding specifically to the particular problem of the objectification of human beings in modernity, Tillich's theology addresses the ontological root of the problem, such as the ambiguity of subject and object. For him, theology formulates the answers, implied in revelation, to the questions implied in human existence.[203] His theology seeks to address existential problems that are general and not their specific manifestations, which differ in different historical periods and cultures. One might say that Tillich's critical interpretation of modernity has taken a "radical" approach, in the sense that it seeks to go to the root (Latin *radix*) of problems. One might also describe it as a "theonomous" approach, as it keeps modernity always open to the answers of theology. Social and psychological problems in modernity might be changed perhaps by social reforms and psychotherapy, but such changes are never "radical," never complete, for such changes, as human endeavors, are not able to affect the existential predicament of human

---

[202] *ST* 2:74. In the same vein, Tillich points out that "the tragic self-destruction of our present world is the result not simply of the particular contradictions bred by that world but also of the contradictions which characterize human life always. . . . History shows that, over and over again, the achievements of humanity, as though by a logic of tragedy, turn against humanity. . . . Therefore the Christian message cannot anticipate a future situation devoid of tragedy even if the demonic forces in the present situation be conquered. The authentic Christian message is never utopian, whether through belief in progress or through faith in revolution" (*TP*, 156).

[203] *ST* 1:61.

beings. The human predicament can only be transformed by the salvific power of the New Being in Jesus as the Christ.[204]

Theonomy as Critical and Constructive Ideal

If we have to identify one theological concept that is most important in Tillich's critical interpretation of modernity, it is theonomy. In the 1920s, the concept of theonomy was already indispensable to his theology of culture, which was an integral part of his religious socialism. Theonomy is the goal for which Tillich's religious socialism strives.[205] The concept continued to play an important role in *Systematic Theology*, especially parts 1 and 4. Theonomy, as "the state of culture under the impact of the Spiritual Presence," is the answer to the question of the ambiguities of culture and morality in part 4 of *Systematic Theology*.[206] For Tillich, theonomy is both the primordial state of culture, the loss of which he mourns, and the fulfillment of the eschatological vision, which he hopes for. Theonomy stands for the union of religion and culture, a situation in which finite culture is transparent to the ultimate and the holy. It also stands for a situation that transcends the split between subject and object. Theonomy is the ideal which forms the basis of his interpretation and critique of modernity.

The importance of the concept of theonomy is most evident from the fact that he regards autonomy as the most crucial principle of modern bourgeois society. To describe the spirit of bourgeois society in terms of autonomy does not only mean that human culture and reason are free from external authority or tutelage. It also means that culture has lost its union with and closed itself off from its religious depth, ultimate meaning, and the infinite. Modernity is "self-sufficient finitude," following only autonomous reason. It is confined to the realm of the finite. The human spirit becomes devoted to the ever-continuing pursuit of finite things. The loss of theonomy in modern culture is, in a sense, Tillich's theological explanation of rationalization and secularization in modernity. It is the ultimate root of the problems and pathologies of modernity. Other problems in modernity that we examined above, such as technical reason that is concerned with the calculation of

---

[204] See *ST*, vol. 2.

[205] *PE*, 55–56, 62–63.

[206] *ST* 3:249, 252–75. In an earlier formulation, Tillich writes: "Theonomy is the answer to the question implied in autonomy, the question concerning a religious substance and an ultimate meaning of life and culture" (*TPE*, 46).

means for taken-for-granted ends and controlling knowledge that leads to objectification of things and of human persons, can also be traced to the loss of theonomy. Thus, while Tillich shows similarities to some social theorists (especially to the leading members of the Frankfurt School) in his critique of technical reason, objectification, and dehumanization, he is distinctive in offering a theological perspective based on the concept of theonomy as a critical and constructive ideal.

Theological Hope: Beyond Social-Theoretical Pessimism

Thus, compared to social theorists to whom Tillich is indebted (such as Weber) or whose ideas are similar to his own (such as members of the Frankfurt School), Tillich is less pessimistic toward modernity. In spite of this difference, however, his diagnosis of modernity is basically in line with the German tradition of sociology.[207]

Weber and the Frankfurt School theorists were quite pessimistic about modernity. While Weber was committed to a value-free historical investigation of the rise of occidental capitalism in *The Protestant Ethic and the Spirit of Capitalism*, he nonetheless shifted to a more prophetic tone at the end of the book, painting a gloomy picture of capitalistic modernity which he depicted as an "iron cage."[208] Horkheimer and Adorno were even more pessimistic, as expressed in *Dialectic of Enlightenment* and later works. In their view, the domination of a calculating, instrumental rationality was so total that they could offer no way of escape or hope for transformation.[209]

In contrast, Tillich the theologian pointed to a way out.[210] Two theological concepts were foremost in enabling Tillich to go beyond the pessimism of Weber, Horkheimer, and Adorno: *kairos* and theonomy. "Kairos is fulfilled time, the moment of time which is invaded by eternity."[211] It refers to "the

---

[207] On the German sociological tradition and the extent to which Tillich shares its insight, see Keith Tester, "Between Sociology and Theology: The Spirit of Capitalism Debate," *SocR* 48 (2000) 43–58. Tester considers Weber and Simmel the major representatives of this tradition.

[208] Weber, *Protestant Ethic and the Spirit of Capitalism*, 181–82.

[209] Horkheimer and Adorno both turned more positive toward religion in their later years, but they did not conceive of religion as bringing this-worldly transformation.

[210] Tester, "Between Sociology and Theology," 45. Tester discusses only Tillich's concept of *kairos* and omits theonomy as another way out.

[211] *RS*, 176. " 'Kairos,' the 'fullness of time,' according to the New Testament use of the word, describes the moment in which the eternal breaks into the temporal, and the temporal is prepared to receive it" (*TPE*, xix).

moment at which history, in terms of a concrete situation, had matured to the point of being able to receive the breakthrough of the central manifestation of the Kingdom of God."[212] The unique *kairos* is "the appearance of Jesus as the Christ" as the center of history, but it can be re-experienced again and again through relative *kairoi* in other moments of history as particular manifestations of the Kingdom of God.[213] Tillich felt that a relative *kairos* was happening after the First World War.[214] He saw that the self-sufficient spirit of bourgeois society was deeply shaken and being challenged from all sides—in art and science, in economics and politics, in religious movements outside and inside the churches. In every sphere there was a turning away from the spirit of self-sufficient finitude. In particular, doubt was cast on the completeness of the rationality of natural science, technology, and capitalist economy.[215] All these challenges were for Tillich the manifestations of a *kairos*.

Tillich's hope for an imminent *kairos* faded away after the rise of the Nazis, his emigration from Germany, and the start of the Second World War, but he nevertheless held to hope in theonomy. In fact, theonomy takes up a pivotal role in part 4 of *Systematic Theology*. Earlier in this chapter we looked at several aspects of theonomy: 1) the general solution to the problems of autonomous modern culture; 2) the particular solution to the problem of the unlimited production of means for ends which in turn become means; 3) the cure for the basic split between subject and object and to the specific ambiguities of technical activity and the problem of objectification; 4) the critical and constructive ideal on which his critique of modernity is based. Here we just need to note that, for Tillich, theonomy can only be fragmentarily realized. The Spiritual Presence overcomes the ambiguities of life by creating a "transcendent union" of essential and existential

---

[212] *ST* 3:369.

[213] *TPE*, xix; *ST*, 3:370. According to Tillich, the unique *kairos* is the manifestation of Jesus as the Christ, that is, as the center of history, but what happened in that unique *kairos* "may happen in a derived form again and again in the process of time, creating centers of lesser importance on which the periodization of history is dependent" (*TPE*, xix). They are the relative *kairoi*, "the continually recurring and derivative *kairoi* in which a religious cultural group has an existential encounter with the central event" (*ST* 3:153). "The relation of one *kairos* to the *kairoi* is the relation of the criterion to that which stands under the criterion and the relation of the source of power to that which is nourished by the source of power" (*ST* 3:370).

[214] *TPE*, xix.

[215] See *RS*, 27, 41, 52, 218–19.

elements of being.[216] Although theonomy, which is created by the Spiritual Presence, is also unambiguous, the realization of theonomy in time and space can nevertheless be fragmentary. "The fulfilled transcendent union is an eschatological concept. The fragment is an anticipation."[217] This is Tillich's version of "already but not yet." If this is applied to the relation between theonomy and the problems of modernity, Tillich would say that theonomy can unambiguously overcome the problems and pathologies of modernity, yet fragmentarily. In this dialectical way characteristic of Tillich, both utopian optimism and cynical pessimism are rejected. For Tillich, Weber's "iron cage" of capitalistic modernity is definitely not the final destiny for humanity. Theonomy can be realized fragmentarily in—and in spite of—the most secular, technological, and capitalistic culture. This theological hope leads one beyond pessimism and despair, but there is, at the same time, no place for naïve optimism. The problems of modernity are not expected to be "solved" once and for all. Thus Tillich's concept of theonomy, as a critical and constructive ideal, is the basis of a nuanced interpretation of modernity and a nuanced attitude to social actions that aim at the transformation of modernity.

In his contribution to the volume *Christian Faith and Social Action*,[218] Tillich warns those who participate in movements that challenge modern, technical society to avoid two "shortcuts." The first is a "realism of resignation" to the realities of technical society. That is, in a state of disappointment, old and young people, "without a revolutionary impetus and without visions concerning the future," simply accept and adapt in a matter-of-fact way

---

[216] *ST* 3:129. In *Systematic Theology,* Tillich distinguishes two basic qualifications or states of being: essential and existential. Everything has its essential nature, which, insofar as it participates in the power of being while being limited by nonbeing, is characterized by finitude. However, essence remains a potentiality if it is not actualized, that is, if it does not exist. Existence means standing out of one's own nonbeing. Standing out involves a separation from that out of which one stands. Thus, the state of existence is the state of estrangement (estranged from one's own essential being and from the ground of being). See *ST* 1:165, 189, 202–4; 2:19–21, 29, 44–45; 3:11–12. For Tillich, life is a concrete unity or "mixture" of essence and existence. The separation and interplay of essential and existential elements produce the ambiguities of life. See *ST* 3:12, 32, 107, 129. The Spiritual Presence brings about a reunion of essential and existential being. In the reunion, "ambiguous life is raised above itself to a transcendence that it could not achieve by its own power" (*ST* 3:129). Thus, Tillich calls this "transcendent union."

[217] *ST* 3:140.

[218] Paul Tillich, "The Person in a Technical Society," in *Christian Faith and Social Action* (ed. John A. Hutchinson; New York: Scribner, 1953) 137–53; collected in *SSOTS*, 123–37.

to the given reality of modernity. Tillich maintains that one can resist this conservative and pessimistic mood "by transcending the whole situation and seeing it from a point beyond it."[219] Tillich would say that theology, and especially his notion of theonomy, offers such a transcendent viewpoint. The other shortcut he warns against is "[using] the Christian message as a *deus ex machina* that solves all problems." Tillich points out that "the church and her message are unable to resist the progressive annihilation of the person within industrial society" because the church itself "has been determined by the categories of life and thought that characterize the industrial society." Dehumanization occurs even within the church.[220] Tillich concludes: "Only from 'beyond' can industrial society and its dehumanizing forces be resisted and finally overcome."[221] Such a nuanced position—combining both a realistic perspective that takes seriously the negative aspects of social reality (the church included) and the difficulties in solving social problems, and, at the same time, a perspective of faith that insists on hope for the transformation of social reality in spite of the negativity and difficulty—expresses an attitude that Tillich calls "belief-ful realism" (*gläubigen Realismus*).[222]

Conclusion

This chapter contributes to the construction of a religious critique of global capitalistic modernity in a number of ways. First, it establishes the claim that Tillich's critique of cultural modernity is the same as his critique of the cultural dimension of capitalism. It thus underscores the inseparable relation of capitalism and modernity and it prepares the way for my constructive proposal in chapter 4 which interprets the relation between capitalism and capitalistic modernity as the relation between religious substance and cultural forms. Second, the present chapter offers a general account of Tillich's interpretation of bourgeois society, its spirit, and its historical development. This gives an important background to any critical interpretation of capitalistic

---

[219] *SSOTS*, 131.

[220] *SSOTS*, 131–32.

[221] *SSOTS*, 132.

[222] As Tillich explains, "belief-ful realism" (*gläubigen Realismus*) is "an unconditioned acceptance of the serious importance of our concrete situation in time and of the situation of time in general in the presence of eternity; such an attitude contains the negation of every kind of romanticism and utopianism but it includes the hope of a social and economic life in which the spirit of capitalism—the symbol of self-sufficient finitude—has been overcome" (*MW/HW* 5:58 = *RS*, 116).

modernity, including the one I offer in this book. Third, the chapter provides a thematic reconstruction and an in-depth examination of Tillich's critical interpretation of capitalistic modernity. These can be incorporated into the critique of the cultural aspects of the quasi-religion of global capitalism in my constructive proposal, subject to the necessary revisions and improvements of its inadequacies, which I will discuss in the next chapter. Fourth, the chapter demonstrates the relevance of Tillich's theological perspective, especially his ideal of theonomy, for the critical interpretation of capitalistic modernity and for offering an eschatological vision, which can be realized only fragmentarily, as a nuanced response to the pathologies of modernity.

CHAPTER THREE

Critical Discussions

In the preceding chapters we examined Tillich's religious critique of capitalism and of capitalistic modernity. In this chapter I evaluate his position and discuss certain ways to reduce or eliminate its weaknesses and inadequacies, in the hope of paving the way for a more adequate theological response to global capitalistic modernity.

My proposal for employing the concept of quasi-religion as a basis for constructing this response requires an adequate understanding of capitalistic modernity and an adequate conception of religion. The first part of this chapter brings in the critical views of Jürgen Moltmann as an alternative perspective by which to assess Tillich's position. In particular, I will argue that Tillich's interpretation of capitalistic modernity is primarily cultural-spiritual and does not pay enough attention to the material-economic dimension, and also that his critical interpretation of capitalistic modernity is Eurocentric and neglects those non-European cultures that are also constitutive of modernity. The second part of the chapter brings in Émile Durkheim's theory of religion, and here I will argue that Tillich's asocial conception of religion in terms of ultimate concern is inadequate for a critique of capitalism as quasi-religion and suggest that his critical concept of quasi-religion can be enhanced by Durkheim's view of religion as a "unified system of beliefs and practices relative to sacred things."[1]

This chapter's focus on inadequacies might be taken to indicate a predominately negative evaluation of Tillich, but this is far from being my position. My general assessment is that Tillich's thought remains largely

---

[1] Émile Durkheim, *The Elementary Forms of Religious Life* (trans. Karen E. Fields; New York: Free Press, 1995) 44.

relevant to the theological critique of global capitalistic modernity, yet it can be enhanced by putting more emphasis on the material-economic dimension, by moving from a Eurocentric to a global perspective, and by adding a social dimension to the concept of quasi-religion. These moves would not be totally alien to Tillich; rather, they entail the extension or intensification of some aspects of his thought.

Enhancing Tillich's Critique of Capitalistic Modernity with Insights from Moltmann

Let me remark at the outset that I am not using Moltmann to argue that Tillich's perspective is inherently flawed, problematic, or inferior. I contend simply that Tillich's perspective is inadequate for the contemporary situation and that Moltmann provides a more adequate critique of capitalism and modernity today. As Tillich does not have the benefit of hindsight that Moltmann has, it is certainly not his fault for not addressing, for example, the globalization of capitalism in the post-Cold War era.

Moltmann's Critique of Capitalistic Modernity: An Overview

Why Moltmann?

There are several reasons to choose Moltmann: 1) Moltmann is a theologian. While Tillich's critique of modernity and capitalism shares many similarities with that of some social theorists, it is in the final analysis a theological critique, and our evaluation of Tillich will be more appropiate if we bring Tillich into dialogue with a theologian. 2) Moltmann belongs to the generation of German Protestant theologians that followed Tillich. He witnessed the intensification and end of the Cold War, the collapse of the communist regimes in Russia and Eastern Europe, and the "victory" of capitalism. Moltmann saw some events that Tillich did not live to see, such as globalization. 3) Moltmann, like Tillich, was influenced by Marxism and neo-Marxism. He takes up Marx's concern for world-transforming praxis and a critical stance toward capitalism. Moreover, Moltmann is influenced by the messianic Marxism of Ernst Bloch and the critical theory of the Frankfurt School (notably Horkheimer, Adorno, and Benjamin). Such intellectual similarities with Tillich make Moltmann an appropriate participant in our critical discussion.[2] Moltmann's theology, no less than Tillich's, is a conscious and intended response to modernity. Moltmann understands the task of theology to be mediation, that is, to relate the Christian tradition "critically and therapeutically" to the modern situation, in which the scientific-technological project of modernity has found itself enmeshed in contradictions.[3] He summarizes his view of the nature and origins of modernity in the following passage:

> The domination of peoples, the seizure of power over nature, and the project of a civilization that makes human beings the subjects of history constitute the millenarian dream of the "modern age." Its reality is the scientific-technological civilization of "modernity," whose inner and outer contradictions we are today suffering and experiencing ever stronger.[4]

I would like to highlight several points here. First, Moltmann understands modernity in terms of "scientific-technological civilization." The rapid advancement of science and technology, marked especially by the industrial revolution, characterizes modern society.[5] Second, science and technology set human beings into an antagonistic relationship to nature in which they treat it as an object.[6] The emergence of the human subject in modernity thus

---

[2] Compared to Moltmann, Tillich seems less influenced by Ernst Bloch, yet he also is familiar with Bloch's works. On 28 March 1965, in the last year of his life, he preached on "The Right to Hope" at Harvard University's Memorial Church (Ronald Stone, "Introduction," *TP*, 23). At the beginning of the sermon, he mentions Bloch's "two-volume work about hope" and describes Bloch as recognizing hope as "a permanent force" and "driving-power" in everyone (*TP*, 182).

[3] Jürgen Moltmann, *Was ist heute Theologie? Zwei Beiträge zu ihrer Vergegenwärtigung* (Freiburg: Herder, 1988) 8, 59, 102 = *Theology Today: Two Contributions towards Making Theology Present* (London: SCM, 1988) viii, 53, 94.

[4] Jürgen Moltmann, *Das Kommen Gottes. Christliche Eschatologie* (Gütersloh: Kaiser, 1995) 215 [translation mine] = *The Coming of God: Christian Eschatology* (trans. Margaret Kohl; Philadelphia: Fortress, 1996) 190.

[5] See Jürgen Moltmann, *Theology of Hope: On the Ground and the Implications of a Christian Eschatology* (trans. James W. Leitch; new preface; Minneapolis, Minn.: Fortress, 1993) 305; *Religion, Revolution, and the Future* (trans. Douglas Meeks; New York: Scribners, 1969) 109; *Creating a Just Future* (trans. John Bowden; Philadelphia: Trinity Press International, 1989) 1; *God in Creation: A New Theology of Creation and the Spirit of God* (trans. Margaret Kohl; Minneapolis, Minn.: Fortress, 1993) xii.

[6] See Moltmann, *Creating a Just Future*, 56.

entails the domination of nature. In fact, even human beings become objects of domination. Further, both types of domination are affected by instrumental reason.[7] Moltmann's position here is similar to that of Horkheimer and Adorno. To a certain extent, it is also similar to that of Tillich, who criticizes, as we have seen, the objectification and dehumanization brought about by technical reason and controlling knowledge. Third—and this is where he differs from Tillich and the Frankfurt School theorists—Moltmann is not just concerned with the domination of nature and of human beings in general; he is also concerned particularly with the domination of non-Western peoples by Europeans and by the other peoples of the First World. Moltmann would even say that the twofold First World domination of the other—a twofold domination that embraces nature and non-European peoples—is a constitutive element of modernity. Fourth, for Moltmann modernity was born out of the spirit of millenarian or messianic hope, which was the driving force behind the above-mentioned twofold domination.[8] Moltmann, thus, like Tillich, underscores the Christian religious background of modernity, yet his emphasis differs from that of Tillich. Moltmann focuses on the eschatological hope of Christianity, while Tillich highlights the prophetic-critical and world-transforming character of Protestantism. Fifth and finally, Moltmann stresses, a bit more than Tillich, the contradictions and crises of modernity.

To supplement Moltmann's view, I will bring in occasionally the thought of Johann Baptist Metz, another postwar German theologian for whom suffering is an important theme. While Moltmann works out the theme of the suffering of the crucified God, Metz highlights the memory of suffering as a challenge to modern rationality. For Metz, even Jürgen Habermas's development of the notion of communicative reason as a corrective to modernity's overemphasis on instrumental reason is inadequate as it still does not take seriously the suffering of past victims. This is an aspect less dealt with in Moltmann's critique of modernity.

---

[7] See Jürgen Moltmann, *God for a Secular Society: The Public Relevance of Theology* (trans. Margaret Kohl; Minneapolis, Minn.: Fortress, 1999) 7–8; *Coming of God*, 185.

[8] See Moltmann, *God for a Secular Society*, 6–11; *Coming of God*, 184–90.

Moltmann's Material-Economic Perspective

In contrast to Tillich, Moltmann emphasizes the material-economic dimension modernity.[9] This emphasis can be seen in the two terms he most often uses to describe modernity: "industrial society" and "scientific-technological civilization." These might be roughly understood as the societal and the cultural aspects of modernity, respectively. For Moltmann, modern society "arose as the result of the industrial revolution and the scientific-technological civilization," and "is in the process of establishing itself throughout our world."[10] In his view, "scientific-technological civilization" has become the great universal human experiment and is becoming the fate of all human beings, whether they like it or not.[11] In this way, Moltmann highlights the crucial significance of technologies of production in the constitution of modernity. While he is far from being an advocate of historical materialism, he nonetheless assigns what Marx would call the "forces of production" a significant role in his interpretation of modernity. Moltmann—unlike Tillich—often underscores the socioeconomic basis of the cultural aspects of modernity. For example, he interprets secularization and historicization in terms of urbanization, industrialization, and "the programmed progress of the development of industrial power."[12]

Consistent with his material-economic emphasis, Moltmann maintains that public criticism on behalf of the victims of the market economy should be the main task of political theology.[13] In his more recent works he has

---

[9] This does not mean Moltmann is concerned only about the material-economic dimension of modernity. In fact, he has underscored the multidimensional nature of the pathologies of modernity.

[10] Moltmann, *Religion, Revolution, and the Future*, 109. Later, he describes three "industrial revolutions": the mechanization, electrification, and then the computerization of production (*Creating a Just Future*, 1).

[11] Jürgen Moltmann, *Der Weg Jesu Christi. Christologie in messianischen Dimensionen* (Munich: Kaiser, 1989) 75 = *The Way of Jesus Christ: Christology in Messianic Dimensions* (trans. Margaret Kohl; Minneapolis, Minn.: Fortress, 1993) 56.

[12] Moltmann, *Theology Today*, 55.

[13] "It is here that the future tasks facing the churches and political theology lie: the duty of maintaining, and maintaining publicly, criticism of capitalism, not in the name of any ideology, but in the name of the victims of the market-economy system; and the task of creating justice for human beings and nature through appropriate social and environmental policies" (Moltmann, *God for a Secular Society*, 60). He acknowledges that his latest theology is "seeking a critical ecclesiology which defines the position of the church of Christ in a globalized market economy," and he wishes he could develop an "economic theology" (Jürgen

moved toward naming the capitalist economy as modernity's primary source of contradictions and pathologies. This course runs in the reverse direction of Tillich and the Frankfurt School.[14] In an early work, Moltmann speaks of five interrelated "vicious circles of death," meaning the economic, political, cultural, ecological, and spiritual dimensions of modern society: poverty, force, racial and cultural alienation, and industrial pollution of nature, as well as senselessness and godforsakenness.[15] More recently, Moltmann has focused more and more on the material-economic dimension of the pathologies of modernity and narrows his diagnosis of modernity to three main problems: economic injustice (primarily Third World poverty), nuclear threat, and ecological crisis.[16] These three issues belong to what he calls "the other side" of the scientific-technological civilization of modernity, which has developed at the expense of its victims, including the Third World and the natural world.[17] With the end of the Cold War and the apparent victory of capitalism, "the global marketing of everything"[18] emerged as a crucial source of problems.

Moltmann, "The Adventure of Theological Ideas," in Douglas M. Meeks, "Jürgen Moltmann's *Systematic Contributions to Theology*," *RelSRev* 22 [1996] 102–5, at 105).

[14] As we saw in ch. 1, Tillich increasingly focuses on the cultural dimension of capitalism; the Frankfurt School moves from the critique of capitalism to the critique of domination, which it sees as taking increasingly direct, noneconomic forms. Capitalism is seen as a specific historical form of domination characteristic of the bourgeois era of Western history. See Martin Jay, *The Dialectical Imagination: A History of the Frankfurt School and the Institute of Social Research, 1923–1950* (Weimar and Now 10; Berkeley, Calif.: University of California Press, 1996) 256.

[15] Jürgen Moltmann, *Der gekreuzigte Gott. Das Kreuz Christi als Grund und Kritik christlicher Theologie* (6th ed.; Gütersloh: Kaiser, 1993) 306–8 = *The Crucified God: The Cross of Christ as the Foundation and Criticism of Christian Theology* (trans. R. A. Wilson and John Bowden; London: SCM, 1974) 330–32. See Jürgen Moltmann, *The Future of Creation: Collected Essays* (trans. Margaret Kohl; Philadelphia: Fortress, 1979) 109–13; Jürgen Moltmann, "Freedom in the Light of Hope," *JCQ* 39 (1973) 157–58. Among the five vicious circles, two are cultural-spiritual (alienation and meaninglessness), and the other three are societal, economic, or material (economic poverty, political oppression, and environmental pollution).

[16] Moltmann, *Creating a Just Future*, 2–4; idem, *Way of Jesus Christ*, 64–68; idem, *Coming of God*, 204–16; idem, *God for a Secular Society*, 11–17, 66–67, 92–95, 153–66. Moltmann does not neglect the cultural problem of alienation and the spiritual problem of godforsakenness (*God for a Secular Society*, 16–20, 135–52).

[17] Moltmann, *Way of Jesus Christ*, 64.

[18] Jürgen Moltmann, *Gott im Projekt der modernen Welt. Beträge zur öffentlichen Relevanz der Theologie* (Gütersloh: Kaiser, 1997) 68, 200 = *God for a Secular Society*, 68, 223. See also *Gott im Projekt der modernen Welt*, 141 = *God for a Secular Society*, 153; Jürgen Moltmann, "Ist der Markt das Maß aller Dinge?," in *Totaler Markt und Menschenwürde.*

Moltmann criticizes Francis Fukuyama, who celebrates the triumph of capitalism as the "end of history," for forgetting "the inward contradictions inherent in the universal marketing of everything: the contradictions between market value and human dignity, between the First World and the Third, as well as between humanity and nature."[19] He writes further:

> These human, economic and ecological contradictions have been brought about by capitalism itself, and it is extremely doubtful whether capitalism can surmount them, since it is through capitalism that they are continually engendered, and all social and ecological corrections are always too late.[20]

I will explain below why I believe a more marked emphasis on the material-economic dimension in general and on capitalism in particular allows a more adequate response to the present global situation.

Global-Critical Perspective of Modernity

Another aspect of Moltmann's contribution to a more adequate critique of capitalism and modernity is a global perspective that goes beyond the Eurocentric perspective that Tillich (along with many other interpreters of modernity) exhibits. All too often, modernity is regarded as a situation resulting from social and cultural developments within European civilization. It does not recognize that non-European civilizations are also constitutive of modernity and does not take seriously the suffering of modernity's victims.

Moltmann sees modernity in terms of a twofold domination of the European subject, or in his words, the "double seizure of power over the world by European civilization."[21] In line with his material-economic perspective, he identifies two "significant pre-Enlightenment sources" of modernity.[22] The first is the *conquista*, discovery and conquest of America from 1492 onwards.[23] For Moltmann, 1492 inaugurated the new world order in which Europe, which had been at the periphery, moved to the center of

---

Herausforderungen und Aufgaben christlicher Anthropologie heute (ed. Rudolf Weth; Neukirchen-Vluyn: Neukirchener, 1996) 75–88.

[19] Moltmann, *Coming of God*, 225.

[20] Ibid.

[21] Ibid., 185.

[22] Moltmann, *God for a Secular Society*, 6.

[23] Ibid., 3–4; *Coming of God*, 185.

the world.[24] As we will see, Moltmann maintains that the domination of Latin America and Africa provided the natural and human resources for the economic development in Europe. "With the conquest of the American continent, European Christianity came forward to missionize the world through colonization, and Europe acquired the resources for its world-wide mercantile and capitalist economic system."[25] For Moltmann, what gave Europe victory was modern reason, that is, the instrumental reason of domination (*instrumentelle Herrschaftsvernunft*).[26] Reason was also effective in the second significant foundation of European modernity: the scientific and technological seizure of power over nature. Modern sciences strip the natural world of its magic and divine mystery. Scientific discovery enables human beings to master things and to become their determining subjects.[27] Modern instrumental reason, aiming at utilization and domination, pushes out receptive reason, becoming active and aggressive:[28] "From science and technology, Europe acquired that instrumentalizing knowledge which enabled it to use the resources of the colonized world to build up a worldwide civilization."[29] While Tillich also regards instrumental reason (which he calls "technical reason") as an important aspect of modernity insofar as it produces objectification and dehumanization, he does not consider in any significant way its involvement in the domination and exploitation of the non-European world.

Moltmann also goes beyond Tillich in stressing that this twofold seizure of power over the world by European civilization is driven by Christian millenarianism.[30] For Moltmann, the Columbus who searched for God's Garden of Eden and the city of gold and the pious immigrants to North America who wiped out the "Indians" were all driven by millenarian

[24] Moltmann, *God for a Secular Society*, 6.

[25] Moltman, *Coming of God*, 185.

[26] Moltmann, *Das Kommen Gottes*, 210 = *Coming of God*, 185. For Moltmann, who was influenced by the Frankfurt School, instrumental reason has brought about the domination of nature and human beings in the dialectic of enlightenment: "Liberty and autonomy are what the Enlightenment promised in the sunrise of its era. In the twilight of that same era, what emerges is the total rule of 'instrumental reason,' the loss of liberty and the dissolution of human subjectivity" (ibid., 220).

[27] Moltmann, *God for a Secular Society*, 7; *Coming of God*, 185.

[28] Moltmann, *God for a Secular Society*, 7–8; *Coming of God*, 185.

[29] Moltmann, *God for a Secular Society*, 8.

[30] Moltmann, *Coming of God*, 185–86.

expectations.[31] The optimistic faith in humanity and progress cherished by the German Enlightenment was, according to Moltmann, also a millenarianism,[32] and such transitions from theological to philosophical millenarianism also occurred in the French and English Enlightenments.[33] All this, however, should not be understood to furnish any real theological justification of modernity, for it "overlooks the victims on the underside of its history—in the Third World, in nature, and among women."[34] It is from the standpoint of the suffering victims on the underside of history that Moltmann offers his critique of modernity.[35]

Moltmann's critique of modernity does not imply an embracing of postmodernity. To throw oneself easily from modernity into postmodernity is for Moltmann a symptom of "our credulous faith in progress." One must pause first and "be clear about the victims of modernity in *sub-modernity*."[36] This "sub-modernity" is the other side of the scientific-technological civilization of modernity. "Every civilization has its reverse side, which is a barbarism; every victorious history has its underside, which is the misery of the defeated; and all progress has its price. This other side is generally neither seen nor heard."[37] This is especially true for the other side of European progress—the

---

[31] Moltmann, *God for a Secular Society*, 8–9. Moltmann gives in-depth accounts of the "political millenarianism" expressed in the ideas of the "Holy Empire" (Europe after Constantine) and of the "Redeemer Nation" (the United States) (Moltmann, *Coming of God*, 159–78).

[32] Moltmann mentions, as examples, Lessing's evolutionary history of the human race as a successful translation of the theological millenarianism of seventeenth-century "prophetic theology" and Kant's teleological view of the kingdom of God realized through the growth of reason and morality as a "philosophical chiliasm" (Moltmann, *Coming of God*, 184–90).

[33] Ibid. This seems to echo Karl Löwith's thesis that modern philosophy of history originates with Hebrew and Christian eschatology and ends with its secularization (*Meaning in History* [Chicago: University of Chicago Press, 1949] 2). However, Moltmann criticizes Löwith's thesis as one-sided because it takes up only "the teleological nature of the kingdom of God and the messianic side of Christian eschatology" while neglecting "the eschatological character of the kingdom of God and the apocalyptic nature of Christian eschatology" (Moltmann, *Coming of God*, 133–34). For Moltmann, this neglected aspect stresses that the end of history is a rupture, not continuous with the course of history nor its fulfillmen: "They do not lend history any meaning, but withdraw from its every legitimation" (ibid.).

[34] Ibid.

[35] Moltmann's focus on the suffering victims of modernity seems to correspond to his christology, especially his theology of the "crucified God," which emphasizes God's co-suffering solidarity with human beings. See Moltmann, *Crucified God*.

[36] Moltmann, *God for a Secular Society*, 11–12 [emphasis in original].

[37] Moltmann, *Way of Jesus Christ*, 64.

often-neglected suffering of the non-Western world. Moltmann maintains that the success story of the First World must always go together with the story of the Third World's suffering.[38] For example, when the Reformation in Germany began, the Spanish were conquering the Aztecs in Mexico, and when the Enlightenment was underway in Europe, hundreds of thousands of slaves were being sold from Africa to America every year.[39]

For Moltmann, modernity in the West has developed at the expense of the Third World, whose people have become the suffering victims of modernity. He contends that "the very genesis of the Third World is causally linked with the beginning of the modern world."[40] In fact, it was "the modern mass enslavement of Africans and the exploitation of America's mineral resources which provided the labour and capital for the development and advancement of the West."[41] The slave trade and the exploitation of the non-European world provided Europe with the investment capital for mercantilism and industrialization.[42]

> From the seventeenth century until well into the nineteenth, Europe's wealth was built up on the basis of a great transcontinental, triangular commerce: slaves from Africa to America; gold and silver from America to Europe, followed by sugar, cotton, coffee, tobacco and rubber; then industrial commodities and weapons to Africa; and so on. This wholesale transatlantic commerce produced the investment capital for the industrialization of Western Europe. Through the slave trade it destroyed the cultures and kingdoms of West Africa, and through monocultures it wrecked the native subsistence economies of Central and South America, making whole peoples the victims of European development.[43]

In other words, the economic transformation of modern Europe from agrarian feudalism to industrial capitalism[44]—hence the development of Western

---

[38] Moltmann, *God for a Secular Society,* 12.

[39] Ibid.

[40] Ibid., 164.

[41] Ibid., 13. The slave trade brought the "de-development" of Africa, the enslavement and death of Africans, and the destruction of African cultures (Moltmann, *Coming of God,* 211–12; *God for a Secular Society,* 13). According to Moltmann's figure, twenty million Africans were enslaved and fifty million died (idem, *Coming of God,* 212).

[42] Ibid., 212–15.

[43] Moltmann, *God for a Secular Society,* 13.

[44] Ironically, as Moltmann points out, it was the emergence of industrial capitalism that brought the abolition of slavery, for industry needs paid workers, not slaves (Moltmann,

capitalistic modernity—was enabled and sustained by the enslavement of Africans and the exploitation of the lands of the native Americans. "From the very beginning, the vanquished countries and subjected peoples in America, Africa and Asia bore the largest share of the human and material costs of European progress."[45] For Moltmann, the current global situation continues to betray the fact that the modernity of the First World developed at the expense of the sub-modernity of the Third World—and at the expense of nature.

Global Problems and Victims of Capitalistic Modernity

Moltmann's analysis of the following problems of capitalism and modernity is informed by both his material-economic perspective and his global perspective. For Moltmann, the primary problem that capitalism brings to the modern world is worsening economic injustice within and between countries. This growing injustice is not temporary, but "a congenital defect of the civilization itself."[46] Moltmann points out that colonial structures of domination and exploitation still exist in today's world: monocultures are enforced for the benefit of the world market; the interest paid to the industrial countries for the servicing of huge debts far exceeds the capital invested in the Third World countries; worse still, new technologies of production allow industry to be less and less dependent on the cheap labor in poorer countries, with the resulting in the increasing superfluousness of Third World peoples; poverty is worsening; ecological destruction of the countryside is driving more and more people into the city slums; the plagues are coming back.[47]

Economic injustices are not confined to Third World countries alone. The recent globalization of the economy brings about what Moltmann calls the "globalization of the Third World," such that injustice and inhumanity are growing in industrialized countries.[48] Technological progress favors capital, not labor.[49] Thus, while economic productivity is growing, unemployment

---

Coming of God, 213).

[45] Moltmann, *Way of Jesus Christ,* 64. Besides the enslavement of Africans and the exploitation of Americans, Moltmann in another place also mentions the colonization of India and the subjugation of China (ibid., 64).

[46] Ibid., 65.

[47] Moltmann, *Coming of God,* 215; *God for a Secular Society,* 13–14, 164.

[48] Moltmann, *God for a Secular Society,* 66.

[49] Moltmann, *Way of Jesus Christ,* 65. See also William Wolman and Anne Colamosca, *The Judas Economy: The Triumph of Capital and the Betrayal of Work* (Reading, Mass.: Addison-Wesley, 1997) esp. 43–54.

is increasing. The percentage of the population living below the poverty line is also rising. For Moltmann, this contradiction "is inherent in the structure of technological development and in the market structure."[50] According to the law of competition and the survival of the efficient, the market becomes a machine that constantly produces victims: weaker businesses fail; weaker and older people are dismissed; and women are discriminated against. On the world market, industrialized nations impose the laws of the market upon the agrarian nations, forcing them into a situation of economic dependence.[51]

As Karl Polanyi observes, modern society is distinguished from premodern societies by the dominance of the separate and self-regulating market based on the motive of gain. "Instead of economy being embedded in social relations, social relations are embedded in the economic system."[52] Tillich also underscores the dominance of the economy in modern society.[53] Yet the dominating role of the market in modernity significantly broadens and intensifies in the new era of global capitalism. Moltmann calls this "the global marketing of everything."[54] The institution of the market penetrates all aspects of life. It has become the philosophy of life (*Weltanschauung*) and the world religion.[55] "The market no longer serves human beings, but

---

[50] Moltmann, *Way of Jesus Christ,* 66.

[51] Moltmann, "Ist der Markt das Maß aller Dinge?" 80.

[52] Karl Polanyi, *The Great Transformation* (Boston: Beacon, 1957) 57. Polanyi's position is not without problems. Studies of Old Assyrian trade (ca. 19th century B.C.E.) in ancient Anatolia reveal that trade between Ashur and Anatolia was highly entrepreneurial, governed by contracts and legal rule (including procedures for dealing with debtors who were unable or refused to pay), and privately financed by a sophisticated system of investment (including the payment of dividends to shareholders, the converting of debts to shares, and the negotiability of shares) (Klaas R. Veenhof, " 'Modern' Features in Old Assyrian Trade," *JESHO* 40 [1997] 336–66; see also idem, "Kanesh: An Assyrian Colony in Anatolia," in *Civilizations of the Ancient Near East* [ed. Jack M. Sasson et al.; New York: Scribners, 1995] 859–71). Thus, Polanyi's claim that the Assyrian trade in Kanesh was a risk-free, "nonmarket trade" cannot be sustained (Polanyi, "Marketless Trading in Hammurabi's Time," in *Trade and Market in the Early Empires: Economies in History and Theory* [ed. Karl Polanyi, Conrad M. Arensberg, and Harry W. Pearson; New York: Free Press, 1957] 17–21). I am indebted to the anonymous HTS reviewer for drawing my attention to the works of Klaas R. Veenhof.

[53] *RS*, 105, 108.

[54] Moltmann, *God for a Secular Society,* 68. See also ibid., 153, 161; idem, "Ist der Markt das Maß aller Dinge?" 85.

[55] Moltmann, *God for a Secular Society,* 162, 153. Even religions are subject to marketing (idem, "Ist der Markt das Maß aller Dinge?" 84–85; idem, *God for a Secular Society,* 223).

human beings serve the market."[56] As an all-dominating social institution it determines all other social relationships and even personal self-esteem.[57] Human dignity is reduced to market value.[58] Mutual recognition as the basis of human self-respect gives way to the value one is assigned in the public market. People are supposed to realize themselves through work and consumption; therefore those who have no work and are poor lose their very selves. The losers usually internalize the winners' value-system, which rests on competition in the market.[59] The principle of competition rewards the strong and punishes the weak; it sets one person against the other, and thus individualizes, isolates, marginalizes, and oppresses people.[60]

Thus, globalization of the market economy not only erodes human dignity, but it also destroys human communities. As Moltmann points out, it leads to a "shortfall of solidarity." Politicians and economists reduce social benefits in an attempt to address the decline in productivity by retreating from unproductive areas; since the subvention of poor, elderly, unemployed, and sick persons is economically unproductive, they receive the sharpest cut.[61] If people are judged by their market value, then, Moltmann contends, the disabled, the elderly and the "useless" might realistically fear for their lives.[62] "Here the

[56] Moltmann, "Ist der Markt das Maß aller Dinge?" 80 [translation mine]. "It is no longer human needs which regulate production; it is the requirements of the market" (idem, *God for a Secular Society,* 162).

[57] Moltmann, "Ist der Markt das Maß aller Dinge?" 79.

[58] The Frankfurt School expresses similar ideas. For example, Horkheimer and Adorno note that in America a person is identical to his economic fate: "All are worth as much as they earn, and earn as much as they are worth. . . . People judge their own selves by their market value and find out who they are from how they fare in the capitalist economy" (Max Horkheimer and Theodor W. Adorno, *Dialectic of Enlightenment: Philosophical Fragments* [ed. Gunzelin Schmid Noerr; trans. Edmund Jephcott; Stanford, Calif.: Stanford University Press, 2002] 175). A similar vein of critique is already present in Marx, who denounces the bourgeoisie for turning personal worth into exchange value (Karl Marx and Friedrich Engels, "Manifesto of the Communist Party," in *The Marx-Engels Reader* [ed. Robert C. Tucker; 2d ed.; New York: Norton, 1978] 475).

[59] Moltmann, "Ist der Markt das Maß aller Dinge?" 80; idem, *God for a Secular Society,* 153, 162–63.

[60] Moltmann, *Creating a Just Future,* 8–9; *The Spirit of Life: A Universal Affirmation* (trans. Margaret Kohl; Minneapolis, Minn.: Fortress, 1992) 251–52.

[61] Moltmann, *God for a Secular Society,* 67; idem, "Ist der Markt das Maß aller Dinge?" 81.

[62] Moltmann, *Gott im Projekt der modernen Welt,* 68 = *God for a Secular Society,* 67 = "Political Theology and Theology of Liberation," in *Liberating the Future: God, Mammon, and Theology* (ed. Joerg Rieger; trans. Virgil Howard; Minneapolis, Minn.: Fortress, 1998) 78.

market society, which rewards only the competent performers and successful, brings with it severe personal and family problems."[63] Families are weakened by the overwork of some members and the long-term unemployment of others.[64] Meanwhile, civil community becomes increasingly polarized into rich and poor, as the middle class is eliminated by "the neo-liberal laws of the market."[65] Democracy, which presupposes a strong middle class, is then further eroded by "marketed politics": citizens become consumers of what political parties offer to sell them. Political participation is increasingly replaced by political apathy and privatization of life.[66] News is marketed as "infotainment," and the media convey a prefabricated reality.[67] Moreover, national community is weakened by the internationalization of production and of the flow of capital that is beyond the control of governments.[68] The destructive impact on human society is far-reaching.

Tillich had already pointed out the "infinite finitude" of the spirit of capitalism; Moltmann likewise criticizes the "capitalist ethos" of limitless growth.[69] Moreover, he criticizes it for leading to the ecological crisis. As he points out, while premodern civilizations were based on equilibrium, modern Western civilization is "being programmed solely towards development, growth, expansion and conquest."[70] Under "the mindless imperialism of the ideology of progress," ancient civilized nations are assessed as "underdeveloped" or "developing." "Zero growth" in the economy is counted as stagnation.[71] Economic growth as a sign of "progress" is driven

---

[63] Moltmann, *God for a Secular Society,* 163.

[64] Ibid., 153.

[65] Ibid., 154. Moltmann is emphatic that capitalism is incompatible with democracy (ibid., 67, 154).

[66] Moltmann, "Ist der Markt das Maß aller Dinge?" 82–83.

[67] Ibid., 83–84. Moltmann in particular mentions that CNN's coverage of the Gulf War used many recordings that had been made previously at practice fields of the military. What was broadcasted was psychological warfare, not enlightenment (ibid.).

[68] Moltmann, *God for a Secular Society,* 154.

[69] Moltmann, *The Church in the Power of the Spirit: A Contribution to Messianic Ecclesiology* (trans. Margaret Kohl; Minneapolis, Minn.: Fortress, 1993) 172–73. "The modern world . . . is fundamentally out for growth, expansion and conquest, without inward moderation and without external scruple" (ibid., 170).

[70] Moltmann, *God for a Secular Society,* 97. See also idem, *God in Creation,* 26; idem, *Creating a Just Future,* 53.

[71] Moltmann, *God in Creation,* 28; idem, *Church in the Power of the Spirit,* 170. "When economic growth stops, we talk of zero growth; for growth simply has to be" (idem, *God for a Secular Society,* 97).

by the constantly accelerating race between demand and satisfaction. Lying behind the ethos of unlimited expansion is "the will to power and the interest to rule."[72] This will to power, or "boundless will towards domination," is responsible for the domination of nature in modernity and the resulting environmental and ecological crisis.[73]

> The fundamental values of society which give birth to [modern] sciences and technologies, and also govern them, are: the acquisition of power, the consolidation of power, and the pursuit of profit. Even if "faith" in progress has been abandoned in the general mind of the public, modern industrial society is still programmed towards growth and expansion . . . . The progress of modern civilization and the acquisition of still further power can be gained only at the cost of the expense of nature.[74]

This economy-driven crisis of the environment is especially evident in the ecological catastrophes of the Third World. For Moltmann, poverty leads to overpopulation (as children are understood to provide security), and overpopulation leads to depletion, resulting in pollution and damage to the environment. While Western countries can preserve a clean environment in their own land by relocating environmentally harmful industries to Third World countries and by selling them toxic wastes, the poverty-stricken countries have no defense. Moreover, global capitalism compels the poor countries to forsake their own subsistence economy and plant monocultures for the world market, as well as to cut down the rain forests and to overgraze their grasslands. "They not only have to sell their products; they have to sell their means of production too—which is to say the foundation from which they live."[75] Thus, both the industrial world and the Third World are caught up in a vicious circle that destroys nature. "The Western world destroys the people of the Third World, compelling its peoples to destroy their natural foundations for living; but the destruction of nature in the Third World, such as the cutting down of the rain forests and the pollution of the seas, then reacts

---

[72] Moltmann, *Church in the Power of the Spirit*, 171.

[73] Moltmann, *God for a Secular Society,* 97 [emphasis omitted]. "The increase of human power and securing of that power provide the driving power of progress. This progress is still always measured quantitatively, in economic, financial and military terms, and its cost is shuffled off on to nature" (ibid., 15).

[74] Moltmann, *Way of Jesus Christ,* 67–68. See also idem, *God in Creation,* 26; idem, *Creating a Just Future,* 53.

[75] Moltmann, *Coming of God,* 210; idem, *God for a Secular Society,* 94.

on the industrial world by way of climatic changes."[76] The result is a "slow but sure and irreversible catastrophe," in which all living things, including human beings, will be gradually destroyed.[77]

Throughout Moltmann's interpretation of modernity there is a strong sense of urgency and crisis. He emphasizes that the contradictions and crises of modern society are getting out of control. Although the project of modernity is created by human beings, it has acquired a logic of its own. In Marx's vivid description, modern bourgeois society—with its gigantic means of production and of exchange—"is like the sorcerer, who is no longer able to control the powers of the nether world whom he has called up by his spells."[78] For Moltmann, the situation of human beings in modernity is like someone riding on a tiger who can hardly get off.[79] The project of modernity carries a "compulsion to progress" which will prove to be fatal.[80] Similar to Tillich's view of the demonic, Moltmann asserts that in the modern world there are evil structures, such as the worldwide economic order that makes the poor poorer and that turns people into victims and perpetrators.[81] He calls these unjust systems "vicious circles of death,"[82] "because unless their very beginnings are resisted they develop a potential of their own, through which the whole system inexorably impels itself towards its own death."[83] In other words, without radical interventions in the project of modernity, the modern world is heading toward self-destruction. This is most evident in the increasing destruction of nature through the mechanisms of capitalism.

> Rising consumption must be followed by rising production, just as, conversely, expanding production must be boosted by rising consumer

---

[76] Moltmann, *Coming of God,* 210.

[77] Ibid., 208–9.

[78] Marx and Engels, "Manifesto of the Communist Party," 478. Somewhat similarly, Giddens describes modernity in terms of the image of the "juggernaut": a runaway engine of enormous power, that crushes those who resist it, that human beings can steer only to some extent, and that threatens to rush out of control and smash itself to pieces (Anthony Giddens, *The Consequences of Modernity* [Stanford, Calif.: Stanford University Press, 1990] 139).

[79] Ibid., 45; see Moltmann, *Man: Christian Anthropology in the Conflicts of the Present* (trans. John Sturdy; Philadephia: Fortress, 1974) 26.

[80] Moltmann, *Coming of God,* 45; idem, *God in Creation,* 28–29; idem, *Church in the Power of the Spirit,* 172; idem, *Man,* 25–26.

[81] Moltmann, *Spirit of Life,* 138–41.

[82] Moltmann, *Crucified God,* 329–32; see also idem, *Church in the Power of the Spirit,* 165.

[83] Moltmann, *Spirit of Life,* 139.

demands. As a result, everywhere processes of growth have come into being which escape our control: growth of industrial production, growth of environmental destruction, growth of populations, growth of the need for raw materials and energy, growth of man's dependence on a flood of outward stimuli, and his inward instability. These different processes of growth goad one another on reciprocally. This results in an ever more comprehensive spiral, whose future today can be seen as . . . the universal death of humanity and organic nature.[84]

Moltmann's "crisis theory" of the contemporary world may help sharpen the critical edge of Tillich's response to capitalistic modernity. His analysis of the vicious circles of death and the self-destructive spiral of growing production and consumption would fit well into Tillich's critique of capitalism as demonic. Moltmann may also help revitalize Tillich's recognition of a *kairos* in the 1920s as he saw that capitalism is heading toward self-destruction.[85]

Beyond Tillich's Cultural-Spiritual Perspective

Inadequacy of Tillich's Cultural View of Capitalistic Modernity

By comparison to Moltmann, Tillich offers a more culturally and spiritually oriented interpretation of modernity, insofar as he analyzes major features of the spirit of bourgeois society, such as the principle of autonomy, self-sufficient finitude, technical reason, and objectification. However, it would be quite incorrect to say that Tillich is concerned only with cultural aspects of capitalism and modern society. In fact, his religious socialist writings largely adopt Marx's political-economic critique of capitalism. Tillich focuses on the critique of the cultural-spiritual dimension of capitalism more than its material-economic aspects. As Ronald Stone points out: "Economics was never of independent, isolated concern to Tillich. The discipline was of importance as related to humanistic needs, and the ethical and psychological implications of economics interested Tillich."[86] This is understandable, as

[84] Moltmann, *Church in the Power of the Spirit,* 172. See also idem, *God in Creation,* 28–29.

[85] After the Second World War, Tillich came to the view that there was no imminent *kairos* in his time but only a "sacred void" (*MW/HW* 3:527). While he could still identify certain features and trends of modernity as pathological and even destructive, the sense of historical crisis, urgency, and concreteness originally associated with the *kairos* concept faded away in his *Systematic Theology.*

[86] Ronald H. Stone, "Conversations in Religous-Socialist Circles," in *Dialogues of Paul*

he takes the view that the economic sphere is complex, interdependent with other social and cultural spheres, and not an isolated phenomenon.[87] Yet this implies only that Tillich holds a complex and nuanced view of the economy; the fact remains that he has a relatively diminuated concern with material-economic problems in the critical interpretation of modernity. John P. Clayton even criticizes Tillich for remaining in certain aspects in the idealist tradition despite Marx's influence:[88] "In many cases when Tillich 'mentions' the social situation, he tends to 'spiritualise' it, in the sense that he tends to transform, say, the capitalist society into the spirit of the capitalist society."[89]

Moreover, while Tillich identifies capitalism as the main culprit of various social and cultural problems, he does not take the problem of economic injustice seriously enough. "Justice was not the central term of Paul Tillich's religious-socialist polemic against capitalism. He did not often judge capitalism by the criteria of justice; rather, he assumed that the contradictions within capitalism were going to destroy it."[90] When Tillich criticizes capitalism, he often focuses, above all, on class struggle, which in his view is inherent in the structure of bourgeois society, and, to a lesser extent, on the economic domination of all aspects of society, as well as on dehumanization and meaninglessness.[91] He rarely mentions economic injustice as a problem of capitalism; rather, economic injustice is significant because

---

Tillich (ed. Mary Ann Stenger and Ronald H. Stone; Macon, Ga.: Mercer University Press, 2002) 181.

[87] *TPE*, 258 = *MW/HW* 3:481. "In the most extended description of my social-political ideas, the book *Die Sozialistische Entscheidung*, I have developed a many-sided image of a transformed society in which the economic element is definitely subordinated. Only within this longer [sic] image is my idea of economic justice understandable, especially the fact that it includes bourgeois as well as feudal elements" (Tillich, "Rejoinder," *The Journal of Religion* 46 [1966] 190).

[88] John P. Clayton, *The Concept of Correlation: Paul Tillich and the Possibility of a Mediating Theology* (Berlin: de Gruyter, 1980) 135.

[89] Clayton, *Concept of Correlation*, 138. Clayton points out Tillich's *Religious Situation* as an example. "For it is the *spirit* of capitalism which is being attacked by Tillich and not the social conditions which—in Marx's view—produce the ideology of capitalism. This is implied in Tillich's characterisation of bourgeois society as an *attitude*" (ibid., 137 [emphasis in original]).

[90] Stenger and Stone, *Dialogues of Paul Tillich*, 193.

[91] See, for example, *PE*, 48–49, 74–75, 77–78; *SD*, 58, 67, 97, 171 n. 6; *RS*, 105–11; *TP*, 47–48, 119, 130–33.

it leads to dehumanization, which is for Tillich more fundamental.[92] He does not give enough attention to the material-economic problems engendered by capitalism: systemic poverty and distributive injustice, hunger, malnutrition, diseases, and other kinds of bodily suffering, as well as environmental crisis.[93] Tillich's relative neglect of the material-economic dimension prevents him from adequately diagnosing the problems of capitalistic modernity and thus also restricts his theological response to these problems. If he had put more emphasis on the material-economic dimension, Tillich could have, for example, elaborated his theological response to the economic injustice of capitalism in terms of the symbol of the kingdom of God, which, with respect to capitalism, implies the application of the criterion of material justice.[94]

Toward a More Material-Economic Perspective

It certainly would have been possible for Tillich to incorporate a material-economic perspective in his critique of capitalistic modernity similar to that of Moltmann, given both his indebtedness to Marx and also his own view of the multidimensional unity of life. Marx maintains that the analysis of human society and history should start from the "real" life-process of human beings, their material conditions of existence, and their practical activity of

[92] When he explicates "the principles of justice, including that of economic justice, that underlay Religious Socialism," Tillich states that the principle of justice means "the prohibition to treat a person as a thing." The economic order of high capitalism denies dignity and rights to the proletariat, thus producing "a large-scale dehumanization among the hired manual workers" (Tillich, "Rejoinder, " 190).

[93] Tillich died before the problem of environmental crisis became a public concern and a significant theological issue; the modern environmental movement, regarded as beginning with the publication of Rachel Carson's *Silent Spring* in 1962, only emerged near the end of Tillich's life. Serious theological concern arose after the publication of Lynn White's article "The Historical Roots of the Ecological Crisis" in 1967. See Stephen B. Scharper, "The Ecological Crisis," in *The Twentieth Century: A Theological Overview* (ed. Gregory Baum; Maryknoll, N.Y.: Orbis, 1999) 220–24. However, Tillich had a lifelong interest in the theology of nature, beginning as early as his dissertation on Schelling. In the early 1960s, Tillich had already anticipated the ecological challenge to Christian theology. See Pan-chiu Lai, "Paul Tillich and Ecological Theology," *JR* 79 (1999) 234, 240.

[94] *TP*, 54. The symbol of the Kingdom of God predominates in part 5 of Tillich's *Systematic Theology*. Tillich points to the social character of the Kingdom of God, which includes ideas of justice and peace, but he does not address the issue of material-economic justice (*ST* 3:358). His concept of justice in *Systematic Theology* and other later writings (such as *Love, Power, and Justice: Ontological Analyses and Ethical Applications* [Oxford: Oxford University Press, 1960]) is primarily social and political, not economical.

production. Culture, religion, ideology, and all that belong to "consciousness" should not be treated as independent from material life.[95] Marx himself applies this approach when he traces the cultural characteristics of modernity (for example, the prevalence of egotistical calculation, the reduction of personal worth to exchange value, the profanization of everything, the "uninterrupted disturbance of all social conditions, everlasting uncertainty and agitation") to the changed and ever-changing means of production and relations of production of modern bourgeois society.[96] Here I am not suggesting that Tillich should have adopted Marx's economic materialism, which he in fact explicitly criticizes.[97] Rather, Tillich's critical interpretation of capitalistic modernity would be more adequate if it came closer to Marx's by taking more seriously the material-economic dimension.

Moreover, such a move would not be adding something alien to Tillich's thought. In fact, it would just bring out more fully the implications of Tillich's own principle of the "multidimensional unity of life."[98] According to this principle, human life is a unity made up of all dimensions of life (inorganic, organic, psychological, spiritual, and historical), and in it all dimensions are actualized.[99] Thus, a human being is not just a spirit or a thinking subject, nor is it just a physical body driven by biological impulses. Any form of anthropological reductionism, be it an idealist or an materialist version, is rejected. At the same time, the dimensions are interrelated, such that a richer and more complex dimension is a constellation of less complex dimensions, which serve as conditioning factors. This is true not only historically in evolution but also at present in any act of life. For example, every act of the spirit (cognitive, moral, and so on) arises out of a constellation of psychological factors; however, psychological factors cannot in themselves produce a spiritual act: "Every act of the spirit presupposes given psychological material and, at the same time, constitutes a leap which

---

[95] See Karl Marx, "The German Ideology: Part I," in *The Marx-Engels Reader* (ed. Robert C. Tucker; 2d ed.; New York: Norton, 1978) 146–200, esp. 149–55.

[96] Marx and Engels, "Manifesto of the Communist Party," 475–76.

[97] *TPE*, xviii, 258; *OB*, 87–88. Tillich characterizes materialism (or reductionist naturalism), which reduces the whole of reality to the inorganic processes, as an "ontology of death" (*ST* 3:19 [emphasis omitted]).

[98] *ST* 3:12, 15–28.

[99] Tillich maintains that all dimensions of life are potentially present in every realm. Even the dimension of the spirit is potentially present in an atom, in which only the inorganic dimension is actualized (*ST* 3:16).

is possible only for a centered self, that is to say, one that is free."[100] The implication of such an understanding for Tillich's approach to modernity is this: Modern culture, constituted by numerous creative acts of the human spirit, presupposes the material conditions of modern society; therefore, an adequate interpretation of cultural modernity should take seriously these material factors. To do so is to accept the logical implications of Tillich's principle of the multidimensional unity of life. At the same time there is no place for any materialistic determinism. Material-economic factors condition, but do not determine, the cultural-spiritual realm.

Beyond Tillich's Eurocentric Perspective

Inadequacy of Tillich's Eurocentric View of Modernity

Another aspect in which Tillich's critique of modernity is inadequate and can be enhanced by Moltmann is Tillich's Eurocentric view of modernity. To be fair to Tillich, he was not unaware of his limitation in perspective; this can be seen in self-critical remarks about his "provincialism" after his emigration to the United States.[101] Yet his rejection of "Western provincialism"—a result of the profound culture shock he experienced during his visit to Japan in 1960,[102] just five years before his death—came too late in his career to effect substantial changes in his thought.

Tillich regards two cultural movements in Western society (the Protestant Reformation and the European Enlightenment) to be the origins of modernity. As we have seen, for him these two historical movements, representing prophetism and autonomy respectively, constituted the double break with the "myth of origins" in traditional society. Through the spread of technology and capital, the spirit of Western bourgeois society spread to other parts of

[100] *ST* 3:27.

[101] *TC*, 159–76.

[102] Tillich wrote shortly after returning from Japan: "Before all the impressions have settled down in me, I cannot formulate what it has meant; and even then probably others will notice the influence of Japan more than I myself. But I know that something has happened: no Western provincialism of which I am aware will be tolerated by me from now on in my thought and work, and I am grateful to the Japanese friends who worked for a long time to make my trip and this insight possible" (Wilhelm Pauck and Marion Pauck, *Paul Tillich: His Life and Thought* [1976; repr., San Francisco, Calif.: Harper & Row, 1989] 260–61. According to the authors, the source of the quotation is Paul Tillich, "On the Boundary Line," *ChrCent* 77 [1960] 1435–37, at 1435, where, the quotation cannot be found). Similar quote in "An Informal Report of a Lecture Trip to Japan–1960," p. 15 [unpubl.; William R. Crout files].

the world.[103] Thus, he understands modernity as an internal development within European (or Western) civilization. Non-European civilizations are related to modernity insofar as they are the recipients of modernity. This is a Eurocentric understanding of modernity, not uncommon among philosophers and social theorists, and is problematic insofar as it overlooks the Other of modernity, i.e., those whose contributions and sacrifices have made possible the development of modernity. Tillich's interpretation of modernity should be corrected and transformed by a global perspective that—as Moltmann's does—acknowledges and takes seriously the contributions and sacrifices of the non-Western world.

Modernity Influenced by Contributions of Non-Western Civilizations

The first step toward a global perspective on modernity is to acknowledge the indispensable contributions of non-Western civilizations (such as the Islamic and the Chinese) to the emergence and development of modernity in Europe. Islamic civilization made particularly significant contributions to the Renaissance, which is the precursor to the two cultural events—the Reformation and the Enlighenment—that Tillich regards as the origins of modernity. Tillich calls the Renaissance "the rebirth of Western society in all aspects: religious, cultural, political."[104] While the background of the Renaissance was still the "Christian substance of Western culture," it broke new ground with the emergence of the new ideal—made possible by the unprecedented interaction of science and technology—of actively controlling and shaping the world.[105] The Renaissance would not have been possible without the significant contributions of Islamic civilization. Tillich acknowledges that the Renaissance was a rebirth of Western society "with the help of the ancient sources of Mediterranean civilization, the classical Greek and Latin writers and the biblical literature."[106] However, he did not take seriously the fact that some of these "ancient sources of Mediterranean

---

[103] In this way his understanding of modernity is similar to that of Anthony Giddens, who defines modernity as "modes of social life or organization which emerged in Europe from about the seventeenth century onwards and which subsequently became more or less worldwide in their influence" (Giddens, *Consequences of Modernity*, 1).

[104] *IRCM*, 26.

[105] Ibid., 27. Such continuous and active shaping of the world, based on controlling knowledge, is for Tillich a significant aspect of modern society.

[106] Ibid., 26–27.

civilization"—predominantly Greek philosophy, mathematics, and the
natural sciences—were preserved, translated, developed, and transmitted
to the West by Islamic civilization, nor did he mention that the culture of
the Mediterranean world (including Italy and Spain), which influenced the
Renaissance and early modern Europe, was itself influenced significantly
by Arabic-Islamic civilization during the Middle Ages.[107]

However, Tillich was not unaware of the contribution of Islamic civilization
to Western culture. He acknowledges the role of "Arabian theologians" in
mediating classical culture to the medieval world and mentions especially the
help of "Arabian philosophers" in the discovery of Aristotle.[108] Yet the Islamic
contribution plays no role in his interpretation of modernity. Further, he
overlooks the fact that Islamic civilization was not only a curator and mediator
of the Hellenistic heritage; it also developed and transformed that heritage
and made original contributions to Western civilization. These include the
contributions of Avicenna and Averroës to philosophy, al-Khwarizmi and
others to mathematics, and still others to theoretical and practical astronomy,

---

[107] The House of Wisdom (Bayt al-Hikmah), founded in Baghdad in the early ninth century
under the sponsorship of the Abbasid caliphate, translated into Arabic various works from
the Hellenic world, including Greek and Syriac texts on philosophy, medicine, mathematics,
and others (excepting literature). These works became accessible to Europeans primarily via
Muslim Spain (al-Andalus), which was an offshoot of Abbasid culture and became the center of
learning for Europeans during the Middle Ages. In the twelfth and thirteenth centuries, Arabic
texts of Hippocrates, Euclid, and others were translated into Latin. The Latin translations of
the works of Aristotle and the commentaries of Averroës gave rise to a growing interest in
Aristotelianism in medieval Europe. See Francesco Gabrieli, "Islam in the Mediterranean
World," in *The Legacy of Islam* (ed. Joseph Schacht with C. E. Bosworth; 2d ed.; Oxford:
Clarendon, 1974) 63–104; Harfiyah Abdel Haleem et al., eds., *The Crescent and the Cross:
Muslim and Christian Approaches to War and Peace* (London: Macmillan, 1998) 2–3; Jane
I. Smith, "Islam and Christendom: Historical, Cultural, and Religious Interaction from the
Seventh to the Fifteen Centuries," in *Oxford History of Islam* (ed. John L. Esposito; Oxford:
Oxford University Press, 1999) 131, 334; *Encyclopaedia Britannica Online*, s.v. "philosophy,
history of," http://www.search.eb.com/eb/article?eu=115381 (accessed 30 October 2002).

[108] *HCT*, 181, 183.

optics, chemistry, medicine, and geography.[109] All this paved the way for the Renaissance and for the rise of modern sciences.[110]

Western modernity has learned from Chinese civilization as well. Knowledge of Chinese scientific and technological discoveries was diffused rapidly throughout Europe as a result of the Mongol invasion in the thirteenth century,[111] while some other discoveries were known even earlier. Much of this knowldge was crucial for the rise of modernity. For example, the three inventions that Francis Bacon considered the greatest contributions to the transformation of the modern world—paper and printing, gunpowder, and the magnetic compass—were Chinese.[112] To this list we should add movable type printing[113] and paper money.[114] The Chinese method of issuing paper money had a profound influence on Western banking. "The old Hamburg Bank and

[109] See Juan Vernet, "Mathematics, Astronomy, Optics," in *The Legacy of Islam*, 461–88; Ahmad Dallal, "Science, Medicine, and Technology: The Making of a Scientific Culture," in *Oxford History of Islam*, 155–214; Martin Plessner, "The Natural Sciences and Medicine," in *The Legacy of Islam*, 425–60; *Encyclopaedia Britannica Online*, s.v. "Khwarizmi, al-," http://www.search.eb.com/eb/article?eu=46427 (accessed 2 November, 2002); s.v. "mathematics, history of," http://www.search.eb.com/eb/article?eu=118177 (accessed 16 October, 2002); s.v. "Europe, history of," http://www.search.eb.com/eb/article?eu=108599 (accessed 24 October 2002).

[110] "Indeed the Renaissance, the very foundation of modern European thought, culture and political structures, could not have happened if Muslims had not preserved, developed and transmitted much more than just Greek philosophy" (Haleem et al., *The Crescent and the Cross*, 3–4).

[111] Vernet, "Mathematics, Astronomy, Optics," 487.

[112] Joseph Needham, introduction to *The Genius of China: 3,000 Years of Science, Discovery, and Invention*, by Robert Temple (New York: Simon and Schuster, 1986) 7. Needham mentions some circumstantial evidence of China's influence on the West. For example, "as late as the seventeenth century all the magnetic compasses of surveyors and astronomers pointed south, not north, just as the compasses of China had always done" (ibid.). *The Genius of China* is based on Joseph Needham's monumental work *Science and Civilisation in China* (7 vols.; Cambridge: Cambridge University Press, 1954–2000).

[113] Movable type was invented in China in mid-eleventh century and is believed to have spread to Europe through Turfan and then through Persia after the Mongol conquest. Gutenberg "invented" movable type printing in 1458, not long after the Mongol army reached the borders of Germany (Temple, *Genius of China*, 115; *Encyclopaedia Britannica*, s.v. "Printing"). "Although no hard evidence exists for its transmission from China, the circumstantial evidence is strong enough to support it" (Temple, *Genius of China*, 115).

[114] Paper money, so important to commercial transactions and to the rise of modern capitalism, was invented by the Chinese at the beginning of the ninth century. In 1023 the government set up its own official agency to issue bank notes backed by cash deposits. Paper money was printed in Persia in 1294 following the Chinese method and its Chinese name eventually entered the Persian language. Marco Polo was so impressed by paper money in

the Swedish banking system were set up on Chinese lines. Thus, some of the fundamental banking procedures of the Western world came from China directly."[115] These are not the only examples of the contributions of Chinese civilization to the emergence of capitalism and modernity.

Nothing said above implies the underestimation of the original contributions of European intellectuals to the formation of modernity, but it does imply that without the contributions of Islamic, Chinese, and many other non-Western civilizations, the West and indeed the whole modern world would be quite different from what we know today. Western modernity is the outcome of a complex history of interregional exchange within what is called the "Afro-Eurasian zone" of civilization.[116] The rise of Western modernity involves the assimilation and appropriation of non-Western cultures, which had been more advanced than the West until the modern age.[117] "The flow of cultural learning was quite one-sided—from China, India, the Middle East, and (above all) the eastern Mediterranean to the Occident, with little going in the opposite direction."[118] This historical fact is, however, rarely acknowledged by Eurocentric interpretations of modernity, including Tillich's. Europe's significance in world history is often exaggerated, just as the size of Europe is greatly exaggerated in world maps drawn according to the Mercator projection.[119]

China that he wrote a whole chapter about its manufacture and circulation (Temple, *Genius of China*, 115–19).

[115] Ibid., 119.

[116] This term is used by Marshall G. S. Hodgson in his posthumously published *Rethinking World History: Essays on Europe, Islam, and World History* (ed. Edmund Burke III; Cambridge: Cambridge University Press, 1993) to stress the interregional continuity and exchanges between what are usually thought of as separate civilizations. The "Afro-Eurasian zone" includes four main regions: Europe, the Middle East, India, and China (Hodgson, *Rethinking World History*, 6).

[117] As Hodgson points out, for a long time in history Western Europe was a "frontier region" playing a rather "peripheral" and "backward" role. Western Europeans began to attain the same creative level of other core-area civilizations only in the High Middle Ages (Hodgson, *Rethinking World History*, 26–27). A Latin American scholar describes pre-1492 Europe as being "peripheral to the Islamic world" (Enrique Dussel, *The Invention of the Americas: Eclipse of "the Other" and the Myth of Modernity* [trans. Michael D. Barber; New York: Continuum, 1995] 88).

[118] Hodgson, *Rethinking World History*, 27.

[119] The Mercator projection exaggerates the size of non-equatorial regions on the world map: the farther a country or region is from the equator, the more its size is exaggerated. Thus, Europe appears much larger than it actually is (Hodgson, *Rethinking World History*, 7–8, 33).

Modernity Developed at the Expense of the Non-Western Other

The second step toward a global perspective of modernity is to take seriously the suffering and sacrifices of non-Western peoples in the development and constitution of modernity. There is a need to trace the origins of capitalistic modernity not only to the Reformation and the Enlightenment,[120] which Tillich rightly regards as historically crucial, but also to what the year 1492 symbolizes: the inauguration of centuries of European expansion, conquest, and colonization beginning with Christopher Columbus's "discovery" of America.[121] This is the view, as we have seen, of Moltmann, and also of Enrique Dussel.[122] Modernity, Dussel maintains, is dialectically constituted by the simultaneous appearance of Europe as the center of the world-system and of non-European alterity as its colonizable periphery.[123]

> While modernity is a undoubtedly a European occurrence, it also originates in a dialectical relation with non-Europe. Modernity appears when Europe organizes the initial world-system and places itself at the center of world history over against a periphery equally constitutive of modernity.[124]

The forgetting of the periphery, Dussel says, has led to a Eurocentric understanding of modernity. Overlooking the constitutive role of the periphery, this paradigm maintains that Europe's own "exceptional internal characteristics" enable it to outdo all other cultures in rationality.[125] According to Dussel, however, this view is untenable.

`
[120] Some thinkers—such as Habermas—would include the French Revolution (Jürgen Habermas, *Philosophical Discourse of Modernity* [trans. Frederick Lawrence; Cambridge, Mass.: MIT Press, 1987] 17).

[121] The year 1492 also marks two events of European exclusion of and violence against the Other: the Spanish conquest of Granada (the last Muslim stronghold in Europe) and the expulsion of Jews from Spain (Karen Amstrong, *The Battle for God* [New York: Ballantine, 2001] 3–5).

[122] Enrique Dussel, "Eurocentrism and Modernity (Introduction to the Frankfurt Lectures)," *Boundary 2* 20 (1993) 65; idem, *The Invention of the Americas*, 12; Moltmann, *Coming of God*, 185; idem, *God for a Secular Society*, 6.

[123] Dussel, *Invention of the Americas*, 9–10. "Modernity began in 1492 with Europe thinking itself the center of the world and Latin America, Africa, and Asia as the periphery" (ibid., 132).

[124] Ibid., 9–10.

[125] Ibid., 10.

> Europe's centrality reflects no internal superiority accumulated in
> the Middle Ages, but it is the outcome of its discovery, conquest,
> colonization, and integration of Amerindia—all of which give it an
> advantage over the Arab world, India, and China. Modernity is the
> result, not the cause, of this occurrence.[126]

Seen in this global perspective, modernity is constituted by the European
domination of and violence against the non-European lands as its Other.
"By controlling, conquering, and violating the Other, Europe defined itself
as discoverer, conquistador, and colonizer of an alterity likewise constitutive
of modernity."[127] The non-European Other is not recognized as constitutive
of modernity. In fact, according to the modern discourse of Orientalism,
which is produced with and shaped by (and also legitimates and exercises)
colonialist and imperialist practices of power, this Other is constructed and
represented as the exact opposite of modernity. Orientalism, as Edward Said
observes, has taught "the absolute and systematic difference between the
West, which is rational, developed, humane, superior, and the Orient, which
is aberrant, undeveloped, inferior."[128] The European domination of the Other
(and the latter's suffering) is at the same time concealed and justified. The
suffering and sacrifices of non-European peoples, through which Western
modernity has come into being, are forgotten. What is called for is a change
from the Eurocentric to a global-critical perspective, as advocated by Dussel
and Moltmann.[129]

As we saw above, Moltmann argues that Western modernity developed
at the expense of the "Third World." In particular, the enslavement of
Africans and the exploitation of Latin American resources provided the
capital for economic development in Europe that eventually led to industrial
capitalism.[130] Besides Africa and Latin America, we might also mention the
exploitation of India for agricultural products, the subjugation of China for
the sake of "free trade" in opium, and the domination of the Middle East for
oil. All this—the history of suffering of various non-European peoples—is
for Moltmann "the other side" of the scientific-technological civilization of

---

[126] Ibid., 11.

[127] Ibid., 12.

[128] Edward W. Said, *Orientalism* (New York: Vintage, 1994) 300. The "Orient" that
Edward is primarily concerned with is the Arabic and Islamic Middle East, but the term can
be applied to other non-European lands.

[129] See Dussel, *Invention of the Americas*, 136–40.

[130] See pages 118–19 above.

modernity. It is partial and distorted to interpret modernity only from the side of its victors and forget "the victims of modernity in *sub-modernity*."[131] No interpretation of modernity from a truly global perspective can afford to ignore the "others" whose suffering under modernity has been constitutive of modernity. Thus, a global and critical perspective of modernity should be guided by the remembrance of the suffering of the others.

Remembrance of others' suffering is the basis of the structure of "anamnestic reason" proposed by Johann Baptist Metz to supplement and transform Habermas's concept of communicative reason, which Metz sees as imposing "a privileging of contemporaneity on the readiness of reason to recognize the Other."[132] "Anamnestic reason opposes the oblivion of past suffering" and is guided by "the memory of someone else's suffering."[133] Only it, argues Metz, can bring to light the pathologies of European modernity.

> In my view we can only reckon with the insights of the dialectic of Enlightenment—for the most part once again forgotten or repressed—in the light that is shed by anamnestic reason. Only in that light can the Enlightenment enlighten itself about the disaster it has brought about; only in that light can it arrive at some understanding of the moral and political exhaustion of the Enlightenment, or, that is to say, of European modernity.[134]

Toward a Global-Critical Perspective

The remembrance of the suffering others in the interpretation of modernity makes possible a global-critical perspective of modernity. By being "critical," this perspective seeks to expose, critique, subvert, and transform various forms of domination, dehumanization, and other pathologies of modernity. By being "global," this perspective views modernity as a world-historical phenomenon from a global point of view, recognizing the contributions and sacrifices of the non-Western Other as constitutive of modernity. This perspective rejects the assumption that modernity is the product of social

[131] Moltmann, *God for a Secular Society,* 12 [emphasis in original].

[132] Johann Baptist Metz, "Anamnestic Reason: A Theologian's Remarks on the Crisis in the *Geisteswissenschaften*," in *Cultural-Political Interventions in the Unfinished Project of Enlightenment* (ed. Axel Honneth et al.; trans. Barbara Fultner; Cambridge, Mass.: MIT, 1992) 191.

[133] Ibid., 192; Metz, *A Passion for God: The Mystical-Political Dimension of Christianity* (ed. and trans. J. Matthew Ashley; New York: Paulist, 1998) 143.

[134] Metz, *A Passion for God*, 142.

and cultural developments only within Western civilizations and recognizes the indispensable contributions of Islamic and Chinese civilizations, among others, in the formation of Western modernity. It remembers these non-Western peoples (as well as victims of modernity in the West) for their suffering and sacrifices that have made possible the development of modernity in the West. By recognizing the other as other, this understanding of modernity is oriented toward universal solidarity, which has as its primary basis not the universality of reason but the universality of suffering.[135]

Adopting a global-critical perspective does not require completely overhauling Tillich's position. His thought already includes elements that suggest an expansion of his critique of capitalistic modernity in the direction of a global-critical perspective. For example, Tillich already criticizes technical reason for its tendency to lead to domination (through controlling knowledge) and to objectification and dehumanization. What is needed is an explicit recognition that the victims of technical reason—or of what Moltmann calls the instrumental reason of domination—include not just peoples in the West but also non-Western peoples, especially those who have suffered from European colonialism and Western imperialism.[136] Tillich's critique of autonomy furnishes another example. In Tillich's conception, autonomy and the related concept of self-sufficient finitude refer to the self-enclosed spirit that excludes and cuts itself off from the ultimate or the divine. His critique of autonomy and self-sufficient finitude can be expanded and reinterpreted to include the critique not only of the exclusion of the divine (the "Wholly Other") in modernity, but also of the exclusion of the human "others" of modernity. Such a reinterpretation is possible because Tillich's thought affirms that finite beings (including human beings) are vehicles of the divine, or of being-itself, in which they participate. However, Tillich's ontology of

---

[135] The idea of the universality of suffering does not reject the universalism advocated by Western modernity, as exemplified by the Enlightenment. It rather reminds us that this universalism is not universal enough, for it fails to remember the others who suffer, especially the victims of Western modernity (ibid., 142–43; see also Edmund Arens, "Interruptions: Critical Theory and Political Theology between Modernity and Postmodernity," in *Liberation Theologies, Postmodernity, and the Americas* [ed. David Batstone et al.; New York: Routledge, 1997] 237). The idea of the universality of suffering highlights the suffering of the non-Western peoples in modernity, yet it does not imply that those peoples experience nothing but suffering in modern times, nor does it overlook their contributions in the past and at present.

[136] His idea of theonomy (and theonomous reason), which overcomes the subject-object split and enables *eros*, is also a useful step, since it attempts to subvert and transform the subject-centered, instrumental reason of domination.

being, which permeates his theology, must still be criticized for failing to recognize the otherness of the others. If one goes beyond the philosophical concern with being to the philosophical concern with otherness, one can then affirm with Moltmann that we should try to perceive God as the Wholly Other in what is "other" and strange, or with Metz that we should seek to "uncover the *traces of God* in the experience of the other's alterity."[137] This affirmation enables our reworking of Tillich's critique of the principle of autonomy in modernity such that it includes the critique of the exclusion of the others who are constitutive of and yet are victimized by modernity. In a similar vein, Tillich's critique of controlling knowledge, objectification, and dehumanization in modernity can be reworked to include the critique of the Western domination, control, and dehumanization of non-Western peoples through oppression, exploitation, and colonization, as well as political, military, economic, and cultural imperialism.

Enhancing Tillich's Concept of Religion with Insights from Durkheim

Tillich's Asocial Conception of Religion

An important aspect of Tillich's critique of capitalism and capitalistic modernity is that he understands them as religious phenomena. As we have seen, Tillich regards capitalism as demonic, which is "sacred antidivine" and carries religious qualities. Also he regards what he calls "the spirit of bourgeois society," that is, the cultural dimension of capitalism or cultural modernity, as the "unconscious, self-evident faith" of capitalist society. As I have suggested in chapter 1, Tillich's concept of quasi-religion is able to bring together these two lines of critique; we can develop a critique of capitalism as quasi-religion. Nevertheless, the concept of quasi-religion remains underdeveloped and problematic in Tillich's writing. His concept of quasi-religion, defined in terms of ultimate concern, is asocial, because he does not work out the full implications of his understanding of quasi-religions as "systems of secular life and thought."[138] In other words, Tillich defines the concept of quasi-religion primarily in terms of his "larger" conception

---

[137] Moltmann, *God for a Secular Society,* 19; Metz, *Passion for God*, 27 [emphasis in original]. Moltmann cites Emmanuel Lévinas while Metz adopts his ideas.
[138] *ERQR*, 9.

of religion and fails to develop it along the line of his "narrower" conception of religion. According to Clayton, "Tillich distinguished with remarkable persistence between two basic senses of 'religion': namely, 'religion' as a pervasive feature of the human spirit and 'religion' as one sphere of human culture amongst others."[139] The first sense, the larger concept of religion,[140] is what Tillich advocated throughout his career and is his distinctive contribution to the conception of religion. In his earlier writings, this first sense of religion is variously defined as the experience of, directedness toward, or being grasped by the unconditioned.[141] Later, in America, he formulated this broader sense of religion in terms of the concept of ultimate concern. Whether in its earlier or later formulation, however, Tillich's broader sense of religion emphasizes the "vertical" or "depth" dimension of religion, that is, the relation to the unconditioned or the ultimate. While this conception of religion has a number of strengths,[142] one of its weaknesses is that it is essentially an asocial and unpractical conception of religion. Of course, Tillich does not deny the social dimension of religion; in fact, he emphasizes that an ultimate concern must express itself socially.[143] Nor does he ignore the dimension of practice in religion. However, the social and practical dimensions are not conceptually necessary in order to define religion in terms of ultimate concern; Tillich would acknowledge that community and praxis are important expressions of religion as ultimate concern, but he would not say that they are constitutive of religion. It follows that quasi-religion, as a special subset of religion, is also essentially asocial and unpractical. This conception is unsatisfactory for understanding social phenomena, such as capitalism, as quasi-religions.

Suppose we were to adopt Tillich's notion of quasi-religion, which is conceptualized asocially in terms of ultimate concern, to analyze capitalism. What would be the ultimate concern of this capitalistic quasi-religion? Money or market or the accumulation of capital might well be the ultimate concern

[139] John P. Clayton, "Introducing Paul Tillich's Writings in the Philosophy of Religion," in *MW/HW* 4:14.

[140] See *TPE*, xvi; *MSA*, 131; *TC*, 7–9.

[141] Clayton, "Introducing Paul Tillich's Writings," 15.

[142] For example, Tillich's broad conception of religion is able to express in nonreligious language the Christian concept of faith. It is also broad enough to include nontheistic religions (such as Confucianism) and secular religions (such as Ethical Humanism).

[143] *TC*, 178. For Tillich, "an ultimate concern is real in the individual; it is also embodied in the institutions of a society and effective in the actions of social groups" (*TC*, 177).

for a number of people, but for many others such capitalistic goals, though highly important, are not really their ultimate concern. Yet, we would still want to count these people as participants or even as none-too-willing adherents of a quasi-religion named capitalism. They are exhausting themselves to earn a bit more, trying hard to increase their competitiveness in the job market, shopping earnestly for the cheapest or most desirable products and services, investing in stocks and mutual funds and being affected in many ways by their rise and fall, and so on. Even more problematic is the case of complex organizations at various levels. For most commercial corporations and for many countries and transnational organizations, the free market, accumulation of wealth, or unlimited economic growth is the topmost priority. Nevertheless, it is difficult to regard any of these goals as their "ultimate concern," which is an existential and therefore individualistic concept, and can hardly be applied to organizations without overstretching its meaning. What we need, then, is an enhancement of the concept of quasi-religion that goes beyond Tillich's individualistic, asocial, and unpractical conception in terms of ultimate concern.

Durkheim's Social Conception of Religion and Its Contributions

Durkheim's Compatibility with Tillich

I suggest we draw from Émile Durkheim's social conception of religion. At first sight, Durkheim the sociologist and Tillich the philosopher-theologian might seem light-years apart.[144] However, they do have some ideas and concerns in common. First, both affirm that religion is a perennial dimension of human society[145] and that religion and society are inseparable. For Tillich,

---

[144] Durkheim's sociological understanding of religion in terms of the projection or apotheosis of society does not invalidate Tillich's philosophical-theological view of religion. The two simply interpret religion from differing perspectives. Durkheim's sociological perspective requires him to deal only with observable social phenomena and gives only social-scientific explanations; such a perspective neither supports nor rules out Tillich's philosophical-theological perspective, for it simply operates within a different, and not necessarily incommensurable, language-game. Durkheim's position might be interpreted as a reductionistic claim that religion is "nothing but" the projection of society itself, but this ontological claim is not an indispensable premise of his sociological interpretation of religion.

[145] Tillich: "The theologian must assume that religion as a structure of symbols of intuition and action—that is, myths and rites within a social group—has lasting necessity for even the most secularized culture and the most demythologized theology. I derive this necessity, the lasting necessity of religion, from the fact that spirit requires embodiment in order to become

religion is the meaning-giving substance of culture and is expressed by the cultural forms of a society. For Durkheim, religion is socially constituted and it in turn constitutes and maintains social solidarity. Second, since religion is perennial, modernity brings not the demise of religion but a situation in which the prominence of traditional religions has given way to new forms of religion. For Tillich, what has become socially and religiously significant in the modern world are the "quasi-religions" that are based on the secularism of the technical civilization.[146] For Durkheim, the new religion of modernity is the "cult of the individual,"[147] in which the humanity that each person embodies is rendered sacred and inviolable. Such religion emerges from and underpins the organic solidarity constituted by the advanced division of labor in modern society.[148] Third, both are interested in analyzing the religious aspects of secular social phenomena in modernity. Tillich examines the "religious situation" of his times primarily by looking at cultural, economic, and social trends in Western bourgeois society. Durkheim's sociology of religion sorts out the basic elements of religion in order to understand "present-day humanity" and he discerns the emergence of a religion at the beginning of the French Revolution.[149]

Moreover, Tillich would not have much of a problem accepting two important insights of Durkheim's, which will be elaborated in detail below.

real and effective" (*CEWR*, 66); Émile Durkheim, *The Elementary Forms of Religious Life* (trans. Karen E. Fields; New York: Free Press, 1995) 429.

[146] *CEWR* 3–4, 8–9.

[147] Durkheim (and his translators) uses various names for this religion, including "the religion of the individual," "the religion of humanity," "cult of personality," or the "cult of man." Here I follow the usage in Anthony Giddens, *Capitalism and Modern Social Theory: An Analysis of the Writings of Marx, Durkheim and Max Weber* (Cambridge: Cambridge University Press, 1971) 80, 115–16, 218; and James J. Chriss, "Durkheim's Cult of the Individual as Civil Religion: Its Appropriation by Erving Goffman," *Sociological Spectrum* 13 (1993) 251–75.

[148] Émile Durkheim, "Individualism and the Intellectuals," in *Durkheim on Religion* (ed. W. S. F. Pickering; trans. S. and J. Lukes; London: Routledge, 1975; repr., American Academy of Religion Texts and Translations 6; Atlanta: Scholars, 1994) 64, 67; Émile Durkheim, *The Division of Labor in Society* (trans. George Simpson; London: Collier Macmillan, 1933; repr., New York: Free Press, 1964) 400; see also Giddens, *Capitalism and Modern Social Theory*, 72, 77, 80. Organic solidarity is based upon a heterogeneous group of human individuals who form a society by functional interdependence. It is a situation "in which the members of a single social group will no longer have anything in common other than their humanity, that is, characteristics which constitute the human person in general" (Durkheim, "Individualism and the Intellectuals," 67).

[149] *RS*; Durkheim, *Elementary Forms of Religious Life*, 215–16.

First, Tillich could readily accept Durkheim's definition of religion in terms of beliefs and practices, for he already has a "narrow" conception of religion defined in terms of myths (beliefs) and rites (practices), beside his "broader" conception of religion in terms of ultimate concern. Second, Tillich could agree with Durkheim that religion helps to create and maintain social solidarity. This can be seen in the case of the quasi-religions which Tillich analyzes, such as nationalism, fascism, socialism, communism, and liberal humanism. They are all powerful systems of thought and life which bring social integration and solidarity to countries and, in the case of communism and liberal humanism, blocs of countries.

Durkheim's Significance for Tillich

We need now to take a closer look at what we can borrow from Durkheim to enrich and enhance Tillich's conception of quasi-religion.[150] I will start from Durkheim's classic definition of religion:[151]

> A religion is a unified system of beliefs and practices relative to sacred things, that is to say, things set apart and forbidden—beliefs and practices which unite into one single moral community called a Church, all those who adhere to them.[152]

Such emphasis on beliefs and practices is not incompatible with Tillich's conception of religion and quasi-religion. Tillich does not overlook the dimensions of belief (myth) and practice (rite or cult) in his conception of

---

[150] Thus I will deal with Durkheim in a circumscribed and highly selective way and not offer a comprehensive or in-depth exposition of his theory of religion.

[151] Before offering the definition as formulated in the *Elementary Forms of Religious Life*, which we are considering here, Durkheim had previously defined religion as an organized whole of religious phenomena consisting of obligatory beliefs and connected with clearly defined practices (Durkheim, *Durkheim on Religion*, 93). For an analysis of Durkheim's change in the definition of religion, see W. S. F. Pickering, *Durkheim's Sociology of Religion: Themes and Theories* (London: Routledge, 1984) 163–92.

[152] Durkheim, *Elementary Forms of Religious Life*, 44 [emphasis omitted]. Here the term "Church" is understood by Durkheim as "a society whose members are united because they imagine the sacred world and its relations with the profane world in the same way, and because they translate this common representation into identical practices" (ibid., 41). As for religious beliefs and practices (rites), Durkheim defines them respectively as "those representations that express the nature of sacred things and the relations they have with other sacred things or with profane things" and "rules of conduct that prescribe how man must conduct himself with sacred things" (ibid., 38).

religion.[153] His philosophy of religion already includes "myth" and "the cultus" as religious categories of the theoretical and practical spheres.[154] In his last public lecture he describes about religion as "a structure of symbols of intuition and action—that is, myths and rites within a social group."[155] Tillich's conception of quasi-religions as "systems of secular *thought* and *life*" that are similar to traditional religions also includes both belief and practice.[156] However, religion defined in terms of beliefs and practices pertains to Tillich's "narrow" conception of religion, which plays a relatively minor role in his writings. The predominant concept in his works is the "broader" definition of religion as "directedness of the spirit toward "the unconditional" or as "ultimate concern," and, as we have seen, it also underlies his conception of quasi-religion.[157] However, as the "depth" dimension of the spirit and as the substance of culture, religion in the broader sense (which includes quasi-religion as its subset) does not necessarily include beliefs and practices. In comparison, Durkheim's conception of religion seems better suited to the critical analysis of capitalism as a quasi-religion. Capitalism might not have an ultimate concern, but it does have a system of beliefs (such as the belief in competition) and practices (such as shopping) relative to things socially revered as "sacred," such as the market and its "invisible hand," limitless economic growth, freedom of choice, right to private property, and so forth.

Another aspect of Durkheim's thought that might contribute to our project is his conception of religion in terms of socially-constructed sacred things. The concept of the sacred or the holy is important to Tillich's philosophy of religion.[158] However, he does not consider the sacred to be intrinsically related to society. Durkheim's theory has two points worth noting in this regard. First, sacred things are characterized as "things set apart and

---

[153] See Clayton, "Introducing Tillich's Writings in Philosophy of Religion," *MW/HW* 4:17.

[154] *WR*, 101–21.

[155] Tillich, "The Significance of the History of Religions for the Systematic Theologian," in *CEWR*, 66.

[156] *ERQR*, 9 [emphasis added].

[157] *WR*, 59; *TC*, 8, 177.

[158] *WR*, 81–85. For the change in Tillich's concepts from the sacred to the Holy, see Gabriel Vahanian, "The Holy and the Secular Versus the Sacred and the Profane," in *Being versus Word in Paul Tillich's Theology? Proceedings of the VII. International Paul Tillich Symposium Held in Frankfurt/Main, 1998* (ed. Gert Hummel and Doris Lax; Berlin: De Gruyter, 1999) 330–41.

forbidden" by the society.[159] They are sacred insofar as they are socially constructed as sacred by collective imagination.[160] Durkheim points out that "society never stops creating sacred things." This includes the consecration of people with high positions by quasi-religious deference as well as the consecration of ideas—he mentions the idea of progress and the principle of free discussion—by regarding them as unquestionable.[161] He also points to the sacralization of the fatherland, liberty, and reason in the first years of the French Revolution, resulting in the emergence of a new religion.[162] Second, Durkheim stresses that religion is constituted by a "plurality of sacred things." A religion is composed of "separate and relatively distinct parts," within which homogeneous groupings of sacred things constitute centers of beliefs and rites.[163] Thus religion is, for Durkheim, a "system of cults that possess a certain autonomy," forming a "confederate organization."[164] In the next chapter I will argue that this conception of religion is more suitable for our critique of capitalism as a quasi-religion than is Tillich's conception of religion as ultimate concern.

Perhaps the most important contribution to our project is Durkheim's emphasis on the social nature of religion and its integrative function. For

---

[159] Durkheim, *Elementary Forms of Religious Life*, 44. Sacred things conceptualized as "things set apart and forbidden" can be empirically studied. This is in line with Durkheim's intention to explain religion from a social-scientific perspective.

[160] Ibid., 349.

[161] Ibid., 215.

[162] "Nowhere has society's ability to make itself a god or to create gods been more in evidence than during the first years of the Revolution. In the general enthusiasm of that time, things that were by nature purely secular were transformed by public opinion into sacred things: Fatherland, Liberty, Reason. A religion tended to establish itself spontaneously, with its own dogma, symbols, altars, and feast days. It was to these spontaneous hopes that the Cult of Reason and the Supreme Being tried to give a kind of authoritative fulfillment" (ibid., 215–16).

[163] Ibid., 38.

[164] Ibid., 39. "When a certain number of sacred things have relations of coordination and subordination with one another, so as to form a system that has a certain coherence and does not belong to any other system of the same sort, then the beliefs and rites, taken together, constitute a religion" (ibid., 38).

him, religion is never a "purely individual thing;"[165] rather, it is eminently "social" or "collective":[166]

> Religious representations are collective representations that express collective realities; rites are ways of acting that are born only in the midst of assembled groups and whose purpose is to evoke, maintain, or recreate certain mental states of those groups.[167]

Religion and society are inseparable.[168] On the one hand, society forms the foundation and content of religious beliefs and practices.[169] On the other hand, religion as a unified system of beliefs and practices creates and maintains social solidarity. Religion both originates from society and binds society together.[170] In Durkheim's view, society owes its existence to shared imagination. "A society is not constituted simply by the mass of individuals who comprise it . . . but above all by the idea it has of itself."[171] Society creates or recreates itself by creating at the same time some kind of ideal by which individuals imagine themselves as its members.[172] It is religion—or, to be precise, religious beliefs as collective representations—that expresses and provides such collective ideal or shared imagination. For Durkheim, "religion is first and foremost a system of ideas by means of which individuals imagine the society of which they are members and the obscure yet intimate

[165] "Even where religion seems to be entirely within the individual, the living source that feeds it is to be found in society. We can now judge the worth of the radical individualism that is intent on making religion out to be a purely individual thing: It misconceives the fundamental conditions of religious life" (ibid., 427).

[166] Ibid., 9, 44.

[167] Ibid., 9.

[168] See ibid., 44.

[169] See Peter B. Clarke and Peter Byrne, *Religion Defined and Explained* (New York: St. Martin's, 1993) 158.

[170] This dialectical relation between religion and society lies behind Durkheim's apparent "equation" of god and society. He asks "if the totem is the symbol of both the god and the society, is this not because the god and the society are one and the same?" His conclusion is that god is the apotheosis of society: "Thus, the god of the clan, the totemic principle, can be none other than the clan itself, but the clan transfigured and imagined in the physical form of the plant or animal that serves as totem" (Durkheim, *Elementary Forms of Religious Life*, 208).

[171] Ibid., 425.

[172] Ibid., 425. Such an ideal is closely related to the sacred world which human beings impose on the real world of profane life (ibid., 424).

relations they have with it."[173] Religion enables human beings to override sense impressions by a new way of imagination which establishes the interconnection between disparate things; this includes the imagination of society and one's belongingness to it.[174] Religious symbolism, such as the totemic emblem, enables society to become conscious of itself and also to perpetuate that consciousness;[175] that is to say, religious symbolism, as an objectified form of religious beliefs, both constitutes and sustains social solidarity.[176] Rituals—Durkheim's "rules of conduct," which prescribe one's action in relation to sacred things[177]—also create and sustain social solidarity. Engendered in the midst of assembled groups, rituals "evoke, maintain, or recreate certain mental states of those groups;" rituals remind or rekindle the communal experience of delirium or ecstasy (what Durkheim calls "collective effervescence") generated at assemblies, in which individuals intensely feel that they are part of the community. They thus reinforce the social solidarity generated and sustained by such experiences.[178] According to Durkheim, maintaining and strengthening at regular intervals the collective feelings that generate social solidarity is something eternal in religion. Thus, for him there is no basic difference between Christians celebrating the principal

---

[173] Ibid., 227. In an earlier formulation, Durkheim defines religion as a "system of symbols by means of which society becomes conscious of itself; it is the characteristic way of thinking of collective existence" (Émile Durkheim, *Suicide: A Study in Sociology* [ed. G. Simpson; trans. J. A. Spaulding and G. Simpson; Chicago: Free Press, 1951] 312, quoted in Pickering, *Durkheim's Sociology of Religion,* 369).

[174] Durkheim, *Elementary Forms of Religious Life,* 239. In totemism, which Durkheim regards as the most primitive form of religion, "the people of the clan, and the various beings whose form the totemic emblem represents, are held to be made of the same essence" (ibid., 238). This makes possible the imagination of the clan, which, in Durkheim's view, is otherwise lacking in social cohesion (ibid., 234). If the clan's name and its symbol (tangibly expressed by its totemic emblem) were taken away, "the clan can no longer even be imagined" (ibid., 235).

[175] Ibid., 233. For Durkheim, symbols are durable media on which the collective feelings of a community—which are strongest when it is in assembly and gradually fade away when the gathering is over—are inscribed (ibid., 232–33).

[176] "Thus, in all its aspects and at every moment of its history, social life is only possible thanks to a vast symbolism" (ibid., 233).

[177] Ibid., 38

[178] Durkheim, *Elementary Forms of Religious Life,* 9, 220, 228, 350, 424, 429. See also Catherine M. Bell, *Ritual: Perspectives and Dimensions* (New York: Oxford University Press, 1997) 24–25; Daniel L. Pals, *Seven Theories of Religion* (New York: Oxford University Press, 1996) 107–10.

dates of Christ's life, Jews celebrating the exodus from Egypt, and citizens commemorating great national events.[179]

In the next chapter, we will see how these insights of Durkheim—emphasis on religion as beliefs and practices, religion as a confederation of socially-constructed sacred things, the function of religion in social integration, the constitution of society by shared imagination—may be used in my own construction of a critical perspective that interprets capitalism as a quasi-religion.

[179] Durkheim, *Elementary Forms of Religious Life*, 429.

CHAPTER FOUR

Capitalism as a Quasi-Religion:
A Constructive and Critical Perspective

We come now to the telos of this dissertation: to develop a critical framework for the interpretation of global capitalism and capitalistic modernity. I draw primarily on Tillich's critique and borrow from the insights of Moltmann and Durkheim in areas where I consider Tillich's critique inadequate. Before putting forth my perspective, I will briefly restate my view of the overall contributions and limitations of Tillich.

Tillich's Contributions and Limitations

In the previous chapter I discussed several limitations of Tillich's response to capitalistic modernity, yet we cannot conclude that Tillich's critique of capitalism and modernity has now become obsolete and irrelevant. In fact, Tillich's critical interpretation of capitalism and modernity has obvious strengths and contributions that we should take seriously.

Contributions

First, Tillich's theology informs and closely correlates with his critical interpretations of modernity. The idea of theonomy—an ideal situation in which religion and culture have an unambiguous union, in which every cultural form expresses the religious substance, and in which God is all in all—is his own contribution to informing the critical interpretation of modernity. Tillich ingeniously formulated this concept both as a critique of and as an answer to what he regarded as the most significant feature of modernity, namely, autonomy. He applies theonomy as well to other problems of capitalistic modernity, such as the loss of ultimate meaning in the production process and the *eros*less relation between humans and technical objects.

Second, Tillich creatively incorporates the leading social theories of his day into his theological critique of capitalistic modernity. In his critique of capitalistic modernity, "rational criticism" and "prophetic criticism" intertwine. As does the Frankfurt School (his friends Horkheimer and Adorno as its major theorists) in this regard, Tillich owes the most to Marx, Weber, and Freud. His debt includes ideas such as objectification, dehumanization, class struggle, as well as the spirit of capitalism, means-ends rationality (or technical reason). Tillich does not usually cite the sources of these ideas, as he has already assimilated them and has integrated them seamlessly and creatively with his own thought. In this way, he stands out as the forerunner of a constellation of later theological movements—including political theology in Germany (such as that of Moltmann and Metz) and liberation theology in Latin America—which integrate critical social theory with theology.[1] Moreover, these theological movements do not supersede his critical interpretation of capitalistic modernity, just as contemporary social theories do not supersede the social theories of Marx and Weber. As I suggested in the previous chapter by drawing on Moltmann, a global perspective with more emphasis on the economic-material dimension provides a necessary corrective to Tillich's inadequate critique of modernity. Nevertheless, the basic tenets of Tillich still prove relevant today, and nothing has rendered them obsolete.

Third, Tillich carves out a proper space for affirming and enhancing the relevance of theology to the social and cultural situation. His theology of culture enables him to work out a critique of capitalism and modernity with special emphasis on the cultural-spiritual dimension. He criticizes capitalism primarily for the meaninglessness and dehumanization that it produces. He sees modernity as problematic because self-sufficient autonomy shuts out the ultimate, and technical reason leads to the loss of meaning and to

---

[1] In an early book, Dorothy Sölle tries to develop a political theology through the critique of the apolitical theology of Rudolf Bultmann. She remarks that such an endeavor is a detour and that "a political theology could be developed far more directly from the early writings of Paul Tillich, who understood religious socialism as 'the radical application of the prophetic-Protestant principle to religion and Christianity'" (Dorothee Sölle, *Political Theology* [trans. John Shelley; Philadelphia: Fortress, 1974] xix). As my analysis shows, even Tillich's later writings, including *Systematic Theology,* are helpful for the development of political theology.

objectification. Moreover, his theological perspective in general and his theology of culture enable him to analyze the religious dimension of social and cultural phenomena. He regards the spirit of bourgeois society as an "unconscious faith" that appears in various social and cultural institutions and movements. He interprets capitalism in terms of the demonic, which carries religious qualities. Finally, he analyzes various ideological systems or "systems of thought and life" as quasi-religions. All this contributes to the "public" relevance of theology.

Fourth, Tillich offers a dialectical critique of modernity. Tillich's theologically informed interpretation of capitalistic modernity resembles, while remaining different from, the critical theory of the Frankfurt School. Like them, Tillich has his own version of the "dialectic of enlightenment": the project of modernity originated as emancipatory yet eventually became dehumanizing. For example, autonomy frees human beings from various forms of heteronomy, which can occur particularly in some premodern epochs, yet it also entails the exclusion of the dimension of depth or the ultimate in modern culture, thereby leading to many problems. Unlike the Frankfurt School, however, Tillich has a less pessimistic attitude toward modernity. Consider again the concept of autonomy, which, for Tillich, represents a state of culture following only the demand of reason and excluding the ultimate. Its problems lie not in what it comprises but in what it lacks; thus, we need not a complete rejection of autonomy (and thence of modernity) but the transformation of it toward theonomy. By contrast, Horkheimer and Adorno do not expect to find a way out of the totalizing domination of instrumental reason.

Fifth, Tillich nuances his critique by calling capitalism demonic. The connotation of the term at first glance suggests something entirely negative and evil, but in that case Tillich would have called it "satanic," that is, something cannot exist in itself but has reality only in the demonic.[2] The demonic denotes a structure of evil with an ambiguous unity of both creativity and destructiveness. For Tillich, capitalism is demonic because on the one hand it is the most effective economic system that has ever existed, while on the other it has brought about many and various destructive results. Such a dialectical view of capitalism is more nuanced than those that condemn

[2] See ch. 1, page 40.

it as entirely evil.[3] Moreover, Tillich's critique of capitalism in terms of the concept of the demonic goes beyond the common critique of capitalism in terms of idolatry.[4] If we consider capitalism as idolatrous,[5] then a correct theological response should entail outright rejection. As Richard Tawney says, "Compromise is as impossible between the Church of Christ and the idolatry of wealth, which is the practical religion of capitalist societies, as it was between the Church and State idolatry of the Roman Empire."[6] The practical stance that such a view entails would result in nothing less than total withdrawal from, resistance to, or subversion of the capitalist system, seriously limiting political options.[7] Further, since we call idolatry a sin, the proper attitude toward it would involve repentance, which includes the reshaping of one's thought and life. However, this response is theologically misguided and practically inadequate, for capitalism is systemic and structural and can hardly be changed by moral effort. Here again, Tillich's critique of capitalism as demonic appears analytically more compelling. As a demonic structure, capitalism has the character of "possession" and, thus, moral acts

[3] In a rebuke of his friend Emmanuel Hirsch, who voiced theological support for National Socialism, Tillich criticized an undialectical view of the capitalist system as demonic. He wrote: "We have never called an age sinful, but we have called powers demonic. And what is more important, we have interpreted the demonic dialectically. It is never destructive but always also creative and sustaining." He continues: "you should have asked further whether in general a political movement in a particular country, however powerfully it prevail, is able at the outset to abolish a social structure in which it is involved and by which it lives. Indeed, if one calls persons, groups, and trends demonic, and moreover in the entirely undialectical sense of wicked, then it is easy, after abolishing them, to prove triumphantly the victory 'over the mass of the demonry.' But one only shows by this that he has understood nothing of the true depth and power of the demonic" (Tillich, "Open Letter to Emmanuel Hirsch," in *The Thought of Paul Tillich,* [ed. James Luther Adams, Wilhelm Pauck, and Roger L. Shinn; San Francisco, Calif.: Harper & Row, 1985] 365).

[4] The advantage of regarding capitalism as idolatrous is that it can be analyzed not just socially and theoretically as an economic system but also theologically as a quasi-religion. Tillich speaks of quasi-religions (although he does not mention capitalism): "Neither their nature nor their success can be explained without the analogy of religion" (*ERQR*, 9). Moreover, such a move allows theologians to draw from biblical and doctrinal traditions—especially the prohibition against the worship of idols to evaluate, criticize, and respond to capitalism.

[5] For example, some critics would regard capitalism as the "service of mammon." But Tillich cautions that one should not reduce the demonic element in capitalism to such religious-moral categories. See ch. 1, page 47.

[6] Richard H. Tawney, *Religion and the Rise of Capitalism* (intro. Adam B. Seligman; New Brunswick, N.J.: Transaction, 1998) 286.

[7] For example, incremental reform of or strategic participation in (with partial resistance to) an "idolatrous" system would certainly be out of the question.

of freedom and goodwill cannot break it; in fact, it can even turn goodwill to its own purposes.

Sixth, Tillich's critique of capitalism and capitalistic modernity avoids both optimism and pessimism.[8] We cannot improve or overcome the demonic structure of capitalism by moral goodwill, nor can we easily reverse the pathological tendencies of capitalistic modernity. Thus, we have no room for the millenarian optimism of, say, Marx's philosophy of history. This does not, however, entail the pessimism of the later thought of Horkheimer and Adorno. Tillich holds the hope that the kingdom of God will finally overcome the demonic powers and other negativities of history and that the kingdom of God will be realized at least fragmentarily in history, by means of, for example, the church's struggle against the principalities and powers.

Limitations

On the other hand, Tillich's critique of capitalism and modernity has some weaknesses and limitations. In the last chapter, I discussed in detail a few major problems, which I will briefly recapitulate here.

First, Tillich's critique of capitalistic modernity, which tends toward a cultural-spiritual emphasis, does not put enough emphasis on the material-economic dimension. In his interpretation, the economic system of capitalism, which is increasingly regarded by Moltmann as the root of the pathologies of modernity, fades into the background. Second, Tillich's interpretation remains Eurocentric and does not take seriously the contributions, sacrifices, and suffering of non-Western peoples in the development and constitution of modernity. Third, Tillich's conception of religion, defined in terms of ultimate concern, remains primarily asocial and thus inadequate for developing a critique of capitalism as a quasi-religion. I suggest borrowing from the insights of Durkheim, who sees religion as a unified system of beliefs and practices in relation to a confederation of sacred things in which religious beliefs and practices create, constitute, and sustain social solidarity. In the next section, I shall elaborate such insights for the development of a more adequate theological critique of global capitalistic modernity. This critique starts with seeing capitalism as a quasi-religion.[9]

[8] This may express Tillich's "belief-ful realism," which I briefly mentioned near the end of ch. 2 (see page 107).

[9] In the following discussions, I will characterize capitalism variously as a religion, a quasi-religion, or a global civil religion, according to context. In calling capitalism a religion,

Capitalism as Quasi-Religion: A Constructive Proposal

Some scholars have pointed out the quasi-religious character of capitalism or its vital components (such as the market or money). Thus, Jürgen Moltmann and John Cobb identify, respectively, the market and "economism" (with wealth as its god) as a world religion or global religion.[10] David Loy and Harvey Cox have offered insightful analyses of the religion of the market.[11] According to Loy, "market capitalism . . . has already become the most successful religion of all time, winning more converts more quickly than any previous belief-system or value-system in human history."[12] Cox sees in market capitalism striking parallels to traditional religions: the "religion of market culture" has an interpretation of the meaning of human history (freedom of choice), a doctrine of sin and redemption, a sacramental system (shopping), a catechetical network (advertising), and, most importantly, the market as a god, who exhibits all the divine attributes of omnipotence, omnipresence, and omniscience.[13] Eugene McCarraher points out that capitalism, instead of being an agent of disenchantment, "might be best understood as a perverse regime of the sacred, an order of things bearing powerful and unmistakable traces of enchantment."[14] For him, "enchantment is the perverse appropriation and practice of sacrament" and capitalism is a "parody of sacramentality."[15]

Not limited to scholars in the field of religion and theology, the view of capitalism as quasi-religious may include Karl Marx's critique of capitalism

---

I am basically using Tillich's broader definition of religion, which includes religions in the conventional sense (such as Christianity, Islam, Buddhism) as well as quasi-religions. I regard civil religion as a type of quasi-religion.

[10] Jürgen Moltmann, *God for a Secular Society: The Public Relevance of Theology* (trans. Margaret Kohl; Minneapolis, Minn.: Fortress, 1999) 153; John Cobb, Jr., "Liberation Theology and the Global Economy," in *Liberating the Future* (ed. Joerg Rieger; Minneapolis, Minn.: Fortress, 1998) 32.

[11] David R. Loy, "The Religion of the Market," *JAAR* 65 (1997) 275; Harvey Cox, "Mammon and the Culture of the Market: A Socio-Theological Critique," in *Meaning and Modernity: Religion, Polity, Self* (ed. Richard Madsen et al.; Berkeley, Calif.: University of California Press, 2002) 124–35.

[12] Loy, "Religion of the Market," 276.

[13] Cox, "Mammon and the Culture of the Market," 126–32.

[14] Eugene McCarraher, "The Enchantment of Mammon: Notes Toward a Theological History of Capitalism," *ModTh* 21 (2005) 429–61, at 430.

[15] Ibid., 431 [emphasis omitted].

in terms of the "fetishism of commodities,"[16] which he explains with the analogy of religion.[17] Walter Benjamin goes further and says that capitalism represents an "essentially religious phenomenon." He points to several definitive characteristics in the "religious structure of capitalism": purely cultic, it has no specific dogma; as a permanent cult, it gives no "weekdays" for escape; the cult leads not to atonement but to guilt and debt.[18] Christoph Deutschmann analyzes capitalism as a new religion that enables humans to take the place of god through the religious qualities of money (or capital). Money embodies power and possibilities, the utopian promise of absolute wealth, and also the quasi-religious imperative of growth, which is acted out by capitalist entrepreneurs relying on technical and organizational "myths."[19]

Unlike those mentioned above, Tillich does not explicitly analyze capitalism using the concept of quasi-religion, which he uses instead for the analysis of "systems of secular life and thought" that have significant influence in the world (e.g., nationalism and socialism). However, I see no reason why we cannot view capitalism as a quasi-religion in Tillich's sense. As I argued in the previous chapter, Tillich's concept of religion and quasi-religion, as defined in terms of ultimate concern, remains asocial and unpractical and thus inadequate for the analysis and critique of capitalism, but this does not mean that we cannot use Tillich's notion of quasi-religion at all. I suggest working out the full implications of his understanding of quasi-religions as "systems of secular life and thought" along the line of Durkheim's definition of religion as a unified system of beliefs and practices in relation to sacred things. We could then see capitalism as one of the most influential quasi-religions in the modern world. It has arguably

---

[16] Marx understands fetishism of commodities to be the process by which the product of human labor existing in definite social relations between human beings "assumes, in their eyes, the fantastic form of a relation between things" (Karl Marx, "*Capital*, Volume One," in *The Marx-Engels Reader* [ed. Robert C. Tucker; 2d ed.; New York: Norton, 1978] 321).

[17] "In that world [of religion] the productions of the human brain appear as independent beings endowed with life, and entering into relation both with one another and the human race. So it is in the world of commodities with the products of men's hands" (ibid.).

[18] Walter Benjamin, "Capitalism as Religion," in *1913–1926* (vol. 1 of *Selected Writings / Walter Benjamin*; ed. Marcus Bullock and Michael W. Jennings; Cambridge, Mass.: Harvard University Press, 1996) 288–89.

[19] Christoph Deutschmann, "Capitalism as a Religion? An Unorthodox Analysis of Entrepreneurship," *EJST* 4 (2001) 387–403; idem, "The Promise of Absolute Wealth: Capitalism as a Religion?" *ThII* 66 (2001) 32–56.

formed the civil religion[20] of global modernity or, in Tillich's language, the religious substance of modern society. I will elaborate on this suggestion when I construct a critical perspective of capitalism as a quasi-religion in the following paragraphs.[21]

Beliefs and Practices of Capitalism

Adopting Durkheim's insights, I regard the quasi-religion of capitalism as a unified system of beliefs and practices in relation to a confederation of sacred things. Capitalism comprises a quasi-religion consisting of a "system of cults" with a number of sacred things.[22] Market, money, and unbounded growth constitute the most significant sacred things in capitalism. We have already seen that some authors, such as Cox and Loy, single out the market as having sacred or quasi-divine status (hence the object of a cult) in contemporary capitalism. Like other sacred things, the market is "set apart and forbidden."[23] Free market (including free trade) is jealously guarded against political and social interferences. This is especially true in the economic neoliberalism promoted by many national governments as well as international organizations such as the World Trade Organization, International Monetary Fund, and the World Bank.[24] Through what Moltmann

[20] While the term "civil religion" goes back to Rousseau, I have in mind Bellah's use in his analysis of "American civil religion," which he describes as "a set of beliefs, symbols, and rituals" shared by the great majority of Americans (Robert N. Bellah, "Civil Religion in America," in *Beyond Belief: Essays on Religion in a Post-Traditionalist World* [Berkeley, Calif.: University of California Press, 1970] 171).

[21] My view of capitalism as a quasi-religion is complementary, not contradictory, to the common understanding of capitalism as an economic system.

[22] See Émile Durkheim, *The Elementary Forms of Religious Life* (trans. Karen E. Fields; New York: Free Press, 1995) 38–39. In a similar vein, John Boli finds that "the sacrality of the economy is generated less by the ritualization of the economy as a whole than by that of its constituent parts—companies, products, consumers, styles, sometimes particular technologies (the computer, the automobile) or economic sectors" (Boli, "The Economic Absorption of the Sacred," in *Rethinking Materialism: Perspectives on the Spiritual Dimension of Economic Behavior* [ed. Robert Wuthnow; Grand Rapids, Mich.: Eerdmans, 1995] 93–116, at 105). Each of these sacred things might have its own cult, its own beliefs and rites, yet, as long as they "have relations of coordination and subordination with one another, so as to form a system that has a certain coherence" (Durkheim, *Elementary Forms*, 38), they form a confederation of sacred things that constitute capitalism as a quasi-religion.

[23] Ibid., 44.

[24] See David Harvey, *A Brief History of Neoliberalism* (New York: Oxford University Press, 2005); Richard Peet et al., *Unholy Trinity: The IMF, World Bank and WTO* (Lon-

calls the "global marketing of everything," market value becomes the supreme good which demands the sacrifice even of human dignity. No less sacred in capitalism, money also has quasi-religious qualities.[25] Unbounded economic growth constitutes the third sacred thing.[26] Under capitalism, a "zero-growth" economy means stagnation, which is considered bad.[27] The market requires corporations not only to make profits but also to keep growing in profits. This "capitalist ethos" of limitless growth is an idol.[28] Other sacred things in capitalism include: individual freedom, rational choice, private property, brand name,[29] efficiency, and competitiveness.[30] The importance, rightness, and desirability of these sacred things are taken-for-granted, unquestionable, and inviolable. To the above list of intangible sacred things we must to add what is more tangible—"sacred spaces," such as shopping malls, which

---

don: Zed, 2003).

[25] As Boli writes, "Money is surely a sacred symbol: we hesitate to deface it, we endow it with great power, we fear the destruction it can wreak on society or our own selves (corruption)" (Boli, "Economic Absorption of the Sacred," 105). Deutschmann also mentions several quasi-religious qualities of money. For example, money, like religion, is based solely on the "trust" of the actors. Also, money is characterized by the quality of infinity, as in the idea of God. Moreover, money, like God, has the same inherent paradox: "it *is* what it signifies, a universal symbol connoting potentially everything (including itself) *as well as* a quantitatively fixed 'substance'—a paradox, which, as I have argued with Marx, transforms itself into the quasi-religious need of capitalist 'growth'" (Deutschmann, "Capitalism as a Religion?," 399 [emphasis in original]). See also idem, "Promise of Absolute Wealth," 38–41).

[26] "The most vital religion of the modern age has been economic progress" (Robert H. Nelson, *Economics as Religion: From Samuelson to Chicago and Beyond* [University Park, Pa.: Pennsylvania State University Press, 2001] 329).

[27] Jürgen Moltmann, *The Church in the Power of the Spirit: A Contribution to Messianic Ecclesiology* (trans. Margaret Kohl; Minneapolis, Minn.: Fortress, 1993) 170; idem, *God in Creation: A New Theology of Creation and the Spirit of God* (trans. Margaret Kohl. Minneapolis, Minn.: Fortress, 1993) 28.

[28] Moltmann, *Church in the Power of the Spirit*, 172–73. For a critique of modern societies' obsession with economic growth, measured in terms of Gross National Product, as "growth fetishism," see Clive Hamilton, *Growth Fetish* (London: Pluto, 2004).

[29] McCarraher asks suggestively: "Might brands be best considered in Durkheimian fashion as the latest version of totems, objects that bear the spirit of a clan?" (McCarraher, "Enchantment of Mammon," 454).

[30] Of these, individual freedom and rational choice are elements of what Durkheim called "the cult of the individual" (see above, page 141 n. 147), which provides moral underpinnings to the contractual solidarity characteristic of capitalistic modernity.

are secular cathedrals of the "religion of the market."[31] George Ritzer, a sociologist, describes such means of consumption as Disney World, fast-food restaurants, chain stores, shopping malls, and casinos as "cathedrals of consumption,"[32] for "they are structured, often successfully, to have an enchanted, sometimes even sacred, religious character. To attract ever larger numbers of consumers, such cathedrals of consumption need to offer, or at least appear to offer, increasingly magical, fantastic, and enchanted settings in which to consume."[33]

Capitalism, like other religions, has a system of beliefs and myths. These beliefs and myths constitute the discourses that market commentators, finance journalists, prominent economists, government officials, company directors, advertisement copywriters, as well as executives of institutions such as the International Monetary Fund and the World Trade Organization continually produce and circulate. According to one fundamental belief, originally articulated by Adam Smith, an individual's self-interested pursuits will unintentionally yet effectively bring economic benefits to all, thanks to the providential "invisible hand" of the market.[34] Promoting this belief, economic neoliberalism advocates the expansion and intensification of the market mechanism everywhere.[35] Advocates of what George Soros and Joseph Stiglitz have called "market fundamentalism"[36] affirm the infallible

---

[31] Jon Pahl, *Shopping Malls and Other Sacred Spaces: Putting God in Place* (Grand Rapids, Mich.: Brazos, 2003) 65–82. Pahl observes that shopping malls use water, light, trees, and other things that commonly serve as religious symbols, as well as words that promise us well-being, to disorient us and "*reorient* us toward one or another of the purveyors of goods" (ibid., 71–73 [emphasis in original]). Pahl draws heavily on Ira G. Zepp, Jr. *The New Religious Image of Urban America: The Shopping Mall as Ceremonial Center* (forew. and intro. Davíd Carrasco; 2d ed.; Niwot, Colo.: University Press of Colorado, 1997).

[32] George Ritzer, *Enchanting a Disenchanted World: Revolutionizing the Means of Consumption* (2d ed.; Thousand Oaks, Calif.: Pine Forge, 2005) 2–20.

[33] Ibid., 7.

[34] This is part of what Tillich calls the modern belief in harmony.

[35] Examples of the expansion and intensification of market mechanism include: privatization of public services, reduction of social welfare, deregulation of industries to promote keener competition, market-oriented management of nonprofit organizations, more "flexible" employment contracts, removal of tariffs and other barriers to free trade, and the free transnational circulation of capital.

[36] Soros writes: "The global capitalist system is supported by an ideology rooted in the theory of perfect competition. According to this theory, markets tend toward equilibrium and the equilibrium position. . . . Any constraints on free competition interfere with the efficiency of the market mechanisms; therefore they should be resisted. In previous discussion, I described this as the laissez faire ideology but market fundamentalism is a better term. . . . I

validity of the free market as the best solution to economic problems in spite of contrary evidence. Besides faith in the invisible hand of the market, capitalism also presupposes a number of other beliefs, such as the "absolute goodness of economic growth,"[37] the rationality and equality of the actors, and the tendency toward equilibrium. All this contributes to the construction of a utopia while accounting for empirical imperfections.[38] Capitalism thus provides a meaning-giving sacred order[39] or symbolic universe that explains life's problems and guides human actions in contemporary society.[40] For example, capitalism often interprets the suffering of the poor either as deserved or necessary. Jung Mo Sung, a Brazilian theologian, points out that "market mechanisms are a secularized version of the theology of retribution," according to which "the poor are seen as guilty of their own poverty and that they are receiving *their* just rewards."[41] Under capitalism,

---

believe that the revival of market fundamentalism can be explained only by faith in a magic quality ("the invisible hand") that is even more important than the scientific base" (George Soros, *The Crisis of Global Capitalism: Open Society Endangered* [New York: PublicAffairs, 1998] 126–27). See also Joseph E. Stiglitz, *Globalization and Its Discontents* (New York: Norton, 2002) 58, 73, 219, 221.

[37] Charles A. Reich, *Opposing the System* (New York: Crown, 1995) 75. For Reich, the uncritical trust in the economic "laws" is a "quasi-religious faith" (ibid., 76). It may be noted that limitless growth is an expression of Tillich's "self-sufficient finitude."

[38] Neil J. Smelser, "Economic Rationality as a Religious System," in *Rethinking Materialism: Perspectives on the Spiritual Dimension of Economic Behavior* (ed. Robert Wuthnow. Grand Rapids, Mich.: Eerdmans, 1995) 73–92. Smelser notes that the economic paradigm constructed by classical economics "contained all the major elements of a religious system: a world view or cosmology; a system of legitimizing values, orderliness, and coherence as a belief system; more or less derivable moral implications; and factual claims about the empirical world" (ibid., 81).

[39] Peter Berger has defined religion as "the establishment, through human activity, of an all-embracing sacred order, that is, of a sacred cosmos that will be capable of maintaining itself in the ever-present face of chaos" (Peter L. Berger, *The Sacred Canopy: Elements of a Sociological Theory of Religion* [Garden City, N.Y.: Doubleday, 1967; repr., New York: Doubleday, 1990] 51).

[40] Boli, "Economic Absorption of the Sacred," 94, 107. Boli sketches how the economic religion (of capitalism) offers answers to basic questions of life: The meaning of life is the "full participation in the exchange economy, as both producer of value and consumer of goods" and the purpose of life is the full development of the individual both through value production and rational consumption, as well as the "pursuit of collective progress and justice" through these economic activities (ibid., 109).

[41] Jung Mo Sung, "Hunger for God, Hunger for Bread, Hunger for Humanity: A Southern Perspective," in *Hope and Justice for All in the Americas: Discerning God's Mission* (ed. Oscar L. Bolioli; New York: Friendship, 1998) 38 [emphasis in original].

social injustices may even be viewed as necessary sacrifices for the proper functioning of the system, since social inequality "provides an incentive for competition among people and is, at the same time, the result of a society based on competition."[42]

Perhaps even more important, capitalism operates as a system of practices and rituals in relation to sacred things. Capitalism as quasi-religion resembles more a form of life than a belief system. Walter Benjamin says that capitalism constitutes a "purely cultic religion" without a specific set of dogmas.[43] He emphasizes the significance and permanence of "cultic" practice in the constitution of capitalism as religion. Most people participate daily in the capitalist economy as producers, consumers, or investors without considering their economic beliefs, but their economic activities constitute religious practices or rituals in the Durkheimian sense through their relation to the sacred things in capitalism. Money-based transaction—so vital and prevalent in capitalism—functions as a ritual, for it reinforces faith in the other sacred things (e.g., the free market, the monetary system, the rational individual) that make it possible.[44] Shopping, involving more than money transaction, forms the central ritual in the sacramental system of consumerist capitalism.[45] Moreover, the shopping spree at holidays and the "irrational exuberance"[46] of the stock market instantiate the "collective effervescence" of the capitalistic religion, which reinforces the individual's feeling of belonging to the capitalist society. Capitalism's rituals abound as part of the modern form of life. As Benjamin describes it, we celebrate the cult of capitalism everyday, as "each day commands the utter fealty of each worshiper."[47] We can consider even the daily productive activities of an employee as quasi-religious practices.

---

[42] Ibid., 39.

[43] Benjamin, "Capitalism as Religion," 288.

[44] Cf. Boli, "Economic Absorption of the Sacred," 103–4. For Boli, the elements of the sacred order that give money its value are the nation, the rational individual, and rationalized public and private organizations (ibid., 104). He also characterizes economic policy and advertising as rituals (ibid., 104).

[45] "This sacramental system focuses on the central act of exercising the freedom to choose by making market decisions: 'I shop therefore I am' " (Cox, "Mammon and the Culture of the Market," 126).

[46] The term "irrational exuberance" was originally used by Alan Greenspan, the thirteenth chairman of the Board of Governors of the U.S. Federal Reserve (1987–2006), in his description of the U.S. stock market in 1996 (Greenspan, "The Challenge of Central Banking in a Democratic Society").

[47] Benjamin, "Capitalism as Religion," 288.

In Tillich's interpretation of American society, productive activity itself functions not just as the means but also as the inner aim of production. "The means are more than means; they are felt as creation, as symbols of the infinite possibilities implied in man's productivity. Being-itself is essentially productive."[48] The fact that people apply the originally religious word "creative" to activities of production without hesitation demonstrates that "the creative process of history is felt as divine."[49] Participants in productive activities experience and express "the courage to be a part in the productive process." Such courage helps overcome various types of anxiety.[50]

Capitalism as Global Civil Religion

As I have just outlined briefly, we can see capitalism in a Durkheimian way, namely, as a religion or as a unified system of beliefs and practices in relation to sacred things—and such a view of capitalism falls within Tillich's understanding of quasi-religions as "systems of secular life and thought." However, I have not as yet fully brought out the implications of Durkheim's insights. I consider it important—and a key to the relation between capitalism and modernity—that through those shared beliefs and collective practices in relation to sacred things capitalism as quasi-religion helps create and sustain social solidarity in the modern world. As Durkheim maintains, a society is constituted "by the idea it has of itself," and religion is primarily a system of ideas through which individuals "imagine the society of which they are members."[51] Capitalism's system of ideas, beliefs, and myths, produced and circulated as discourse, constructs and maintains a sacred order or

[48] *CTB*, 108. Although Tillich was analyzing the "democratic conformism" of American society, the validity of his analysis is not limited to the United States.

[49] *CTB*, 109.

[50] See *CTB*, 109–11. Dreisbach interprets what Tillich says in *CTB*: "Economic progress is creative, and so is a manifestation of the power of being. By participating in a society that is inventive and economically productive, we more deeply integrate ourselves into a culture that has saving power, that is, that responds to our anxiety. Participation in the productive process is experienced as sharing in the creative power of God or being itself, and so empowers the participant to confront the threats of non-being" (Donald F. Dreisbach, "History and Economics in *The Courage to Be*," in *Truth and History: A Dialogue with Paul Tillich* [ed. Gert Hummel; Berlin: de Gruyter, 1998] 178). Arguing from a different perspective, Walter Benjamin also asserts that "capitalism serves essentially to allay the same anxieties, torments, and disturbances to which the so-called religions offered answers" (Benjamin, "Capitalism as Religion," 288).

[51] Durkheim, *Elementary Forms*, 227, 425.

symbolic universe by means of which individuals imagine modern society and themselves as its members.[52] At the same time, the practices and rituals of capitalistic religion affirm what it holds as sacred and create and reinforce the feeling of belonging to the capitalist society. The constitution of modern society owes a substantial debt to the beliefs and practices of capitalism, which functions like an economic version of civil religion.[53] This means that the capitalist quasi-religion helps construct and maintain social solidarity in modernity.[54] In the following explication of my view, I will focus on the market, which is one of the most sacred things in capitalism.

The market functions as one key social "imaginary" institution, which helps to constitute modern society. Scholars such as Cornelius Castoriadis, Benedict Anderson, Craig Calhoun, and Charles Taylor have recognized, in differing ways, the important role of social imagination in the constitution of modern society.[55] For Taylor, three crucial "social imaginaries" underpin the rise of Western modernity: the market economy, the public sphere, and the citizen-state.[56] Modernity emerges first of all with the view of society in

---

[52] This of course does not mean that capitalism as a system of ideas exclusively provides the shared imagination of modern society. There is a plurality of quasi-religions complementing or competing with each other in the construction of our modern social reality. Yet, given the dominance of the economy in modern society, capitalism plays a large part in shaping our shared imagination.

[53] I share Boli's view that the notion of "economic religion" (with the economy as the sacred order) is "an elaboration of Bellah's concept of civil religion" (Boli, "Economic Absorption of the Sacred," 107). Yet economic religion differs from civil religion in that the "deep-structured commonality (of the sacred order and its derivatives) serves as a foundation for distinctiveness," a distinctiveness of radically conformist individualism (ibid., 107–8).

[54] This position can be compared to that of Robert Nelson, an economist, who stresses that the economic religion (of capitalism) has become a world religion in modernity and that it is important in sustaining social solidarity. "The most vital religion of the modern age has been economic progress" and the modern nation-state "has been a church of progressive faith" (Nelson, *Economics as Religion,* 329, 335). By promoting a culture of civic commitment to the market system, economists have summoned the power of religion to fence off modern evils, such as opportunistic and predatory forces that undermine the market (ibid., 335).

[55] Cornelius Castoriadis, *The Imaginary Institution of Society* (trans. Kathleen Blamey; Cambridge, Mass.: Polity, 1987); Benedict Anderson, *Imagined Communities: Reflections on the Origins and Spread of Nationalism* (rev. ed.; London: Verso, 1991); Craig Calhoun, "Indirect Relationships and Imagined Communities: Large-Scale Integration and the Transformation of Everyday Life," in *Social Theory for a Changing Society* (ed. Pierre Bourdieu and James S. Coleman; Boulder, Colo.: Westview, 1991) 95–121; Charles Taylor, "Modern Social Imaginaries," *PCul* 14 (2002) 91–124.

[56] Taylor, "Modern Social Imaginaries," 92, 111, 116. For Taylor, the social "imaginary" is "what enables, through making sense of, the practices of a society" (ibid. 91). It refers to

terms of mutual benefit through profitable exchange, or, the view of society as a market economy.[57]

> And so perhaps the first big shift wrought by this new idea of order, both in theory and in social imaginary, consists in our coming to see society as an "economy," an interlocking set of activities of production, exchange, and consumption, which form a system with its own laws and dynamic. Instead of being merely the management, by those in authority, of the resources we collectively need, in household or state, the economic now defines a way in which we are linked together, a sphere of coexistence that could in principle suffice to itself, if only disorder and conflict didn't threaten.[58]

The market becomes a crucial "social imaginary," which contributes to the social cohesion, integration, and solidarity of modern capitalist society. As an imagined institution, the market brings together a group of people—producers, consumers, traders, investors, regulators, and so forth—who become associated with each other and mutually dependent economically through the relation of profitable exchange. People hold the idea that they are interconnected and interdependent economically by means of the market, and they keep that idea alive by ongoing practices. The result is a market-mediated social solidarity,[59] a solidarity formed by functional interdependence.[60] This kind of social solidarity has become more salient in contemporary capitalist society (or as called by some, "market society") in which the relation of individuals to one another and to the society as a whole becomes more

---

"the ways in which people imagine their social existence, how they fit together with others, how things go on between them and their fellows, the expectations that are normally met, and the deeper normative notions and images that underlie these expectations" (ibid. 106). Largely implicit and pretheoretical, the social imaginary has the nature of background understanding that both makes possible and is carried by practices (ibid., 107).

[57] Ibid., 96–100.

[58] Ibid., 105.

[59] Relationship through market activities is momentary and precarious, but this does not mean it cannot create and sustain social solidarity. Market-mediated social solidarity is produced not by this or that exchange relation, but by recurrent and unceasing engagement in exchange relations.

[60] Craig Calhoun, "Imagining Solidarity: Cosmopolitanism, Constitutional Patriotism, and the Public Sphere," *PCul* 14 (2002) 147–71, at 161. Other forms of social solidarity include categorical identities (such as nation, race, and class), direct social relations, and publics (ibid., 161–62).

and more defined in terms of economic exchange.[61] We need to note that the market itself, as I said above, constitutes one of the most sacred things in the quasi-religion of capitalism. The social imaginary of the market and the associated practices comprise the beliefs and rituals of its cult. In this sense, we can see capitalism, with the market as an important sacred thing and an important basis of social solidarity, as an economic version of civil religion.

Robert Bellah describes civil religion as "a collection of beliefs, symbols, and rituals with respect to sacred things and institutionalized in a collectivity."[62] His Durkheimian view of religion resembles the view that I use in analyzing capitalism as a quasi-religion. While civil religion in Bellah's sense contributes to the solidarity of political society, the quasi-religion of capitalism helps sustain the solidarity of economic society. However, I see a significant difference between civil religion in the ordinary sense and capitalism as an economic version of civil religion. Civil religion, in general, helps sustain the social solidarity of a nation; it stays within the national boundary.[63] Capitalist quasi-religion, on the other hand, sustains social solidarity (including market-mediated solidarity) not just nationally but also internationally and, in recent decades, throughout the globe. Capitalism by its nature has an international orientation; the market knows no boundary in its pursuit of the unlimited expansion for the accumulation of capital.[64] In Tillich's day, other quasi-religions, such as fascism and communism, checked the ability of capitalism as quasi-religion to constitute social solidarity at the global level. Fascism suffered defeat in the Second World War, and communism crumbled after 1989. Nationalism propelled postwar decolonization movements; in recent years it has reasserted its presence in many places. However, capitalism, more than anything else, dominates the contemporary world. Informed by the discourse of globalization (itself

---

[61] For example, wage labor is commodified for sale in the "labor market." Market-oriented management practices are initiated in many not-for-profit organizations. Even religions become marketable commodities.

[62] Bellah, "Civil Religion in America," 175.

[63] I say "in general" for the sake of not ruling out the possibility of a global civil religion. One sociologist contends that Durkheim has international civil religion as his ideal (Ruth A. Wallace, "Émile Durkheim and the Civil Religion Concept," *RRelRes* 18 [1977] 287–90).

[64] See Karl Marx and Friedrich Engels, "Manifesto of the Communist Party," in *The Marx-Engels Reader* (ed. Robert C. Tucker; 2d ed.; New York: Norton, 1978) 476.

emanated from capitalism) and aided by the spread of communication technology, capitalism as quasi-religion has become global.

I do not say primarily that capitalism has spread globally but that it gives people around the world a global consciousness, a collective imagination that "we" (individuals as well as nations) are economically interconnected and interdependent with "them" in other parts of the world through the market (including trade and investment).[65] In other words, capitalism as quasi-religion helps to construct social solidarity at the global level. Such global solidarity finds reinforcement in events of international effervescence and melancholy, such as the 1998 Asian financial crisis, the boom and bust of technology stocks at the turn of the millennium, and the repercussions of the U.S. subprime mortgage crisis in 2007–2008. Exchange rate, trade deficit, and global competitiveness comprise the lexicon of the collective imagination of the capitalist quasi-religion. Thus, we can say that capitalism has become a global quasi-religion—indeed a dominant global civil religion in the twenty-first century.[66]

Capitalism as the Religious Substance of Modernity

Up to now I have elaborated my view of capitalism as a quasi-religion primarily in Durkheimian terms. Now I bring Tillich back in to articulate the relation between capitalism and modernity. I venture to suggest that capitalism as a quasi-religion—indeed a global civil religion—is the religious substance of modernity.

Tillich uses the term "substance" in two ways. In one usage, it constitutes one of the four ontological categories that make up forms of finitude expressing the union of being and nonbeing.[67] "Substance points to something underlying the flux of appearances." Characterized as "remaining unity in change," substance "underlies a process of becoming and gives it unity, making it into

---

[65] This global consciousness underlies and legitimizes the "international division of labor," which Giddens includes as one of the four dimensions of globalization. Anthony Giddens, *The Consequences of Modernity* (Stanford, Calif.: Stanford University Press, 1990) 70–77.

[66] I have been saying that capitalism is *a*, not *the*, global quasi-religion or global civil religion. Like traditional world religions in the modern world, capitalism as a quasi-religion has many adherents; however, also like traditional religions, it is not universally accepted. Thus the social solidarity it helps construct and maintains is partial, fragmented, and precarious.

[67] *ST* 1:197–98. The other ontological categories are time, space, and causality (*ST* 1:192–97).

a definite, relatively lasting thing."[68] This usage resembles that of the German term *Substanz* in philosophy. In its second usage, "substance" resembles the English equivalent of *Gehalt*, which is one of the three elements in Tillich's theological analysis of culture: *Inhalt* (content, subject matter), *Form* (form), and *Gehalt* (substance, import).[69] In his analysis, however, Tillich reduces the triad of content, form, and substance into a dialectic of form and substance, by assimilating content into form and rendering it insignificant.[70] "Substance" is the meaning and the spiritual substantiality that gives significance to form.[71] It is implicitly given and presupposed in a cultural creation: "It is unconsciously present in a culture, a group, an individual, giving the passion and driving power to him who creates and the significance and power of meaning to his creation."[72] Thus, religious substance is the "inexhaustible source of meaning," which gives fundamental meaningfulness to culture.[73] On the other hand, religious substance in the sense of *Substanz* means that which gives unity to culture amidst changes.[74] In fact, Tillich uses the words

[68] *ST* 1:197; 3:314.

[69] See *MW/HW* 2:76 = *VS* 27; *ST* 3:60. For a perceptive analysis of the dialectic of *Inhalt*, *Form*, and *Gehalt*, see John P. Clayton, *The Concept of Correlation: Paul Tillich and the Possibility of a Mediating Theology* (Berlin: de Gruyter, 1980) 191–99. See also Victor Nuovo's analysis in *VS*, 73–74; Michael Palmer, "Paul Tillich's Theology of Culture," in *MW/HW* 2:12–15; and James Luther Adams, *Paul Tillich's Philosophy of Culture, Science, and Religion* (New York: Harper & Row, 1965) 77–79.

[70] Clayton, *Concept of Correlation*, 197.

[71] *VS*, 27. Tillich's notion of substance (*Gehalt*) is elusive. "Tillich's notorious lack of precision in the way he uses key terms is nowhere more evident than in the case of *Gehalt*" (Clayton, *Concept of Correlation*, 197 n. 17).

[72] *ST* 3:60. According to Nouvo, Tillich uses the term *Gehalt* (substance) to signify an extraordinary content, a metaphysical content of meaning that cannot be comprehended or rationally expressed, the ground or infinite power to mean something unconditionally (*VS*, 182–83 n. 33).

[73] *ST* 3:97. In a 1924 article, "Kirche und Kultur" (*MW/HW* 2:101–14), translated as "Church and Culture" in *IH*, 219–41, Tillich views culture as the subjective side of "the system of all possible systems of meaning" (*IH*, 222). It is the totality of interconnected meanings from which an individual act of meaning derives its significance. Also, every act of meaning implicitly presupposes "unconditional meaning" or the ultimate meaningfulness of the whole. Religion is the direction of the spirit toward such basis (and abyss) of all meaning, which Tillich calls God (*IH*, 221–22; see also Palmer, "Paul Tillich's Theology of Culture," 11).

[74] See Clayton, *Concept of Correlation*, 143.

Substanz and *Gehalt* synonymously.[75] For example, in the German edition of the final volume of *Systematic Theology* (which, besides being a translation, functions in some sense as Tillich's "second edition"[76]), Tillich renders the triad of subject matter, form, and substance as "*Gegenstand (Material), Form* und *Gehalt (Substanz)*."[77]

Given the above analysis of Tillich's notion of religious substance as the ultimate source of meaning and the basis of the unity of culture, it would appear demonstrable that the quasi-religion of capitalism constitutes the religious substance of modernity. Capitalism as a religion comprises a unified system of beliefs and practices. Its ideas, beliefs, and myths construct and maintain a sacred order that explains life's problems and guides human actions.[78] Moreover, this constructed sacred order, which includes the "social imaginary" of the market, is a principal means by which men and women construe modern society and their belongingness to it; they thereby find their place in the complex whole called society and thus make sense of their life. Meanwhile, the rituals and practices of capitalism affirm and actualize this sacred order and recurrently create the feeling of belongingness. Because of the dominance of economy in modernity, this sacred order, sustained by the system of beliefs and practices of the quasi-religion of capitalism, becomes the basic source of meaning and meaningfulness of life in modern society. At the same time, capitalism as a religion is a unified system of beliefs and practices. With the social imaginary that it constructs and the social solidarity that it constitutes, capitalism gives unity (hence identity) to modern culture and society in the midst of and in spite of the ceaseless changes that it generates. In this twofold sense—capitalism as the source of

---

[75] Translating both *Gehalt* and *Substanz* as "substance," Nuovo notes that Tillich's notion of substance can be understood in the sense used by Spinoza as "a unique and metaphysically ultimate reality, which is the infinite ground of all existence"; it should also be thought of in a Kantian sense as a category (a part of the conceptual scheme that makes human understanding possible), "as the fundamental and ultimate category of meaning"; and also in a romantic sense as unfathomable mystery (*VS*, 73–74).

[76] Clayton, *The Concept of Correlation*, 20. According to Clayton, the translation "afforded Tillich the opportunity to make corrections and additions to the texts to clarify ambiguities—whether theological or grammatical—and inconsistencies which had so characterised the third volume in particular." Tillich played a less active role in the translation of other volumes of *Systematic Theology* (ibid., 20–21).

[77] Paul Tillich, *Systematische Theologie* (4th ed.; Berlin: de Gruyter, 1987) 3:75. For the English version, see *ST* 3:60.

[78] See n. 38 above.

meaning and meaningfulness in modern society and as the basis of unity of modern culture and society—the quasi-religion of capitalism is the religious substance of modern society.

Furthermore, following Tillich's conception of the relation between religion and culture, we can say that the cultural forms by which we recognize cultural modernity express the quasi-religion of capitalism as the religious substance of modern society. In chapter 2, I claimed that Tillich's critique of cultural modernity is basically the same as his critique of the cultural dimension of capitalism. Now we can see the relationship between capitalism and modernity in a clearer light as the relationship between, respectively, religious substance and cultural form. The major principles or features of modernity as analyzed by Tillich—autonomy, self-sufficient finitude, technical reason, controlling knowledge, objectification—all express the capitalistic religious substance. For example, the spirit of self-sufficient finitude expresses the capitalist logic of the infinite pursuit of finite things, the "unending, ever-increasing, life-consuming activity in the service of unlimited wants"[79] and "the endless production of means without an end."[80] Also, objectification results from the domination of nature and human beings through technical reason and controlling knowledge in the service of capitalism. Thus, my constructive proposal incorporates Tillich's critique of cultural modernity, which we have already seen in chapter 2.

Various aspects of cultural modernity, including religion in the narrow sense as a particular sphere of culture, express capitalism as the religious substance of modern society. Thomas Luckmann's analysis of "invisible religion" in modern society supports this claim. For Luckmann, a new form of religion, without institutional specialization, emerges in modernity. Religion is privatized and becomes subject to a "pervasive consumer orientation." As a consumer, the "autonomous" modern individual shops from the assortment of available religious representations to construct his or her own system of "ultimate" significance.[81] The "privatized syncretism" of the New Age movement exemplifies this new social form of "invisible religion."[82] Luckmann might also have observed that even traditional, institutional,

---

[79] *MW/HW* 5:54–55 = *RS*, 107–9.

[80] *SSOTS*, 79–80.

[81] Thomas Luckmann, *The Invisible Religion: The Problem of Religion in Modern Society* (New York: Macmillan, 1967) 90–91, 98–102. See also idem, "Shrinking Transcendence, Expanding Religion?" *SocAn* 50 (1990) 132–34.

[82] Luckmann, "Shrinking Transcendance," 136–37.

and "visible" religions may develop in ways that express the religiosity of capitalism as the religious substance of modern culture. Rationalization constitutes one important aspect of the logic of capitalism. Extending Weber's theory of rationalization, George Ritzer coined the term "McDonaldization" to describe "the process by which the principles of the fast-food restaurant are coming to dominate more and more sectors of American society as well as of the rest of the world."[83] Consisting of four dimensions—efficiency, calculability, predictability, and control[84]—"McDonaldization" permeates contemporary society, including the churches. John Drane, working in the same vein, mentions the "pre-packaged 'welcome' " to newcomers, the proliferation of "how-to" books on Christian life, the stress on quantity in the Church Growth movement, the homogenized understanding of Christian discipleship and lifestyle, the use of "counsellors" at evangelistic crusades, and the emergence of the megachurches as examples of the "McDonaldization" of the church.[85]

If rationalization pertains to capitalistic production (of goods and services), then commodification pertains to capitalistic consumption. Under the impact of capitalism as the religious substance of modernity, elements of religion become commodities for sale in the market. Televangelism, the retailing of Christian goods and services, the Church Growth movement, and the megachurches provide some examples in American Protestantism.[86] This trend demonstrates that "if you do not commodify your religion yourself,

[83] George Ritzer, *The McDonaldization of Society* (rev. ed.; Thousand Oaks, Calif.: Pine Forge, 2004) 1, 25.

[84] Ibid., 12–15.

[85] John Drane, *The McDonaldization of the Church: Spirituality, Creativity, and the Future of the Church* (London: Darton, Longman & Todd, 2000); idem, "From Creeds to Burgers: Religious Control, Spiritual Search, and the Future of the World," in *McDonaldization: The Reader* (ed. George Ritzer; 2d ed.; Thousand Oaks, Calif.: Pine Forge, 2006) 197–202.

[86] John A. Coleman, S.J., "Selling God in America: American Commercial Culture as a Climate of Hospitality to Religion," in *Meaning and Modernity: Religion, Polity, Self* (ed. Richard Madsen et al.; Berkeley, Calif.: University of California Press, 2002) 141–42. Such an intertwining of religion and market already occurred in the nineteenth century when American Protestantism attempted to compete with secular entertainment. Coleman draws on the historical analysis of R. Laurence Moore, *Selling God: American Religion in the Marketplace of Culture* (New York: Oxford University Press, 1994). According to Coleman, American culture has followed "a dominant market logic of commodification and consumerism" and religion, as a component of culture, also "conforms to this dominant market-driven logic" (Coleman, "Selling God," 136). George Ritzer includes the megachurches among the cathedrals of consumption. He points out: "although the cathedrals of consumption have a

someone will do it for you."[87] We see fragments of religious traditions (sacred music, for example) commodified and marketed in popular culture for consumption in order to meet the therapeutic needs of the baby-boomer generation.[88] All the above are ways in which contemporary Christianity, as a religion in the narrow sense (that is, a particular sphere of modern culture) expresses the capitalistic religious substance of modern society.

Contributions to Critique

How does the perspective outlined above contribute to a theological critique of global capitalism and capitalistic modernity?

First, my perspective reveals the unavoidably religious nature of capitalism. To borrow what Tillich says about other quasi-religions, neither the nature of capitalism nor its success can be explained without the concept of quasi-religion.[89] Not only an economic system, capitalism also functions as a quasi-religion, that is, a system of secular thought and life analogous to traditional religions. It holds sway over us as it constructs a sacred order that explains (and explains away) problems in modern society; it guides, coordinates, and gives meaning to human practices; it constructs and maintains social solidarity by providing the symbolic means for the imagination of modern society; it offers a kind of secular salvation.[90] A sound and realistic response to capitalism depends on a sound and realistic understanding of its quasi-religious nature. What David Loy says below about the market applies to capitalism in general:

> The market is not just an economic system but a religion—yet not a very good one, for it can thrive only by promising a secular salvation that it never quite supplies. Its academic discipline, the "social science" of economics, is better understood as a theology pretending to be a science. This suggests that any solution to the problems thus created must also have a religious dimension. This is a matter not of turning

---

quasi-religious character, religion has begun to emulate those cathedrals" (Ritzer, *Enchanting a Disenchanted World*, 23).

[87] Moore, *Selling God*, 11.

[88] See Vincent J. Miller, *Consuming Religion: Christian Faith and Practice in a Consumer Culture* (New York: Continuum, 2005) 73–94.

[89] *ERQR*, 9.

[90] For secular salvation, see Loy, "Religion of the Market," 289; Nelson, *Economics as Religion*, 266–67. Yet, Nelson and Loy both point out that capitalism (or capitalist economics) has been incapable to deliver what it promises to supply.

from secular to sacred values but of the need to discover how our
secular obsessions have become symptomatic of a spiritual need that
they cannot meet. . . . The solution to the environmental catastrophe
that has already begun and to the social deterioration we are already
suffering from will occur when we redirect this repressed spiritual
urge back into its true path. For the time being, that path includes
struggling against the false religion of our age.[91]

In viewing capitalism as a religious phenomenon, we affirm the contribution
of theology, as the normative study of religion, for the analysis and critique
of capitalism. What Tillich has done may not suffice, but it puts us on the
right track.

Second, the perspective outlined above emphasizes that we cannot separate the critique of capitalism (as the religious substance of modernity)
and the critique of modernity (as the cultural expression of capitalism). On
the one hand, we cannot change the cultural pathologies of modernity, if
capitalism as the religious substance that infuses them with its logic remains
intact. Thus the critique of the material-economic dimension of modernity,
which Moltmann emphasizes, remains indispensable. On the other hand,
the critique of capitalism entails the critique of cultural modernity, which
expresses it. Seen in this light, Tillich's critique of cultural modernity from the
perspective of theonomy remains an important development of his religious-
socialist critique of capitalist political economy. His contention that modern
culture—characterized by autonomy, self-sufficient finitude, technical reason,
objectification, and so on—has cut itself off from its divine ground and
produces meaninglessness and dehumanization indirectly critiques capitalist
quasi-religion, which these cultural forms express. My perspective embraces
these two inseparable approaches of critique in Tillich's works (as analyzed
in chapters 1 and 2) and integrates them into a holistic view.

Third, this perspective recognizes our deep entanglement with capitalism,
while also affirming that capitalism can be changed.[92] We can, therefore,
follow Tillich's attitude of "belief-ful realism," which I mentioned in chapter
2.[93] On the one hand, I am underscoring the vital importance of capitalism as
an economic version of civil religion in the construction and maintenance of

[91] Loy, "Religion of the Market," 289.

[92] As Tillich emphasizes, capitalism is embedded in an all-encompassing system of life
and is interdependent with all other spheres, it can only be overcome together with this
system (*MW/HW* 3:199; *TPE*, 258; *SD*, 116).

[93] See above, page 107.

social solidarity at local and global levels and as the religious substance that provides the meaning of modern society. As essentially finite, existentially estranged, and actually ambiguous,[94] we live embedded in and dependent upon capitalism. We also contribute to its continuation and should not underestimate the serious difficulty of transforming it. We should view with skepticism utopian or romantic solutions that promise to get rid of capitalism once and for all. For revolutions that attempt to demolish the capitalist system may end up causing more social suffering than that which they intended to eradicate. Attempts to eliminate the evils of capitalism simply by means of moral goodwill take too lightly the reality of individual egotism and structural sin. On the other hand, we have no place for an attitude of resignation that regards capitalism as a given, unchangeable reality. The perspective outlined above highlights the importance of social imagination. Capitalism, after all, is a human construct, existing through human participation. Perhaps the way to change it, as Ivan Petrella suggests, is "neither revolution (the wholesale change of one structure for another) nor reform (the humanization of the existing structure) but revolutionary reform: the step by step change of the formative context of society."[95]

Fourth, my perspective elaborates Tillich's critique of capitalism as demonic. As we have seen in chapter 1, Tillich characterizes the demonic as the ambiguous mix of creation and destruction, the holy antidivine, the self-elevation that causes split, and as possession. As a quasi-religion, capitalism comprises a confederation of sacred things, including the market, money, unbounded growth, and "cathedrals of consumption," such as shopping malls, theme parks, and casinos that offer magical, enchanted, and ecstatic experiences. Thus, capitalism carries a certain sacred quality. Its sacredness, however, appears antidivine, for it has the spirit of self-sufficient, infinite finitude, seen in the endless production and consumption of means, that

---

[94] For Tillich's analysis of the finitude of human beings, see *ST* 1:186–201; for his analysis of human beings in the state of estrangement, see *ST* 2:44–78; for his analysis of the ambiguities of human life, see *ST* 3:30–106.

[95] Ivan Petrella, *The Future of Liberation Theology: An Argument and Manifesto* (London: SCM, 2006) 108. He advocates Roberto Unger's practice of "institutional imagination," which he sees as "the step-by-step imaginative construction of political and economic institutions" (ibid., 94). An example of institutional imagination in the setting of the capitalist economy is "flexible specialization," which involves "the disaggregation of property and ownership into its diverse parts—use rights, income rights, control rights and transfer rights—enabling the creation of associational networks within the economy that allows small firms to tap large resources" (ibid., 109).

excludes the divine or the dimension of depth and thus results in various social and psychological pathologies. Such a view remains in line with Tillich's characterization of the demonic as "holy antidivine."

As "holy antidivine," the demonic shares the creative power of the divine but at the same time brings destruction. As a global civil religion and as the religious substance of modernity, capitalism plays a vital role for the maintenance of social solidarity at the global level as well as for the provision of meaning. Any blanket condemnation of capitalism fails to understand the ambiguity of the demonic; meanwhile, we should not overlook the destructiveness of capitalism. We may supplement Tillich's analysis with Moltmann's crisis theory: the notion of the "vicious circles of death" and self-destructive spiral of growing production and consumption. As I discussed in chapter 3, in adopting Moltmann's global-critical perspective, I am going further than Tillich did in recognizing the destructive effects of capitalism in global problems, such as the worsening of economic injustice both within and between countries, the "global marketing of everything," and the worldwide ecological crisis. The pernicious effects of capitalism lie especially in the victimization of the "others" in the modern world. Capitalistic modernity has developed at the expense of its "others": the "Third World," the "weak," and nature. The colonial history of conquest, enslavement, and exploitation of "Third-World" peoples has its postcolonial continuation in poverty, hunger, disease, and crushing debt. Many people in the "First World" suffer from chronic unemployment, overwork, and growing insecurity of jobs as a result of "flexible" strategies of management. The omnipresence of the market as a sacred thing in the capitalistic quasi-religion reduces human dignity to market value and marginalizes and victimizes those who are weak in competition (the poor, the sick, and the elderly). The capitalist logic of boundless growth and the spiral of production and consumption lead to the destruction of nature. Capitalism legitimates all these practices and makes them inevitable—necessary sacrifices offered to and in the service of the sacred things of the quasi-religion of capitalism. This provides an instance of what Tillich calls the "distortion of self-transcendence" through the absolutization of finite things characteristic of the demonic. They also exemplify Tillich's characterization of the demonic as a self-elevation to infinity that leads to split, schism, and conflict. When people elevate the market, money, or economic growth to the status of the highest, most sacrosanct, absolute priority, there results a deepening rift between the rich and poor nations, between the privileged class and the underclass, and between dominating human beings and exploiting nature.

Capitalism has a further characteristic of the demonic—the quality of possession. As I have mentioned above, we remain deeply entangled in the quasi-religion of capitalism. As a global civil religion, it plays a vital role in the maintenance of social solidarity in modern society. As the religious substance of modern society, it is played out in various facets of modern culture. We experience capitalism as something given and can hardly escape it. Moreover, like possession, it carries a quality of inevitability. We see this in the "vicious circles of death" and the spiral of growing production and consumption mentioned by Moltmann.

Summary of Theological Response

Under the critical perspective sketched out above, my theological response to and assessment of capitalism as a demonic quasi-religion develop from Tillich's groundwork and involve the following elements. Here I reproduce in summary form the elements that I have already spelled out in detail elsewhere in previous chapters.

1. We can interpret capitalism as a quasi-religion through Tillich's normative view of religion: "religion is being ultimately concerned about that which is and should be our ultimate concern."[96] While Tillich does not specify how we should find out what "should be" our ultimate concern, we can still say with confidence that, if something is not truly ultimate, it should not be our ultimate concern. According to Tillich, the truly ultimate overcomes the ordinary subject-object scheme, such that the subjective and the objective sides of ultimate concern become one. This serves as a criterion for "distinguishing true and false ultimacy."[97] An ultimate concern with something finite (Tillich mentions nation and success) will not be truly ultimate, for the finite reality remains an object and cannot go beyond the subject-object scheme.[98] Moreover, the elevation of the preliminary and finite

---

[96] *TC*, 40.

[97] *DF*, 11. For Tillich, the union of the subjective and objective sides of ultimate concern "is symbolically expressed by the mystics when they say that their knowledge of God is the knowledge God has of himself; and is expressed by Paul when he says (1 Corinthians 13) that he will know as he is known, namely, by God" (ibid.).

[98] Ibid.

to ultimacy and infinity constitutes idolatry.[99] "The more idolatrous a faith the less it is able to overcome the cleavage between subject and object."[100] The quasi-religion of capitalism is not concerned with that which is truly ultimate. As expressed in the culture of autonomy, capitalism shuts itself out from the truly ultimate, the divine, or the ground of being and meaning. Its spirit is that of self-sufficient finitude. Its aspect of infinity, such as limitless production and consumption, remains within the realm of the finite and offers no ultimacy.[101] Moreover, capitalism excludes not only the divine but also the other, where one can find the traces of God in its alterity.

2. I analyze the capitalistic quasi-religion as a demonic structure (see chapter 1) in which modern men and women remain deeply entangled. It constitutes an instance of the "principalities and powers" (Eph 3:10; Col 2:15) that take away human freedom and subjugate human beings. The kingdom of God struggles against, and will ultimately overcome, the demonic powers in history. The churches, as the ambiguous representatives of the kingdom of God in history,[102] stand at the frontline of the struggle against the "principalities and powers," which include the demonic quasi-religion of capitalism. As Tillich emphasizes, we cannot overcome the demonic as a structure of evil by acts of moral goodwill but only by a divine structure, that is, what he calls a structure or *Gestalt* of grace. For Tillich, the church—or what he later calls the Spiritual Community—provides a crucial instance of that structure or *Gestalt* of grace.[103] Insofar as they are the ambiguous embodiments of the Spiritual Community as a structure of grace,[104] the churches may be able to overcome, albeit fragmentarily, the demonic powers. However, Tillich does not spell out how this might come about. For our present discussion, I venture to suggest that the key lies in the churches as communities of alternative practices and values. The logic of grace prevails in the churches, in their acceptance, celebration, and proclamation of God's unconditional

---

[99] *ST* 1:13.

[100] *DF*, 12.

[101] For Tillich, true religion should include in itself the principle of self-negation (*PE*, 65). The finite things in a religion must gives up themselves for the infinite.

[102] *ST* 3:374–77.

[103] *TPE*, xxi, 212–13; *PE*, 25.

[104] Tillich distinguishes between "the church," which is the Spiritual Community, and "the churches," which, as simultaneously sociological and theological realities, participate paradoxically both in "the ambiguities of life in general and religious life in particular," and in "the unambiguous life of Spiritual Community." The Spiritual Community is the Spiritual essence of the churches (*ST* 3:162–67).

acceptance of the unacceptable, in their practices of praise and gifting, in worship (especially the Eucharist). In so doing, the churches constitute an alternative economy that problematizes, resists, and challenges the prevailing logic of market exchange and other constitutive aspects of capitalism.[105] This provides a basis for working for the transformation of capitalism through what Tillich calls the relating functions of the churches, namely, silent interpenetration (priestly influence), critical judgment (prophetic criticism), and political establishment (royal direction).[106] Nevertheless, Tillich allows no place for any naïve optimism. Besides participating in the unambiguous life of the Spiritual Community, the churches also participate in the ambiguities of religious life.[107] They are, for example, not immune to the prevailing influence of consumerism in religious culture, which is an expression of the capitalistic religious substance. The churches should therefore constantly judge and reform themselves in light of the vision of theonomy, lest they succumb to the dominant logic of the market.[108]

3. Theonomy, created by the Spiritual Presence, answers the problems of capitalistic modernity or the cultural dimension of capitalism (see chapter 2). Theonomy serves as a critical and constructive ideal for the transformation of autonomy or the spirit of self-sufficient finitude. On the one hand, theonomy (as a "self-transcending autonomy"[109]) shows how autonomy excludes

---

[105] On the church's functioning as an alternative economy that practices the logic of grace through praise and gifting, see M. Douglas Meeks, "Economy and the Future of Liberation Theology in North America," in *Liberating the Future: God, Mammon, and Theology* (ed. Joerg Rieger; Minneapolis, Minn.: Augsburg, 1998) 43–59, at 52–59. Meeks focuses on how the logic of grace is at work in the church, rather than how an economy of grace can be put to work in society. Kathryn Tanner pursues the latter path in her *Economy of Grace* (Minneapolis, Minn.: Fortress, 2005).

[106] *ST* 3:212–16. Tillich is quick to emphasize the mutual relation between the churches and society. The churches themselves are as much being influenced, judged, and directed by society as they are influencing, judging, and directing society (ibid.).

[107] *ST* 3:165.

[108] According to Tillich, other communities, religious and secular, can represent the Spiritual Community in latency (*ST* 3:152–55). These communities—which today would include environmentalist groups—can thus also become embodiments of structures of grace, fighting against the demonic quasi-religion of capitalism. These communities, however, are, in Tillich's view, even more vulnerable than the churches to the ambiguities of religion, for "the Spiritual Community in its latency is open to profanization and demonization without an ultimate principle of resistance, whereas the Spiritual Community organized as a church has the principle of resistance in itself and is able to apply it self-critically" (*ST* 3:154).

[109] *TPE*, xvi.

the dimension of the ultimate; on the other hand, it fulfills autonomy by opening up its self-enclosed, self-sufficient spirit to its own inexhaustible depth and ground. As Tillich describes, a theonomous culture affirms "the autonomous forms of the creative process" while it also communicates "the experience of holiness, of something ultimate in being and meaning, in all its creation."[110] Further, theonomy critiques and answers the problems arising from technical reason—such as controlling knowledge, objectification, and the meaninglessness of the endless production of means for no ultimate end—as it overcomes the split between subject and object, brings about an *eros*-relation of human beings to things and to other human beings, and provides technical production with an ultimate end and meaning.

4. The incarnation, crucifixion, and resurrection of Jesus as the Christ also inform and guide our theological response. Divine participation in bodily (hence material) human existence underscores the importance of the material-economic dimension, which we should consider crucial in any critique of capitalism and capitalistic modernity. As the symbol of divine participation in human predicament, we interpret the cross of Christ as the co-suffering solidarity of God with the victims of capitalistic modernity. The cross reminds us to remember the suffering and victimization of others, including the "others" of capitalistic modernity (such as the "Third World," the poor, the "weak," and nature). It exposes and protests against injustices and the structures that give rise to them as well as against the demonic forces that lead to such suffering and victimization. The resurrection, then, anticipates the ultimate victory of the kingdom of God (1 Corinthians 15) over—as well as the ultimate divine transformation of—suffering, injustices, and demonic forces, including those related to capitalism and capitalistic modernity. As Tillich reminds us, in the present struggle against the demonic, we have no certainty of success.[111] At present, theonomy and the kingdom of God can only be fragmentarily realized in culture and in history. Nevertheless, the resurrection of Christ gives us the eschatological certainty that demonic forces will ultimately be overcome and transformed, and this hope informs and empowers our present struggles.

---

[110] *ST* 3:251.
[111] *IH*, 122.

Conclusion

This book paves the way for constructing a religious critique of global capitalistic modernity by means of a reconstruction, examination, and evaluation of Tillich's critical interpretation of capitalism and modernity. It contributes to scholarship in several ways. First, it provides an interpretive framework that emphasizes the continuity of Tillich's critique of capitalism and modernity throughout his career. Second, it critically examines Tillich's religious critique of capitalism as demonic and analyzes its theoretical and practical implications as well as its contemporary relevance. Third, it thematically reconstructs, probably for the first time, Tillich's critical interpretation of capitalistic cultural modernity and his theological response. Fourth, drawing on the insights of Moltmann and Durkheim, it critically assesses Tillich's critique of capitalism and modernity and his concept of religion, with a view to enhancing the adequacy of that critique for the contemporary world. Fifth, it puts forward a constructive framework which critically interprets capitalism as a global civil religion and the religious substance of the cultural forms of modernity.

Tillich's critique of capitalism and modernity is a persistent theme in his work, from his early writings on religious socialism to the third volume of *Systematic Theology*. Like Marx and Weber, to whom he is indebted, Tillich considers capitalism and modernity as closely connected and jointly embodied in bourgeois society. Tillich accepts Marx's political-economic critique of capitalism and bourgeois society. Yet he pays more attention to the cultural-spiritual dimension of capitalism. For various reasons (including his apprehension of political dangers such as McCarthyism), the direct critique of capitalism fades out in his American writings, especially in the years after World War II. But his critique of capitalism continues as he sharpens his critique of its cultural dimension, which is also a critique of cultural modernity. Thus, the bifurcation of an "early Tillich" who was socially-critical and a "later Tillich" who was not should be rejected.

The strengths and contributions of Tillich's critique of capitalism and modernity are numerous. First, it unites "rational criticism" and "prophetic criticism," as he assimilated leading social theories of his time and integrated them creatively with his theological thought. Like the Frankfurt School theorists, Tillich attempts to synthesize Marx and Weber (later adding Freud) in formulating his social critique. Tillich shares with the Frankfurt School a cultural focus and a similar diagnosis of capitalistic modernity, including the prevalence of technical (instrumental) reason, domination, and dehumanization. Yet his theological perspective in general and the ideas of theonomy and *kairos* in particular make him less pessimistic than the Frankfurt School about overcoming the pathologies of capitalistic modernity, even though their diagnoses are similar.

Second, Tillich's theological perspective informs and closely correlates with his critical interpretation of capitalistic modernity. His theology of culture enables him to affirm the relevance of theology to the social and cultural situation. A key theological concept for Tillich is theonomy, an ideal situation in which religion and culture are in unambiguous union, in which every cultural form expresses the religious substance, in which God is all in all. Theonomy is ingeniously formulated as both the critique of and answer to what Tillich regards as the most significant feature of modernity, namely, autonomy, as well as other problems of capitalistic modernity. Autonomy is a state of culture that follows reason as its law, cuts itself off from its own depth or religious substance, and becomes "self-sufficient finitude." Persons and things no longer mediate holiness and ultimate meaning. Relations of *eros* and mystical communion are replaced by those of rational control and domination by technical reason and controlling knowledge. Technical reason is concerned only with means, not with ends. In capitalism it leads to the endless production of means without ends, bringing emptiness and meaninglessness. Controlling knowledge tends toward objectification. The object of knowledge becomes a calculable thing which is dominated by the knowing subject. Even human beings are dehumanized as things among things. For Tillich, theonomy is the answer to these problems of modernity, as it reunites persons and things with their divine ground, sets limits to unlimited production of means, and overcomes the general ambiguity of subject-object split.

Third, Tillich's critique of modernity and capitalism is nuanced and dialectical. Modernity has a Janus face. Its principle of autonomy frees human beings from various heteronomies, such as feudal authoritarianism. Yet autonomy also brings meaninglessness as it has lost its connection with the religious depth. Technology and technical reason bring liberating effects to many aspects of modern life. Yet they also bring objectification and dehumanization. The same ambiguity is found in capitalism which thus requires nuanced critique. Tillich characterizes capitalism as demonic. As an ambiguous union of creative and destructive powers, it does not warrant unreserved or uncritical commendation by theology. Its strengths and benefits must be considered alongside the critique of its weaknesses and harms. Capitalism is the most successful economic system in world history, and yet it has brought extensive destruction. As a structure of evil, capitalism cannot be reduced to human sinfulness (such as idolatry) and it cannot be changed simply by good will and moral repentance. This analysis undermines humanistic optimism. Yet it does not lead to pessimism, for capitalism as a demonic structure can be overcome by a structure of grace.

Nevertheless, as a man of his time, Tillich has his own limitations and inadequacies, which can be illuminated by using Moltmann's critique of capitalistic modernity and Durkheim's theory of religion as critical lenses.

First, Tillich's critical interpretation of capitalistic modernity is Eurocentric and forgets the "others" as constitutive of modernity. For Tillich, modernity comes from social and cultural developments within Western civilization. He overlooks the indispensable contributions of non-Western (such as Islamic and Chinese) civilizations to science, technology, and other fields of knowledge that enabled the modernization of Europe. Moreover, he does not take seriously the fact that modernity has developed through Europe's conquest, colonization, and domination of the non-European world, which becomes its victim. It was the mass enslavement of African peoples and the exploitation of the resources of the Americas that provided the labor and capital for the social and economic development of modern Europe. Without the contributions and sacrifices of the "others" of Europe, capitalistic modernity would not have been possible. Thus, it is necessary to work out a global-critical perspective (like that which I attempt here) that includes the "others" and recognizes their sufferings and contributions as constitutive of capitalistic modernity.

Second, Tillich's critical interpretation of capitalistic modernity is primarily cultural-spiritual, and the material-economic dimension is not given enough attention. Even in the direct critique of capitalism in his earlier works, he locates the demonic character of capitalism in economic insecurity and meaninglessness, but he overlooks the material-economic problems of poverty, injustice, and bodily sufferings. This is even more true of the "later Tillich," who sharpens his focus on the critique of cultural modernity as the cultural dimension of capitalism. This hinders him from adequately diagnosing the problems of capitalistic modernity and thus also limits the use of rich social-theoretical and theological ideas (such as justice and the kingdom of God) in his critique. There is a need to develop a critical perspective (such as that which I suggest here) to take more seriously the material-economic dimension of capitalistic modernity and the inseparable interrelation between modernity and capitalism.

Third, Tillich could have interpreted capitalism not just as a demonry but also as a quasi-religion. He could then have analyzed and critiqued capitalism in a manner similar to that which he employs in his analysis other quasi-religions. But even if he did, the religious interpretation of capitalism would still be inadequate, for the social nature of capitalism cannot be adequately grasped by his asocial conception of religion in terms of ultimate concern, which stresses the "vertical" or "depth" dimension. While Tillich recognizes that an ultimate concern always expresses itself socially, the social dimension is neither essential nor constitutive of it. Tillich's concept of quasi-religion can be enhanced by Durkheim's conception of religion as "a unified system of beliefs and practices relative to sacred things." This conception is not alien to Tillich, who already defines quasi-religions as "systems of secular thought and life" (hence beliefs and practices) analogous to traditional religions.

My constructive proposal for a critical perspective on capitalism tries to build on Tillich's strengths while going beyond his weaknesses by enhancing his thought with the insights of Moltmann and Durkheim. I suggest that capitalism should be understood, analyzed, and unmasked as a quasi-religion, with its own beliefs and practices in relation to a confederation of sacred things, including the market, unlimited growth, and "sacred spaces" such as shopping malls. Functioning like a global civil religion, capitalism, with the "social imaginary" of the market, substantially constitutes and maintains—at the expense of its often-forgotten sacrificial victims—the social solidarity of modern society even at the global level. Capitalism as quasi-religion is thus the meaning-giving and solidarity-constituting religious substance of modern society. This is expressed in various features of cultural modernity, which Tillich analyzed critically with perceptive insights. Even religion in the narrow sense, as a particular sphere of culture, expresses capitalism as the religious substance of modern society. This view of capitalism as a quasi-religion paves the way for a more adequate theological critique of capitalism and capitalist modernity in a global perspective.

Bibliography

Works by Paul Tillich

Books

Main Works/Hauptwerke. Edited by Carl Heinz Ratschow. 6 volumes. New York: de Gruyter; Berlin: Evangelisches Verlagswerk, 1987–1998.

The Irrelevance and Relevance of the Christian Message. Edited by Durwood Foster. Cleveland, Ohio: Pilgrim, 1996.

Christianity and the Encounter of World Religions. Foreword by Krister Stendahl. Minneapolis, Minn.: Fortress, 1994.

Theology of Peace. Edited by Ronald H. Stone. Louisville: Westminster/John Knox, 1990.

The Encounter of Religions and Quasi-Religions. Edited by Terence Thomas. Lewiston, N.Y.: Edwin Mellen, 1990.

Paul Tillich on Creativity. Edited by Jacquelyn Ann Kegley. Lanham, Md.: University Press of America, 1989.

The Spiritual Situation in Our Technical Society. Edited by J. Mark Thomas. Macon, Ga.: Mercer University Press, 1988.

On Art and Architecture. Edited by John Dillenberger and Jane Dillenberger. New York: Crossroad, 1987.

Visionary Science: A Translation of Tillich's "On the Idea of a Theology of Culture," with an Interpretive Essay. Translated by Victor Nuovo. Detroit, Mich.: Wayne State University Press, 1987.

Dynamics of Faith. New York: Harper & Row, 1957. Repr., New York: Harper Torchbooks, 1985.

The System of Sciences according to Objects and Methods. Translated by Paul Wiebe. London: Associated University Press, 1981.

The Socialist Decision. Translated by Franklin Sherman. New York: Harper & Row, 1977.

Gesammelte Werke. 14 volumes. Stuttgart: Evangelisches Verlagswerk, 1959–1975.

A History of Christian Thought: From Its Judaic and Hellenistic Origins to Existentialism. Edited by Carl E. Braaten. New York: Simon & Schuster, 1972.

Political Expectation. Edited by James L. Adams. New York: Harper & Row, 1971. Repr., Macon, Ga.: Mercer University Press, 1981.

What is Religion? Edited by James L. Adams. New York: Harper & Row, 1969.

My Search for Absolutes. Edited by Ruth N. Anshen. New York: Simon & Schuster, 1967.

On the Boundary: An Autobiographical Sketch. New York: Scribners, 1966.

Ultimate Concern: Tillich in Dialogue. Edited by D. Mackenzie Brown. New York: Harper & Row, 1965.

Systematic Theology. 3 volumes. Chicago: University of Chicago Press, 1951–1963. Repr., London: SCM, 1978. *Systematische Theologie.* 4th ed. Berlin: de Gruyter, 1987.

Love, Power, and Justice: Ontological Analyses and Ethical Applications. Oxford: Oxford University Press, 1960.

Theology of Culture. Edited by Robert C. Kimball. New York: Oxford University Press, 1959.

The Courage to Be. New Haven, Conn.: Yale University Press, 1952.

The Protestant Era. Translated by James L. Adams. Chicago, Ill.: University of Chicago Press, 1948.

The Interpretation of History. Translated by Nicholas A. Rasetzki and Elsa L. Talmey. New York: Scribners, 1936.

The Religious Situation. Translated by H. Richard Niebuhr. New York: Henry Holt, 1932. Repr., New York: Meridian Books, 1956.

Articles and Papers

"Open Letter to Emmanuel Hirsch." Pages 353–88 in *The Thought of Paul Tillich.* Edited by James L. Adams, Wilhelm Pauck, and Roger L. Shinn. San Francisco, Calif.: Harper & Row, 1985.

"Rejoinder." *The Journal of Religion* 46 (1966) 184–96.

"Between Utopianism and Escape from History." *Colgate Rochester Divinity School Bulletin* 31 (1959).

"Past and Present Reflections on Christianity and Society." Transcript of Tillich's notes for his remarks to the New York Christian Action retreat, May 1955. Box 409:005, Paul Tillich Papers, Andover-Harvard Theological Library, Harvard University, Cambridge, Mass.

"The Spiritual Situation in Our Technical Society." Manuscript, [1954]. Box 408:039, Paul Tillich Papers, Andover-Harvard Theological Library, Harvard University, Cambridge, Mass.

"Theology of Politics." Manuscript, n.d. Box 408:022, Paul Tillich Papers, Andover-Harvard Theological Library, Harvard University, Cambridge, Mass.

"The Person in a Technical Society." Pages 137–53 in *Christian Faith and Social Action*. Edited by John A. Hutchinson. New York: Scribner, 1953.

"Autobiographical Reflections." Pages 3–21 in *The Theology of Paul Tillich*. Edited by Charles W. Kegley and Robert W. Bretall. New York: Macmillan, 1952.

"Beyond Religious Socialism." *Christian Century* 66 (1949) 732–33.

"How Much Truth Is There in Karl Marx?" *Christian Century* 65 (1948) 906–8.

"Nietzsche and the Bourgeois Spirit." *Journal of the History of Ideas* 6 (1945) 307–9.

"The Church and Communism." *Religion in Life* 6 (1937) 347–57.

Works by Other Authors

Adams, James L. "Introduction: The Storms of Our Times and *Starry Night*." Pages 1–28 in *The Thought of Paul Tillich*. Edited by James L. Adams, Wilhelm Pauck, and Roger L. Shinn. San Francisco, Calif.: Harper & Row, 1985.

———. *Paul Tillich's Philosophy of Culture, Science, and Religion*. New York: Harper & Row, 1965.

———, Wilhelm Pauck, and Roger L. Shinn, eds., with the assistance of Thomas J. S. Mikelson. *The Thought of Paul Tillich*. San Francisco, Calif.: Harper & Row, 1985.

Anderson, Benedict. *Imagined Communities: Reflections on the Origins and Spread of Nationalism*. Rev. ed. London: Verso, 1991.

Angrosino, Michael. "Civil Religion Redux." *Anthropological Quarterly* 75 (2002) 239–67.

Arens, Edmund. "Interruptions: Critical Theory and Political Theology between Modernity and Postmodernity." Pages 222–42 in *Liberation Theologies, Postmodernity, and the Americas*. Edited by David Batstone et al. New York: Routledge, 1997.

Armstrong, Karen. *The Battle for God*. New York: Ballantine Books, 2001.

Barber, Benjamin R. *Jihad vs. McWorld*. New York: Ballantine Books, 1996.

Beck, Ulrich, Anthony Giddens, and Scott Lash. *Reflexive Modernization: Politics, Tradition, and Aesthetics in the Modern Social Order*. Cambridge: Polity, 1994.

Bell, Catherine M. *Ritual: Perspectives and Dimensions*. New York: Oxford University Press, 1997.

Bellah, Robert N. "Civil Religion in America." Pages 168–89 in *Beyond Belief: Essays on Religion in a Post-Traditionalist World*. Berkeley, Calif.: University of California Press, 1970.

Benhabib, Seyla. *Critique, Norm, and Utopia*. New York: Columbia University Press, 1986.

Benjamin, Walter. "Capitalism as Religion." Pages 288–91 in *1913–1926*. Vol. 1 of *Walter Benjamin: Selected Writings*. Edited by Marcus Bullock and Michael W. Jennings. Cambridge, Mass.: Harvard University Press, 1996.

Berger, Peter L. *The Sacred Canopy: Elements of a Sociological Theory of Religion*. Garden City, N.Y.: Doubleday, 1967. Repr., New York: Doubleday, 1990.

Berman, Marshall. *All That Is Solid Melts into the Air: The Experience of Modernity*. New York: Penguin, 1988.

Betz, Hans D. et al. *Religion in Geschichte und Gegenwart. Handwörterbuch für Theologie und Religionswissenschaft*. 4th ed. Tübingen: Mohr Siebeck, 1998–2005.

Boli, John. "The Economic Absorption of the Sacred." Pages 93–116 in *Rethinking Materialism: Perspectives on the Spiritual Dimension of Economic Behavior*. Edited by Robert Wuthnow. Grand Rapids, Mich.: Eerdmans, 1995.

Calhoun, Craig. "Imagining Solidarity: Cosmopolitanism, Constitutional Patriotism, and the Public Sphere." *Public Culture* 14 (2002) 147–71.

———. "Indirect Relationships and Imagined Communities: Large-Scale Integration and the Transformation of Everyday Life." Pages 95–121 in *Social Theory for a Changing Society*. Edited by Pierre Bourdieu and James S. Coleman. Boulder, Colo.: Westview, 1991.

Cameliou, Christian. *The Impasse of Modernity: Debating the Future of the Global Market Economy*. Translated by Patrick Camiller. London: Zed Books, 2002.

Carey, John J. *Paulus Then and Now: A Study of Paul Tillich's Theological World and the Continuing Relevance of His Work*. Macon, Ga.: Mercer University Press, 2002.

————, ed. *Theonomy and Autonomy: Studies in Paul Tillich's Engagement with Modern Culture*. Macon, Ga.: Mercer University Press, 1984.

Carroll, John M. *A Concise History of Hong Kong*. Hong Kong: Hong Kong University Press, 2007.

Castoriadis, Cornelius. *The Imaginary Institution of Society*. Translated by Kathleen Blamey. Cambridge: Polity, 1987.

Champion, James W. "Tillich and the Frankfurt School: Parallels and Differences in Prophetic Criticism." *Soundings* 69 (1986) 512–30.

Chriss, James J. "Durkheim's Cult of the Individual as Civil Religion: Its Appropriation by Erving Goffman." *Sociological Spectrum* 13 (1993) 251–75.

Clarke, Peter B. and Peter Byrne. *Religion Defined and Explained*. New York: St. Martin's, 1993.

Clary, Betsy Jane. "Paul Tillich on the Institutions of Capitalism." *Review of Social Economy* 52 (1994) 361–76.

Clayton, John Powell. "Introducing Paul Tillich's Writings in the Philosophy of Religion." Pages 9–28 in *Writings in the Philosophy of Religion*. Vol. 4 of *Main Works / Haptwerke*. Edited by Carl Heinz Ratschow. New York: de Gruyter; Berlin: Evangelisches Verlagswerk, 1987–1998.

————. *The Concept of Correlation: Paul Tillich and the Possibility of a Mediating Theology*. Berlin: de Gruyter, 1980.

Coates, David. *Models of Capitalism: Growth and Stagnation in the Modern Era*. Cambridge: Polity, 2000.

Cobb, John, Jr. "Liberation Theology and the Global Economy." Pages 27–42 in *Liberating the Future: God, Mammon, and Theology*. Edited by Joerg Rieger. Minneapolis, Minn.: Fortress, 1998.

Coleman, John A., S.J. "Selling God in America: American Commercial Culture as a Climate of Hospitality to Religion." Pages 136–49 in *Meaning and Modernity: Religion, Polity, Self*. Edited by Richard Madsen et al. Epilogue by Robert N. Bellah. Berkeley, Calif.: University of California Press, 2002.

Copleston, Frederick, S.J. *Modern Philosophy: From the Post-Kantian Idealists to Marx, Kierkegaard, and Nietzsche*. Vol. 7 of *A History of Philosophy*. New York: Image Books, 1994.

Cox, Harvey. "Mammon and the Culture of the Market: A Socio-Theological Critique." Pages 124–35 in *Meaning and Modernity: Religion, Polity, Self*. Edited by Richard Madsen et al. Epilogue by Robert N. Bellah. Berkeley, Calif.: University of California Press, 2002.

Cruz, Eduardo. "The Demonic for the Twenty-first Century." *Currents in Theology and Mission* 28 (2001) 420–28.

Dallal, Ahmad. "Science, Medicine, and Technology: The Making of a Scientific Culture." Pages 155–214 in *Oxford History of Islam*. Edited by John L. Esposito. Oxford: Oxford University Press, 1999.

Deutschmann, Christoph. "Capitalism as a Religion? An Unorthodox Analysis of Entrepreneurship." *European Journal of Social Theory* 4 (2001) 387–403.

————. "The Promise of Absolute Wealth: Capitalism as a Religion?" *Thesis Eleven* 66 (2001) 32–56.

Dirlik, Arif. "Global Modernity? Modernity in an Age of Global Capitalism." *European Journal of Social Theory* 6 (2003) 275–92.

Donnelly, Brian. *The Socialist Émigré: Marxism and the Later Tillich*. Macon, Ga.: Mercer University Press, 2003.

Dorrien, Gary J. *Reconstructing the Common Good: Theology and the Social Order*. Maryknoll, N.Y.: Orbis, 1990.

Drane, John. "From Creeds to Burgers: Religious Control, Spiritual Search, and the Future of the World." Pages 197–202 in *McDonaldization: The Reader*. Edited by George Ritzer. 2d ed. Thousand Oaks, Calif.: Pine Forge, 2006.

————. *The McDonaldization of the Church: Spirituality, Creativity, and the Future of the Church*. London: Darton, Longman & Todd, 2000.

Dreisbach, Donald F. "History and Economics in *The Courage to Be*." Pages 176–86 in *Truth and History: A Dialogue with Paul Tillich*. Edited by Gert Hummel. Berlin: de Gruyter, 1998.

Durkheim, Émile. *The Elementary Forms of Religious Life*. Translated by Karen E. Fields. New York: Free Press, 1995.

————. "Individualism and the Intellectuals." Translated by S. and J. Lukes. Pages 59–73 in *Durkheim on Religion*. Edited by W. S. F. Pickering. Boston: Routledge, 1975. Repr., Atlanta: Scholars Press, 1994.

————. *The Division of Labor in Society*. Translated by George Simpson. 1933. Repr., New York: Free Press, 1964.

Dussel, Enrique. *The Invention of the Americas: Eclipse of "the Other" and the Myth of Modernity*. Translated by Michael D. Barber. New York: Continuum, 1995.

———. "Eurocentrism and Modernity (Introduction to the Frankfurt Lectures)." *boundary 2* 20 (1993) 65–76.

Eisenstadt, Shmuel N. "Multiple Modernities." *Daedalus* 129 (2000) 1–29.

Fulcher, James. *Capitalism: A Very Short Introduction*. Oxford: Oxford University Press, 2004.

Gabrieli, Francesco. "Islam in the Mediterranean World." Pages 63–104 in *The Legacy of Islam*. Edited by Joseph Schacht and C. E. Bosworth. 2d ed. Oxford: Clarendon, 1974.

Gabus, Jean-Paul. "Paul Tillich et l'Ecole de Francfort. Bilan d'une recherche." *Revue d'Histoire et de Philosophie Religieuses* 78 (1998) 313–31.

Giddens, Anthony. *The Consequences of Modernity*. Stanford, Calif.: Stanford University Press, 1990.

———. *Capitalism and Modern Social Theory: An Analysis of the Writings of Marx, Durkheim and Max Weber*. Cambridge: Cambridge University Press, 1971.

Gilkey, Langdon. *Gilkey on Tillich*. New York: Crossroad, 1990.

Greenspan, Alan. "The Challenge of Central Banking in a Democratic Society," remarks at the Annual Dinner and Francis Boyer Lecture of The American Enterprise Institute for Public Policy Research. Washington, D.C., 5 December 1996. http://www.federalreserve.gov/boarddocs/speeches/1996/19961205.htm (accessed 17 February 2003).

Habermas, Jürgen. "Modernity: An Unfinished Project." Pages 38–55 in *Habermas and the Unfinished Project of Modernity: Critical Essays on* The Philosophical Discourse of Modernity. Edited by Maurizio Passerin d'Entrèves and Seyla Benhabib. Cambridge, Mass.: MIT Press, 1997.

———. *Philosophical Discourse of Modernity: Twelve Lectures*. Translated by Frederick G. Lawrence. Cambridge, Mass.: MIT Press, 1987.

———. *Reason and Rationalization of Society*. Vol.1 of *The Theory of Communicative Action*. Translated by Thomas McCarthy. Boston: Beacon, 1984.

Haleem, Harfiyah Abdel et al., eds. *The Crescent and the Cross: Muslim and Christian Approaches to War and Peace*. London: Macmillan, 1998.

Hall, Peter A. and David Soskice. "An Introduction to the Varieties of Capitalism." Pages 1–68 in *Varieties of Capitalism: The Institutional Foundations of Comparative Advantage*. Edited by Peter A. Hall and David Soskice. Oxford: Oxford University Press, 2001.

Hall, Stuart, David Held, Don Hubert, and Kenneth Thompson, eds. *Modernity: An Introduction to Modern Societies*. Oxford: Blackwell, 1996.

Hamilton, Clive. *Growth Fetish*. London: Pluto, 2004.

Hammond, Guy B. "Tillich and the Frankfurt School on Protestantism and the Bourgeois Spirit." Pages 327–37 in *Religion et Culture*. Edited by Michel Despland, Jean-Claude Petit, and Jean Richard. Laval, Québec: Les Presses de l'Université Laval, 1987.

———. "Tillich and the Frankfurt Debates about Patriarchy and the Family." Pages 89–110 in *Theonomy and Autonomy: Studies in Paul Tillich's Engagement with Modern Culture*. Edited by John J. Carey. Macon, Ga.: Mercer University Press, 1984.

Harvey, David. *A Brief History of Neoliberalism*. New York: Oxford University Press, 2005.

———. *The Condition of Postmodernity: An Enquiry into the Origins of Cultural Change*. Cambridge, Mass.: Blackwell, 1990.

Hinchman, Lewis. "Autonomy, Individuality, and Self-Determination." Pages 488–516 in *What is Enlightenment? Eighteenth-Century Answers and Twentieth-Century Questions*. Edited by James Schmidt. Berkeley, Calif.: University of California Press, 1996.

Hinkelammert, Franz J. *The Ideological Weapons of Death: A Theological Critique of Capitalism*. Translated by Philip Berryman. Maryknoll, N.Y.: Orbis, 1986.

Hodgson, Marshall G. S. *Rethinking World History: Essays on Europe, Islam, and World History*. Edited by Edmund Burke III. Cambridge: Cambridge University Press, 1993.

Horkheimer, Max. *Critique of Instrumental Reason*. Translated by Matthew J. O'Connell et al., 1974. Repr., New York: Continuum, 1996.

———. *Eclipse of Reason*. New York: Continuum, 1974.

——— and Theodor W. Adorno. *Dialectic of Enlightenment: Philosophical Fragments*. Edited by Gunzelin Schmid Noerr. Translated by Edmund Jephcott. Stanford, Calif.: Stanford University Press, 2002.

Hummel, Gert. "Hope for a New World: The Rappites' Eschatological Settlements." Translated by Doris Lax. Pages 1–17 in *Paul Tillich's Theological Legacy: Spirit and Community*. Edited by Frederick J. Parrella. Berlin: de Gruyter, 1995.

James, Robison B. *Tillich and World Religions: Encountering Other Faiths Today*. Macon, Ga.: Mercer University Press, 2003.

Jay, Martin. *The Dialectical Imagination: A History of the Frankfurt School and the Institute of Social Research, 1923–1950*. Berkeley, Calif.: University of California Press, 1996.

Kegley, Jacquelyn Ann K. Prefatory note to "The Class Struggle and Religious Socialism." Pages 93–94 in *Paul Tillich On Creativity*. Edited by Jacquelyn Ann K. Kegley. Lanham, Md.: University Press of America, 1989.

Kucheman, Clark A. "Professor Tillich: Justice and the Economic Order." *Journal of Religion* 46 (1966) 165–83.

Lai, Pan-chiu. "Paul Tillich and Ecological Theology." *Journal of Religion* 79 (1999) 233–49.

Lau, Siu-kai. "Confidence in the Capitalist Society." Pages 93–114 in *Indicators of Social Development: Hong Kong 1999*. Edited by Lau Siu-kai et al. Hong Kong: Hong Kong Institute of Asia-Pacific Studies, The Chinese University of Hong Kong, 2001.

———— and Kuan Hsin-chi. *The Ethos of the Hong Kong Chinese*. Hong Kong: The Chinese University Press, 1988.

Leibrecht, Walter, ed. *Religion and Culture: Essays in Honor of Paul Tillich*. Freeport, N.Y.: Books for Libraries, 1972.

Livingston, James C. et al. *Modern Christian Thought*. 2d ed. Upper Saddle River, N.J.: Prentice Hall, 1997–2000.

Löwith, Karl. *Max Weber and Karl Marx*. Edited by Tom Bottomore and William Outhwaite. New preface by Bryan S. Turner. London: Routledge, 1993.

————. *Meaning in History*. Chicago: University of Chicago Press, 1949.

Loy, David R. "The Religion of the Market." *Journal of the American Academy of Religion* 65 (1997) 275–99.

Luckmann, Thomas. "Shrinking Transcendence, Expanding Religion?" *Sociological Analysis* 50 (1990) 132–34.

————. *The Invisible Religion: The Problem of Religion in Modern Society*. New York: Macmillan, 1967.

Lyon, David. *Postmodernity*. Minneapolis, Minn.: University of Minnesota Press, 1994.

Macquarrie, John. *Twentieth-Century Religious Thought*. New ed. Harrisburg, Pa.: Trinity Press International, 2002.

Mallow, Vernon R. *The Demonic: A Selected Theological Study: An Examination into the Theology of Edwin Lewis, Karl Barth, and Paul Tillich*. Lanham, Md.: University Press of America, 1983.

Marsden, John Joseph. *Marxism and Christian Utopianism: Toward a Socialist Political Theology*. New York: Monthly Review, 1991.

Marx, Karl. "Capital, Volume One." Pages 294–438 in *The Marx-Engels Reader*. Edited by Robert C. Tucker. 2d ed. New York: Norton, 1978.

———. "The German Ideology: Part I." Pages 146–200 in *The Marx-Engels Reader*. Edited by Robert C. Tucker. 2d ed. New York: Norton, 1978.

———. "Theses on Feuerbach." Pages 143–45 in *The Marx-Engels Reader*. Edited by Robert C. Tucker. 2d ed. New York: Norton, 1978.

——— and Friedrich Engels. "Manifesto of the Communist Party." Pages 469–500 in *The Marx-Engels Reader*. Edited by Robert C. Tucker. 2d edition. New York: Norton, 1978.

McBride, James. "Paul Tillich and the Supreme Court: Tillich's 'Ultimate Concern' as a Standard in Judicial Interpretation." *Journal of Church and State* 30 (1988) 245–72.

McCarraher, Eugene. "The Enchantment of Mammon: Notes toward a Theological History of Capitalism." *Modern Theology* 21 (2005) 429–61.

Meeks, M. Douglas. "Economy and the Future of Liberation Theology in North America." Pages 43–59 in *Liberating the Future: God, Mammon, and Theology*. Edited by Joerg Rieger. Minneapolis, Minn.: Augsburg, 1998.

Mendieta, Eduardo. Introduction to *Religion and Rationality: Essays on Reason, God, and Modernity*. Jürgen Habermas. Edited by Eduardo Mendieta. Cambridge, Mass.: MIT Press, 2002.

Metz, Johann Baptist. *A Passion for God: The Mystical-Political Dimension of Christianity*. Edited and translated by J. Matthew Ashley. New York: Paulist, 1998.

———. "Anamnestic Reason: A Theologian's Remarks on the Crisis in the *Geisteswissenschaften*." Pages 189–94 in *Cultural-Political Interventions in the Unfinished Project of Enlightenment*. Edited by Axel Honneth et al. Translated by Barbara Fultner. Cambridge, Mass.: MIT Press, 1992.

Miller, Vincent J. *Consuming Religion: Christian Faith and Practice in a Consumer Culture*. New York: Continuum, 2005.

Moltmann, Jürgen. *God for a Secular Society: The Public Relevance of Theology*. Translated by Margaret Kohl. Minneapolis, Minn.: Fortress, 1999.

———. "Political Theology and Theology of Liberation." Pages 60–80 in *Liberating the Future: God, Mammon, and Theology*. Edited by Joerg Rieger. Translated by Virgil Howard. Minneapolis, Minn.: Fortress, 1998.

———. *Gott im Projekt der modernen Welt. Beträge zur öffent-lichen Relevanz der Theologie*. Gütersloh: Kaiser, 1997.

———. "The Adventure of Theological Ideas." In "Jürgen Moltmann's *Systematic Contributions to Theology*" by Douglas M. Meeks. *Religious Studies Review* 22 (1996) 102–5.

———. *The Coming of God: Christian Eschatology*. Translated by Margaret Kohl. Minneapolis, Minn.: Fortress, 1996.

———. "Ist der Markt das Maß aller Dinge?" Pages 75–88 in *Totaler Markt und Menschenwürde. Herausforderungen und Aufgaben christlicher Anthropologie heute*. Edited by Rudolf Weth. Neukirchen-Vluyn: Neukirchener, 1996.

———. *Das Kommen Gottes. Christliche Eschatologie*. Gütersloh: Kaiser, 1995.

———. *The Church in the Power of the Spirit: A Contribution to Messianic Ecclesiology*. Translated by Margaret Kohl. Minneapolis, Minn.: Fortress, 1993.

———. *Der gekreuzigte Gott. Das Kreuz Christi als Grund und Kritik christlicher Theologie*. 6th ed. Gütersloh: Kaiser, 1993.

———. *God in Creation: A New Theology of Creation and the Spirit of God*. Translated by Margaret Kohl. Minneapolis, Minn.: Fortress, 1993.

———. *Theology of Hope: On the Ground and the Implications of a Christian Eschatology*. Translated by James W. Leitch. Minneapolis, Minn.: Fortress, 1993.

———. *The Way of Jesus Christ: Christology in Messianic Dimensions*. Translated by Margaret Kohl. Minneapolis, Minn.: Fortress, 1993.

———. *The Spirit of Life: A Universal Affirmation*. Translated by Margaret Kohl. Minneapolis, Minn.: Fortress, 1992.

Moltmann, Jürgen. *Creating a Just Future: The Politics of Peace and the Ethics of Creation in a Threatened World*. Translated by John Bowden. London: SCM; Philadelphia, Pa.: Trinity Press International, 1989.

———. *Der Weg Jesu Christi. Christologie in messianischen Dimensionen*. Munich: Kaiser, 1989.

———. *Theology Today: Two Contributions towards Making Theology Present*. London: SCM Press, 1988.

———. *Was ist heute Theologie? Zwei Beiträge zu ihrer Vergegenwärtigung*. Freiburg: Herder, 1988.

———. *The Future of Creation: Collected Essays*. Translated by Margaret Kohl. Philadelphia, Pa.: Fortress, 1979.

———. *The Crucified God: The Cross of Christ as the Foundation and Criticism of Christian Theology*. Translated by R. A. Wilson and John Bowden. London: SCM, 1974.

———. *Man: Christian Anthropology in the Conflicts of the Present*. Translated by John Sturdy. Philadephia, Pa.: Fortress, 1974.

———. "Freedom in the Light of Hope." *Japan Christian Quarterly* 39 (1973) 157–58.

———. *Religion, Revolution, and the Future*. Translated by Douglas Meeks. New York: Scribners, 1969.

Moore, R. Laurence. *Selling God: American Religion in the Marketplace of Culture*. New York: Oxford University Press, 1994.

Murphy, John W. "Paul Tillich and Western Marxism." *American Journal of Theology & Philosophy* 5 (1984) 13–24.

Needham, Joseph. *Science and Civilisation in China*. 7 volumes. Cambridge: Cambridge University Press, 1954–2000.

———. Introduction to *The Genius of China: 3,000 Years of Science, Discovery, and Invention,* by Robert Temple. New York: Simon and Schuster, 1986.

Nelson, Robert H. *Economics as Religion: From Samuelson to Chicago and Beyond*. University Park, Pa.: Pennsylvania State University Press, 2001.

Ng, Chun-hung. "After the Crises: Changes in Social Ethos." Pages 265–84 in *Indicators of Social Development: Hong Kong 2004*. Edited by Lau Siu-kai et al. Hong Kong: Hong Kong Institute of Asia-Pacific Studies, The Chinese University of Hong Kong, 2005.

O'Keeffe, Terence M. "Paul Tillich and the Frankfurt School." Pages 67–87 in *Theonomy and Autonomy: Studies in Paul Tillich's Engagement with Modern Culture*. Edited by John J. Carey. Macon, Ga.: Mercer University Press, 1984.

———. "Ideology and the Protestant Principle." *Journal of the American Academy of Religion* 51 (1983) 283–305.

Otto, Rudolf. *The Idea of the Holy: An Enquiry into the Non-Rational Factor in the Idea of the Divine and Its Relation to the Rational*. Translated by John W. Harvey. 2d ed. London: Oxford University Press, 1958.

Pahl, Jon. *Shopping Malls and Other Sacred Spaces: Putting God in Place*. Grand Rapids, Mich.: Brazos, 2003.

Palmer, Michael. "Paul Tillich's Theology of Culture." Pages 1–31 in *Writings in the Philosophy of Culture*. Vol. 2 of *Main Works/Hauptwerke*. Edited by Carl Heinz Ratschow. New York: de Gruyter; Berlin: Evangelisches Verlagswerk, 1987–1998.

Pals, Daniel L. *Seven Theories of Religion*. New York: Oxford University Press, 1996.

Pauck, Wilhelm. "To Be or Not to Be: Tillich on the Meaning of Life." Pages 29–43 in *The Thought of Paul Tillich*. Edited by James L. Adams, Wihelm Pauck, and Rogert L. Shinn, with the assistance of Thomas J. S. Mikelson. San Francisco, Calif.: Harper & Row, 1985.

——— and Marion Pauck. *Paul Tillich: His Life and Thought*. New York: Harper & Row, 1976. Repr. San Francisco, Calif.: Harper & Row, 1989.

Peet, Richard et al. *Unholy Trinity: The IMF, World Bank and WTO*. Kuala Lumpur: SIRD; London: Zed Books, 2003.

Pellicani, Luciano. *The Genesis of Capitalism and the Origins of Modernity*. Translated by James G. Colbert. New York: Telos, 1994.

Petrella, Ivan. *The Future of Liberation Theology: An Argument and Manifesto*. London: SCM, 2006.

Pickering, W. S. F. *Durkheim's Sociology of Religion: Themes and Theories*. London: Routledge, 1984.

Plessner, Martin. "The Natural Sciences and Medicine." Pages 425–60 in *The Legacy of Islam*. Edited by Joseph Schacht and C. E. Bosworth. 2d ed. Oxford: Clarendon, 1974.

Polanyi, Karl. *The Great Transformation*. Boston: Beacon, 1957.

Polanyi, Karl. "Marketless Trading in Hammurabi's Time." Pages 12–26 in *Trade and Market in the Early Empires: Economies in History and Theory*. Edited by Karl Polanyi, Conrad M. Arensberg, and Harry W. Pearson. New York: Free Press, 1957.

Reich, Charles A. *Opposing the System*. New York: Crown, 1995.

Reisz, H. Frederick, Jr. "The Demonic as a Principle in Tillich's Doctrine of God: Tillich and Beyond." Pages 135–56 in *Theonomy and Autonomy: Studies in Paul Tillich's Engagement with Modern Culture*. Edited by John J. Carey. Macon, Ga.: Mercer University Press, 1984.

Ritzer, George. *Enchanting a Disenchanted World: Revolutionizing the Means of Consumption*. 2d ed. Thousand Oaks, Calif.: Pine Forge, 2005.

———. *The McDonaldization of Society*. Rev. ed. Thousand Oaks, Calif.: Pine Forge, 2004.

Said, Edward W. *Orientalism*. New York: Vintage Books, 1994.

Sayer, Derek. *Capitalism and Modernity: An Excursus on Marx and Weber*. London: Routledge, 1991.

Scharf, Uwe C. "Dogmatics between the Poles of the Sacred and the Profane: An Essay in Theological Methodology." *Encounter* 55 (1994) 269–86.

Scharlemann, Robert. "Tillich's Religious Writings." Pages 1–12 in *Writings on Religion*. Vol. 5 of *Main Works / Hauptwerke*. Edited by Carl Heinz Ratschow. New York: de Gruyter; Berlin: Evangelisches Verlagswerk, 1987–1998.

Scharper, Stephen B. "The Ecological Crisis." Pages 219–27 in *The Twentieth Century: A Theological Overview*. Edited by Gregory Baum. Maryknoll, N.Y.: Orbis, 1999.

Schwöbel, Christoph. "Tillich, Paul (1883–1965)." In *The Blackwell Encyclopedia of Modern Christian Thought*. Edited by Alister McGrath. Oxford: Blackwell, 1993.

Shaw, Elliot H. "The Americanisation of Paul Tillich, 1945–1955." Ph.D. dissertation. University of Lancaster, 1993.

Shinn, Roger L. "Tillich as Interpreter and Disturber of Contemporary Civilization." Pages 44–62 in *The Thought of Paul Tillich*. Edited by James L. Adams, Wilhelm Pauck, and Roger L. Shinn. San Francisco, Calif.: Harper & Row, 1985.

Simpson, Gary M. *Critical Social Theory: Prophetic Reason, Civil Society, and Christian Imagination*. Minneapolis, Minn.: Fortress, 2002.

Slater, Peter. "Dynamic Religion, Formative Culture, and the Demonic in History." *Harvard Theological Review* 92 (1999) 95–110.

Smelser, Neil J. "Economic Rationality as a Religious System." Pages 73–92 in *Rethinking Materialism: Perspectives on the Spiritual Dimension of Economic Behavior*. Edited by Robert Wuthnow. Grand Rapids: Eerdmans, 1995.

Smith, Jane I. "Islam and Christendom: Historical, Cultural, and Religious Interaction from the Seventh to the Fifteen Centuries." Pages 305–46 in *Oxford History of Islam*. Edited by John L. Esposito. *Oxford History of Islam*. Oxford: Oxford University Press, 1999.

Sölle, Dorothee. *Political Theology*. Translated by John Shelley. Philadelphia, Pa.: Fortress, 1974.

Soros, George. *The Crisis of Global Capitalism: Open Society Endangered*. New York: Public Affairs, 1998.

Stendahl, Krister. Foreword to *Christianity and the Encounter of World Religions*. Paul Tillich. Minneapolis, Minn.: Fortress, 1994.

Stenger, Mary Ann and Ronald H. Stone. *Dialogues of Paul Tillich*. Macon, Ga.: Mercer University Press, 2002.

Sternberg, Ernest. "Transformations: The Forces of Capitalist Change." Pages 3–30 in *Twenty-First Century Economics: Perspectives of Socioeconomics for a Changing World*. Edited by William E. Halal and Kenneth B. Taylor. New York: St. Martin's, 1999.

Stiglitz, Joseph E. *Globalization and Its Discontents*. New York: Norton, 2002.

Stone, Jerome A. "Tillich and Schelling's Later Philosophy." Pages 11–44 in *Kairos and Logos: Studies in the Roots and Implications of Tillich's Theology*. Edited by John J. Carey. Macon, Ga.: Mercer University Press, 1984.

Stone, Ronald H. *Paul Tillich's Radical Social Thought*. Atlanta: John Knox, 1980.

Stumme, John R. *Socialism in Theological Perspective: A Study of Paul Tillich, 1918–1933*. American Academy of Religion Dissertation Series 21. Missoula, Mont.: Scholars, 1978.

———. Introduction to *The Socialist Decision*. Paul Tillich. New York: Harper & Row, 1977.

Sturm, Erdmann. "'Holy Love Claims Life and Limb': Paul Tillich's War Theology (1914–1918)." *Zeitschrift für neuere Theologiegeschichte/ Journal for the History of Modern Theology* 2 (1995) 60–84.

Sung, Jung Mo. "Hunger for God, Hunger for Bread, Hunger for Humanity: A Southern Perspective." Pages 35–42 in *Hope and Justice for All in the Americas: Discerning God's Mission*. Edited by Oscar L. Bolioli. New York: Friendship, 1998.

Tanner, Kathryn. *Economy of Grace*. Minneapolis, Minn.: Fortress, 2005.

Tawney, Richard H. *Religion and the Rise of Capitalism*. Introduction by Adam B. Seligman. New Brunswick, N.J.: Transaction, 1998.

Taylor, Charles. *Modern Social Imaginaries*. Durham, N.C.: Duke University Press, 2004.

———. "Modern Social Imaginaries." *Public Culture* 14 (2002) 91–124.

Tester, Keith. "Between Sociology and Theology: The Spirit of Capitalism Debate." *Sociological Review* 48 (2000) 43–58.

Thatcher, Adrian. *The Ontology of Paul Tillich*. Oxford: Oxford University Press, 1978.

Thomas, J. Mark. "Ambiguity in Our Technical Society." Pages 337–44 in *Religion in the New Millennium: Theology in the Spirit of Paul Tillich*. Edited by Raymond F. Bulman and Frederick J. Parrella. Macon, Ga.: Mercer University Press, 2001.

———. Introduction to *The Spiritual Situation in Our Technical Society*, by Paul Tillich. Macon, Ga.: Mercer University Press, 1988.

Thomas, Terence. *Paul Tillich and World Religions*. Cardiff, U.K.: Cardiff Academic Press, 1999.

Tracy, David. *The Analogical Imagination: Christian Theology and the Culture of Pluralism*. London: SCM, 1981.

Troeltsch, Ernst. *Protestantism and Progress: The Significance of Protestantism for the Rise of the Modern World*. Translated by W. Montgomery. 1912. Repr., Philadelphia, Pa.: Fortress, 1986.

Tsang, Steve. *A Modern History of Hong Kong*. Hong Kong: Hong Kong University Press, 2004.

Tucker, Robert C., ed. *The Marx-Engels Reader*. 2d ed. New York: Norton, 1978.

Vahanian, Gabriel. "The Holy and the Secular versus the Sacred and the Profane." Pages 330–41 in *Being versus Word in Paul Tillich's Theology? Proceedings of the VII. International Paul Tillich Symposium Held in Frankfurt/Main, 1998*. Edited by Gert Hummel and Doris Lax. Berlin: de Gruyter, 1999.

Vaughn, Karen I. "Theologians and Economic Philosophy: The Case of Paul Tillich and Protestant Socialism." *History of Political Economy* 24 (1992) 1–29.

Veenhof, Klaas R. " 'Modern' Features in Old Assyrian Trade." *Journal of the Economic and Social History of the Orient* 40 (1997) 336–66.

———. "Kanesh: An Assyrian Colony in Anatolia." Pages 859–71 in *Civilizations of the Ancient Near East*. Edited by Jack M. Sasson et al. New York: Scribners, 1995.

Vernet, Juan. "Mathematics, Astronomy, Optics." Pages 461–88 in *The Legacy of Islam*. Edited by Joseph Schacht and Clifford E. Bosworth. 2d ed. Oxford: Clarendon, 1974.

Wallace, Ruth A. "Emile Durkheim and the Civil Religion Concept." *Review of Religious Research* 18 (1977) 287–90.

Weber, Max. *The Protestant Ethic and the Spirit of Capitalism*. Translated by Talcott Parsons. Introduction by Anthony Giddens. London: Routledge, 1992.

———. *Wirtschaft und Gesellschaft. Grundriss der verstehenden Soziologie*. Edited by Johannes Winckelmann. 5th ed. 2 vols. Tübingen: Mohr Siebeck, 1985.

———. *Economy and Society: An Outline of Interpretative Sociology*. Edited by Guenther Roth and Claus Wittich. Translated by Ephraim Fischoff et al. 2 vols. Berkeley, Calif.: University of California Press, 1978.

Whitley, Richard. "The Institutional Structuring of Market Economies." Pages 1.ix–xxvii in *Competing Capitalisms: Institutions and Economies*. Edited by Richard Whitley. Cheltenham, U.K.: Edward Elgar, 2002.

Wiggershaus, Rolf. *The Frankfurt School: Its History, Theories, and Political Significance*. Translated by Michael Robertson. Cambridge, Mass.: MIT Press, 1994.

Wolman, William and Anne Colamosca. *The Judas Economy: The Triumph of Capital and the Betrayal of Work*. Reading, Mass.: Addison-Wesley, 1997.

Wuthnow, Robert, ed. *Rethinking Materialism: Perspectives on the Spiritual Dimension of Economic Behavior*. Grand Rapids, Mich.: Eerdmans, 1995.

Zepp, Ira G., Jr. *The New Religious Image of Urban America: The Shopping Mall as Ceremonial Center*. 2d ed. Foreword and Introduction by David Carrasco. Niwot, Colo.: University Press of Colorado, 1997.

Zucker, Wolfgang M. "The Demonic: From Aeschylus to Tillich." *Theology Today* 26 (1969) 34–50.

Index

Harvard Theological Studies

64. Nasrallah, Laura, Charalambos Bakirtzis, and Steven J. Friesen, eds. *From Roman to Early Christian Thessalonikē: Studies in Religion and Archaeology*, 2010.

63. Short, J. Randall. *The Surprising Election and Confirmation of King David*, 2010.

61. Schifferdecker, Kathryn. *Out of the Whirlwind: Creation Theology in the Book of Job*, 2008.

60. Luijendijk, AnneMarie. *Greetings in the Lord: Early Christians and the Oxyrhynchus Papyri*, 2008.

59. Yip, Francis Ching-Wah. *Capitalism As Religion? A Study of Paul Tillich's Interpretation of Modernity*, 2010.

58. Pearson, Lori. *Beyond Essence: Ernst Troeltsch as Historian and Theorist of Christianity*, 2008.

57. Hills, Julian V. *Tradition and Composition in the* Epistula Apostolorum, 2008.

56. Nickelsburg, George W. E. *Resurrection, Immortality, and Eternal Life in Intertestamental Judaism and Early Christianity*. Expanded Edition, 2006.

55. Johnson-DeBaufre, Melanie. *Jesus Among Her Children: Q, Eschatology, and the Construction of Christian Origins*, 2005.

54. Hall, David D. *The Faithful Shepherd: A History of the New England Ministry in the Seventeenth Century*, 2006.

53. Schowalter, Daniel N., and Steven J. Friesen, eds. *Urban Religion in Roman Corinth: Interdisciplinary Approaches*, 2004.

52. Nasrallah, Laura. *"An Ecstasy of Folly": Prophecy and Authority in Early Christianity*, 2003.

51. Brock, Ann Graham. *Mary Magdalene, The First Apostle: The Struggle for Authority,* 2003.

50. Trost, Theodore Louis. *Douglas Horton and the Ecumenical Impulse in American Religion*, 2002.

49. Huang, Yong. *Religious Goodness and Political Rightness: Beyond the Liberal-Communitarian Debate*, 2001.

48. Rossing, Barbara R. *The Choice between Two Cities: Whore, Bride, and Empire in the Apocalypse*, 1999.

47. Skedros, James Constantine. *Saint Demetrios of Thessaloniki: Civic Patron and Divine Protector, 4th–7th Centuries C.E.*, 1999.

46. Koester, Helmut, ed. *Pergamon, Citadel of the Gods: Archaeological Record, Literary Description, and Religious Development*, 1998.

45. Kittredge, Cynthia Briggs. *Community and Authority: The Rhetoric of Obedience in the Pauline Tradition*, 1998.

44. Lesses, Rebecca Macy. *Ritual Practices to Gain Power: Angels, Incantations, and Revelation in Early Jewish Mysticism*, 1998.

43. Guenther-Gleason, Patricia E. *On Schleiermacher and Gender Politics*, 1997.

42. White, L. Michael. *The Social Origins of Christian Architecture* (2 vols.), 1997.

41. Koester, Helmut, ed. *Ephesos, Metropolis of Asia: An Interdisciplinary Approach to its Archaeology, Religion, and Culture*, 1995.

40. Guider, Margaret Eletta. *Daughters of Rahab: Prostitution and the Church of Liberation in Brazil*, 1995.

39. Schenkel, Albert F. *The Rich Man and the Kingdom: John D. Rockefeller, Jr., and the Protestant Establishment*, 1995.

38. Hutchison, William R. and Hartmut Lehmann, eds. *Many Are Chosen: Divine Election and Western Nationalism*, 1994.

37. Lubieniecki, Stanislas. *History of the Polish Reformation and Nine Related Documents*. Translated and interpreted by George Huntston Williams, 1995.

 – Davidovich, Adina. *Religion as a Province of Meaning: The Kantian Foundations of Modern Theology*, 1993.

36. Thiemann, Ronald F., ed. *The Legacy of H. Richard Niebuhr*, 1991.

35. Hobbs, Edward C., ed. *Bultmann, Retrospect and Prospect: The Centenary Symposium at Wellesle*y, 1985.

34. Cameron, Ron. *Sayings Traditions in the Apocryphon of James*, 1984. Reprinted, 2004.

33. Blackwell, Albert L. *Schleiermacher's Early Philosophy of Life: Determinism, Freedom, and Phantasy*, 1982.

32. Gibson, Elsa. *The "Christians for Christians" Inscriptions of Phrygia: Greek Texts, Translation and Commentary*, 1978.

31. Bynum, Caroline Walker. Docere Verbo et Exemplo*: An Aspect of Twelfth-Century Spirituality*, 1979.

30. Williams, George Huntston, ed. *The Polish Brethren: Documentation of the History and Thought of Unitarianism in the Polish-Lithuanian Commonwealth and in the Diaspora 1601–1685*, 1980.

29. Attridge, Harold W. *First-Century Cynicism in the Epistles of Heraclitus*, 1976.

28. Williams, George Huntston, Norman Pettit, Winfried Herget, and Sargent Bush, Jr., eds. *Thomas Hooker: Writings in England and Holland, 1626–1633*, 1975.

27. Preus, James Samuel. *Carlstadt's* Ordinaciones *and Luther's Liberty: A Study of the Wittenberg Movement, 1521–22*, 1974.

26. Nickelsburg, George W. E. *Resurrection, Immortality, and Eternal Life in Intertestamental Judaism*, 1972.

25. Worthley, Harold Field. *An Inventory of the Records of the Particular (Congregational) Churches of Massachusetts Gathered 1620–1805*, 1970.

24. Yamauchi, Edwin M. *Gnostic Ethics and Mandaean Origins*, 1970.

23. Yizhar, Michael. *Bibliography of Hebrew Publications on the Dead Sea Scrolls 1948–1964*, 1967.

22. Albright, William Foxwell. *The Proto-Sinaitic Inscriptions and Their Decipherment*, 1966.

21. Dow, Sterling, and Robert F. Healey. *A Sacred Calendar of Eleusis*, 1965.

20. Sundberg, Jr., Albert C. *The Old Testament of the Early Church*, 1964.

19. Cranz, Ferdinand Edward. *An Essay on the Development of Luther's Thought on Justice, Law, and Society*, 1959.

18. Williams, George Huntston, ed. *The Norman Anonymous of 1100 A.D.: Towards the Identification and Evaluation of the So-Called Anonymous of York*, 1951.

17. Lake, Kirsopp, and Silva New, eds. *Six Collations of New Testament Manuscripts*, 1932.

16. Wilbur, Earl Morse, trans. *The Two Treatises of Servetus on the Trinity: On the Errors of the Trinity, 7 Books, A.D. 1531. Dialogues on the Trinity, 2 Books. On the Righteousness of Christ's Kingdom, 4 Chapters, A.D. 1532*, 1932.

15. Casey, Robert Pierce, ed. Serapion of Thmuis's *Against the Manichees*, 1931.

14. Ropes, James Hardy. *The Singular Problem of the Epistles to the Galatians*, 1929.

13. Smith, Preserved. *A Key to the Colloquies of Erasmus*, 1927.

12. Spyridon of the Laura and Sophronios Eustratiades. *Catalogue of the Greek Manuscripts in the Library of the Laura on Mount Athos*, 1925.

11. Sophronios Eustratiades and Arcadios of Vatopedi. *Catalogue of the Greek Manuscripts in the Library of the Monastery of Vatopedi on Mt. Athos*, 1924.

10. Conybeare, Frederick C. *Russian Dissenters*, 1921.

9. Burrage, Champlin, ed. *An Answer to John Robinson of Leyden by a Puritan Friend: Now First Published from a Manuscript of A.D. 1609*, 1920.

8. Emerton, Ephraim. *The* Defensor pacis *of Marsiglio of Padua: A Critical Study*, 1920,

7. Bacon, Benjamin W. *Is Mark a Roman Gospel?* 1919.

6. Cadbury, Henry Joel. 2 vols. *The Style and Literary Method of Luke*, 1920.

5. Marriott, G. L., ed. Macarii Anecdota: *Seven Unpublished Homilies of Macarius*, 1918.

4. Edmunds, Charles Carroll and William Henry Paine Hatch. *The Gospel Manuscripts of the General Theological Seminary*, 1918.

3. Arnold, William Rosenzweig. *Ephod and Ark: A Study in the Records and Religion of the Ancient Hebrews*, 1917.

2. Hatch, William Henry Paine. *The Pauline Idea of Faith in its Relation to Jewish and Hellenistic Religion*, 1917.

1. Torrey, Charles Cutler. *The Composition and Date of Acts*, 1916.

Harvard Dissertations in Religion

In 1993, Harvard Theological Studies absorbed
the Harvard Dissertations in Religion series.

31. Baker-Fletcher, Garth. *Somebodyness: Martin Luther King, Jr. and the Theory of Dignity*, 1993.

30. Soneson, Jerome Paul. *Pragmatism and Pluralism: John Dewey's Significance for Theology*, 1993.

29. Crabtree, Harriet. *The Christian Life: The Traditional Metaphors and Contemporary Theologies*, 1991.

28. Schowalter, Daniel N. *The Emperor and the Gods: Images from the Time of Trajan*, 1993.

27. Valantasis, Richard. *Spiritual Guides of the Third Century: A Semiotic Study of the Guide-Disciple Relationship in Christianity, Neoplatonism, Hermetism, and Gnosticism*, 1991.

26. Wills, Lawrence Mitchell. *The Jews in the Court of the Foreign King: Ancient Jewish Court Legends*, 1990.

25. Massa, Mark Stephen. *Charles Augustus Briggs and the Crisis of Historical Criticism*, 1990.

24. Hills, Julian Victor. *Tradition and Composition in the* Epistula apostolorum, 1990. Reprinted, 2008.

23. Bowe, Barbara Ellen. *A Church in Crisis: Ecclesiology and Paraenesis in Clement of Rome*, 1988.

22. Bisbee, Gary A. *Pre-Decian Acts of Martyrs and* Commentarii, 1988.

21. Ray, Stephen Alan. *The Modern Soul: Michel Foucault and the Theological Discourse of Gordon Kaufman and David Tracy*, 1987.

20. MacDonald, Dennis Ronald. *There Is No Male and Female: The Fate of a Dominical Saying in Paul and Gnosticism*, 1987.

19. Davaney, Sheila Greeve. *Divine Power: A Study of Karl Barth and Charles Hartshorne*, 1986.

18. LaFargue, J. Michael. *Language and Gnosis: The Opening Scenes of the Acts of Thomas*, 1985.

12. Layton, Bentley, ed. *The Gnostic Treatise on Resurrection from Nag Hammadi*, 1979.

11. Ryan, Patrick J. *Imale: Yoruba Participation in the Muslim Tradition: A Study of Clerical Piety*, 1977.

10. Neevel, Jr., Walter G. *Yāmuna's* Vedānta *and* Pāñcarātra: *Integrating the Classical and the Popular*, 1977.

9. Yarbro Collins, Adela. *The Combat Myth in the Book of Revelation*, 1976.

8. Veatch, Robert M. *Value-Freedom in Science and Technology: A Study of the Importance of the Religious, Ethical, and Other Socio-Cultural Factors in Selected Medical Decisions Regarding Birth Control*, 1976.

7. Attridge, Harold W. *The Interpretation of Biblical History in the* Antiquitates judaicae *of Flavius Josephus*, 1976.

6. Trakatellis, Demetrios C. *The Pre-Existence of Christ in the Writings of Justin Martyr*, 1976.

5. Green, Ronald Michael. *Population Growth and Justice: An Examination of Moral Issues Raised by Rapid Population Growth*, 1975.

4. Schrader, Robert W. *The Nature of Theological Argument: A Study of Paul Tillich*, 1976.

3. Christensen, Duane L. *Transformations of the War Oracle in Old Testament Prophecy: Studies in the Oracles Against the Nations*, 1975.

2. Williams, Sam K. *Jesus' Death as Saving Event: The Background and Origin of a Concept*, 1972.

1. Smith, Jane I. *An Historical and Semantic Study of the Term "Islām" as Seen in a Sequence of Qur'an Commentaries*, 1970.